A Little Dab...

Will Do You UNDER

DIANE C. SHORE

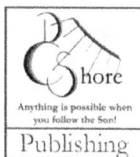

hore
Anything is possible when
you follow the Son!
Publishing

DCShore Publishing
dcshorepublishing.com

ISBN-13: 978-1-7362449-2-0

1.13

"Lord, is there anything in me that is not according to Your will, that has not been ordered by You, or that is not entirely given up to You?"

Andrew Murray
"Absolute Surrender"

CONTENTS

INTRODUCTION

This book can be read as a whole, or subject by subject. It does tend to build on itself, but it can also be separated out as to what might interest you the most on any particular day. The gift of discernment was not strong in my life. Hebrews 5:14 says: *But solid food is for the mature, whose perceptions are trained by practice to discern both good and evil.* We need to be on solid food, not milk. I needed to take off my rose-colored glasses and practice discerning the good and evil around me. The research and study I did for this book helped me be more aware. Now, I hope it helps you in whatever way you might need.

We live in a world full of deception. We can't get around it! We can't escape not being exposed to it. But we can recognize it and be wise to it when we know Jesus as our Savior and Lord. Our one true God is where we must start when surrounded with all the lies on a daily basis—lies in the news, lies in churches, lies in government, lies in our homes... I hope this book helps us all live in the Light as we are called to as the sons and daughters of God Almighty. Our Father in Heaven doesn't want us to be deceived...deception pulls us farther away from our relationship with God. Our Father wants us to see deception for what it is and know that it has already been overcome by the blood of Jesus Christ of Nazareth.

Much of what this book contains is a compilation of Scripture, sermons, videos, personal thoughts, quotations, and more, all brought together in one place to make it easier for those searching for Truth. Some of the words are mine, some are quotes and comments from others. Some of those people have been recognized for their efforts along the way, as I identify them, others have not. I hope those who go unnamed will forgive me since footnotes are not my strong suit. But in the end, I pray the glory is all God's as we all grow together in wisdom and Truth as one body in Christ. I give thanks for all those who came before me and shared their knowledge. There is no way I can cover all the ways of deception in the world today, but I hope when you finish reading this, you will be more aware of what is out there and be able to discern and avoid the many traps the enemy has set for us.

On the Cross, Jesus said, "It is finished". We can believe that Truth and live in it every single day. How? It seems we should start at the very beginning…which is a very good place to start. At least it was….

CHAPTER ONE

BEGINNING

Chapter one, verse one of Genesis in the Bible says, *"In the beginning God created the heavens and the earth."* That is the VERY FIRST miracle we see in God's Word, and it's more than amazing…it is so amazing that we wouldn't be here without it! Let's stop for a moment and absorb that reality, that TRUTH!! Yes, let's start at the very beginning with Truth before we dive into the darkness that the ruthless enemy of God inflicts upon this world and us. Let's stop…let's pray. Let's give thanks and praises for Christ's redemption:

Father in Heaven, You were before the beginning, and You will be until the very end. You are the Alpha and the Omega. We are nothing without You. It is because of You that we even exist. We give You all the praise and glory for what will unravel in this book…for all the places You will take us so we will all walk in more and more of Your Light each day. Lord, we need You! So much! We can get deceived so easily. When non-truth is infused with just a little dab of Your Truth, or even when Your Truth is infused with a little dab of non-truth, we can be drawn to it, tempted into it thinking it could all be okay… "Look, there's God right there…I see Him"—but that little dab of Truth, or that little dab of lie, can do us under if we aren't cautious. We must be a Berean…one who studies the Scriptures to find out if what is being taught is in alignment with

Your Word. (Acts 17:11) Even with this book, please, Lord, draw the readers to Your Word first and foremost, checking on all that is written here. We need all of You, and all of Your Truth to see us through this life until we meet You face to face. In the name of the Lord Jesus Christ we pray. Amen.

I'm serious, that is my heartfelt prayer as we dive into deception here. Chapter by chapter, I believe God is going to bring little dabs of darkness into the Light of Jesus that need to be talked about. I believe some of these things will shock all of us, me included. Things we thought were so needed, so right on, so holy…aren't. It reminds me of the story of the young bride who cut the ends off of her ham before placing it in the pan and putting it in the oven. Her husband asked her why she did that? He had never seen it prepared that way before. She told him she didn't know, that's just the way her mom cooked a ham. So, she asked her mom one day why she cut the ends off the ham? Her mom didn't know, she said that's the way her mom cooked it. So, she asked her grandma why she cut the ends off the ham? Her grandma's response was, "I didn't have a pan large enough to hold the ham, so I had to cut the ends off before cooking it."

We do things, lots of things, without complete understanding. It's just the way it's always been done…in our homes, in our churches, in our relationships. We believe things, lots of things, and don't even know the reason why many times.

Sometimes there is a need for going back to the basics of our Christianity. Why do we believe what we believe? And what is it, exactly, that we *do* believe? We all need to start back at the very beginning from time to time so as to not get lost in the present that we walk in…to understand the Gospel again as a child would. *"Let the little children come to me, and do not hinder them, for the kingdom of heaven belongs to such as these."* Matthew 19:14 (NIV) The Kingdom of Heaven belongs to the adopted sons and daughters of God (believers). We must come as little children to our Father's Throne room, enter into His Word to understand what it is we believe, and then learn to embrace the Lord Jesus Christ from there without reservation. Let's do that, dispelling the darkness along the way…throwing out the papers and the trash that don't line up with God's Word…walking together into God's amazing Light of Truth! As Psalm 119:105 (NKJV) says, *Your word is a lamp to my feet and a light to my path.*

Many who have come before us searched for Truth and found it because that is what they wanted. They weren't searching for their own happiness, their own satisfaction, their own contentment...they were searching for what they truly wanted...the Truth found in God's Word. Maybe that's because they tried so many other things and found there was no satisfaction in them. Oh, in the beginning other things can seem to offer what we're looking for. But in the end there will be consequences we don't want to deal with. How about that chocolate chip cookie? It sure looks good! I think I'll have another, and another...until years later, or maybe just months, we aren't who we want to be. We are in the grips of the enemy who is making us feel bad about our weight. Okay, maybe that's just my struggle. Maybe yours is video games, or shopping. Retail therapy starts off making many feel good. But when the bills come in...LOOK OUT! How about those video games played late into the night, and all day long? Not much harm there, right? Wrong! Those games can take our minds places they don't belong. If we think it doesn't change us from the inside out, let's try putting them down for a week and feel the burn...the pull back to it. Now, instead, pick up our Bible and read it...for every minute/hour we spent playing video games let's read our Bible. Tell me we don't notice a change in our attitude and our focus then. How about...alcohol? Yes, that beer after work that turned into two, then three...then became the comfort we needed when we got fired, when our friend betrayed us...that's using alcohol for comfort when God was calling us instead. We couldn't hear God because He was drowned out by the liquid comfort we chose instead. As I see a million-dollar house down the street go up for sale, with an expensive car sitting in the driveway, I know hearts are broken, a marriage has dissolved because of alcohol for one.... Consequences? YES! Sometimes too many to count.

A little dab of darkness can do us under because little dabs start to add up over time. One pair of shoes becomes twenty. One cookie becomes ten. One glass of wine becomes a bottle. One painkiller becomes ineffective to dull the senses. We want/need more and more! A little dab of Light is never enough either. If we aren't searching for complete Truth in God's Word and are willing to settle for less...then the darkness of deception can move in and overtake even the little light we have. We need to be very careful with what we listen to and believe. Salvation is a gift, faith is a gift, but if we don't strive to walk in it fully as Scripture spells it out, then we can become weak, timid, and overwhelmed and give in to the things of this world that Satan is offering to us.

I know, I know, this book is a downer right now…it's not lifting your spirits the way you hoped it would. It's just making you feel guilty, depressed, and condemned. That's because it's calling all of us to the carpet, me included. And for good reason! Because, GOD IS GOOD! And He wants to get our attention, and soon! Our Father wants to rescue us from the darkness that we are tempted to live in and show us the way to walk free. That's why Jesus came, died, and rose again!! That's why He's coming back again! Jesus is calling us into FREEDOM with His full Gospel Truth. Be warned, a partial Gospel is no Gospel at all. We will talk much more about that in upcoming chapters.

Our joy in the Lord is an eternal life filled with Truth that can start today! Not when we die. Today! Walking free here on this beautiful Earth God created, there in Genesis 1:1, *"In the beginning…"* **But** *"In the beginning…"* along came… not John… that's New Testament! Along came that serpent. The snake… a snake that talks. Seems unbelievable, doesn't it? Well, how many "voices" do we hear every day that sound "snake-ish?" Like, "Eat that pan of chocolate chip cookies." "Buy that pair of shoes." "Play another hour or two of that video game." "Have a drink." "What harm will any of that do?" Yes, those are the voices of the very snake heard in the Garden after everything that God had made that was good and very good. Let's look at Genesis 3:1-5 (NKJV):

Now the serpent was more cunning than any beast of the field which the Lord God had made. And he said to the woman, "Has God indeed said, 'You shall not eat of every tree of the garden'?"

And the woman said to the serpent, "We may eat the fruit of the trees of the garden; but of the fruit of the tree which is in the midst of the garden, God has said, 'You shall not eat it, nor shall you touch it, lest you die.'"

Then the serpent said to the woman, "You will not surely die. For God knows that in the day you eat of it your eyes will be opened, and you will be like God, knowing good and evil."

How many times in life have we dealt with people who connive like this and we think to ourselves, "What a snake!" Well, we know where that comes from…the original Garden snake. That very first snake probably seemed harmless just like our garden snakes do today. If he had shown up as a rattler, Adam and Eve might have run. But he showed up as a wolf in sheep's clothing—he was a rattler in garden snakeskin. He was one of the "wild" animals. We can see that now.

Did you see how the snake brought "God" into the discussion? Why? Because it seems when God is brought into anything it should be a very good thing. And many churches today do bring God into the discussions, the sermons, the songs…but is the true Jesus really there? Is the Good News of Jesus Christ talked about? Is Jesus our focus even in our worship songs? Or is God just an obscure entity who is out there, looking over all of us…from a distance? If we are not specific about which God it is that we are worshipping, which God is in our sermons…a little dab of God/god can do us under right quick. We need the one true God in Heaven—the Father whose Son left His Throne to come to Earth to save humanity from the destruction that the snake caused in the Garden. We need Jesus the Christ, the One who restores us into a right relationship with our Father. When someone mentions God, be sure who it is they are talking about. And then still be very cautious, because Satan even had the right God…but it still went very wrong. Let's continue with the little "dabs" that will do us under in our own lives…

The world thinks the church lives by rules and regulations because that is what makes us holy. Then they view us as holier than thou when we resist the darker side of life, and they want nothing to do with a God like that. Again, see the little dab of lie that hurts the reality of what it is we do believe and why we believe it? We don't stay away from sin to get into Heaven, we stay away from sin because we are going to Heaven and our heart's desire is to please our Father in Heaven. Children should desire to please their parents. We, as adult children, should be no different.

The snake LIED, once again…just a little bit when he asked, *"You shall not eat of every tree of the garden?"* He stretched what God said just enough to bring in some doubt and confusion. He knew very well what God had said, and which tree it was. Now Eve did

5

battle back quite convincingly, didn't she? She told that old snake that it's not that they couldn't eat any of the fruit. Yes. They may eat from the trees. That was the truth. She told him it's just the fruit from the tree in the middle of the Garden that they are not allowed to eat. More truth. Good going, Eve. But then…she added in a little dab of her own white lie for impact. She told that snake that they weren't even allowed to eat or "touch" the tree in the middle of the Garden. When did God say that? Let's look back… Genesis 2:16-17 (NET):

Then the Lord God commanded the man, "You may freely eat fruit from every tree of the orchard, but you must not eat from the tree of the knowledge of good and evil, for when you eat from it you will surely die."

Did you see anything in there about not touching the tree? Why do we think we need to add to God's Word to make it more powerful? We don't! We don't need to go outside of the guidelines of the Bible to walk in the authority we have been given within those guidelines. Those dabs of Truth combined with little dabs of lies, will get us bit as when the snake then fires back, *"You won't die!"* Do you think this had Eve rethinking things? I suspect so, since she did take a bite after that. The snake did speak a little Truth again. He knew they weren't going to physically die…so why not play on that? That one drink won't kill us. That one hour on the video game won't fill our brain to overflowing with darkness. That one innocent cup of coffee with that person who is not our spouse won't lead to anything. That one pair of shoes isn't all that expensive. It won't break the bank. On and on…we listen to lies with some truth. It sounds right. It seems innocent enough. And we agree, we shouldn't be restricted like that. We're adults, after all. We can make wise decisions at the mall, at the coffee shop, at the liquor store….NO! Get out of there! Fast! How many have we known who messed with things they shouldn't have, and we watched their downfall? Too many…they are all around us. But we're different. We're stronger. We're smarter. Uh…pride? To be dealt with in another chapter…

It says the serpent "replied" to the woman. If I were writing it, I would have taken off the "rep" and simply written, "The serpent *lied* to the woman," because he did! Yes, he replied. Yes, he responded.

But listen cautiously when a "snake" responds to you…it's probably a lie. Listen between the lines and you will hear the hiss. It's not a pretty sound. It's full of venom. Should we stick around long enough to then let him bite us? The enemy is only out to steal, kill, and destroy us. Just like he did that very first time in the Garden. We have to understand that's Satan's job, his assignment, as well as all the other angels who were kicked out of Heaven with him when Lucifer tried to exalt himself above God.

Let's listen, cautiously, as Satan talks about God again in verse five. We might think we can relax when we are in the midst of a "God discussion". NOT! Satan's putting God in the sentence while he's hissing underneath his breath, "…*God knows that in the day you eat of it your eyes will be opened, and you will be like God, knowing good and evil.*" Uh…Satan tried that and look what happened to him. Misery loves company. "Come join me," he's saying. He knows he blew it. Now he'd like Eve to join him.

A little dab of venom was injected under Eve's skin with that. It's just enough that she's about to fall for it; and fall bigtime! Don't do it, EVE!!! Oh, too late! Now we're living in the fallen world that started there in the Garden. We know the end of that story, and we also know the end of ours as believers in Jesus Christ. Thankfully, Jesus came to rescue us from that fall.

So, please know we can truly be of good cheer as we work our way through each new deception in this book. Once again, this is not to depress us. This is to make us aware so we understand that we can, *tread on snakes and scorpions and on the full force of the enemy, and nothing will hurt you.* Jesus said this in Luke 10:19 (NET). The victory is already ours in Christ Jesus. Just because the enemy continues to lie to us, doesn't mean we have to believe, fall for, partake in, or have anything to do with his deception. We can turn and walk away at any time…as Eve should have done. But let's not get down on Eve, or even Adam, as they did what we do far too many times. Instead, let's learn from past mistakes and move forward in the victory we have been given.

As we continue on, we know that when the serpent tempted Eve to want to be like God, it's exactly what Satan did to get himself kicked out of his own gardenlike setting in Heaven. The snake, who made the gravest error of his existence, isn't learning from his mistakes and then turning around and helping someone not do what he did. Instead, he is tempting Eve to do what he did. And he's going to get her kicked out, too, along with Adam, into the hard work of toiling the soil and painful childbirth—something that God didn't intend for His children. You and I will one day enjoy what God did intend for us when we arrive in Heaven, free from all this malarkey the "snake" is causing all around us—all the distractions Satan brings into our lives to keep us from a close relationship with God…because that's what he's doing. It's exactly what he did in the Garden. Watch what happened in Genesis 3:6 (NET).

When the woman saw that the tree produced fruit that was good for food, was attractive to the eye, and was desirable for making one wise, she took some of its fruit and ate it. She also gave some of it to her husband who was with her, and he ate it.

Have you ever been convinced of something, by someone, that it was going to be good, but it didn't turn out quite that good? We all have! We listen, and we think, "Yeah, I'll give that a try," and there we go…down a road that has lots of bumps and turns we could have avoided had we been just a bit wiser. Oh, speaking of wisdom, isn't that what the snake is convincing Eve of? "You're gonna know stuff…come on, give it a try." We fall for those insinuations that threaten our manhood, or our womanhood. We decide to take a look… Eve *saw*. She turned to look at that tree. She looked right into the face of temptation instead of looking away. Once we turn and look at something a second time, a third time, a fourth time, it can/will get to us. It will bite us because we have already taken nibbles of extra looks at it. Eve had already seen the tree. If she had decided to not even look in its direction again, maybe she could have avoided it. But she listened to the snake, and she "saw" what the snake was talking about, and it did "look" beautiful. It was so enticing standing there in the middle of the Garden.

Don't you wonder why God would put it in the middle of the Garden? The Tree of Life was also in the center of the Garden, not just the Tree of the Knowledge of Good and Evil. The two trees were there together…it makes me think about God giving us a choice. Which will we choose? His Word says He sets before us life and death. As for me and my house, I want to say we will choose the Lord. Without free will, we would not be able to freely choose to love God. And love that is not freely given and received isn't love at all, is it? Just as today we have to choose between the darkness of this world and the Light of Jesus…Adam and Eve had the same choice to make, even if it's not a lot. It says Eve ate some. There's that "little dab" that we think won't make much difference. Heresy in churches today is not being totally off the mark of Truth. It usually has lots of Truth in it or no one would fall for it.

Let's continue…after Eve ate some, she then gave some to Adam who was with her. We do that, don't we… "Hey, I'm enjoying this, want 'some'?" Lucifer tried to be like God, and now he's getting them to want to be like God. Isn't it interesting later in the Bible where we are taught to be Christlike? The snake says in the NLT Bible, *"…you will become just like God."* When we are called to be Christlike, we won't be just like Christ. No one can be just like Christ. Jesus was perfect, is perfect, and will always be perfect. What being Christlike is, is to use Jesus as our model for what a loving, compassionate, forgiving person we are to be in this world. That's a tall order, and only made even remotely possible through the power of the Holy Spirit who lives within each believer. And that is what we should want to give to others. To give them what we have received as a child of God. To receive as many of Christ's qualities into our own lives as possible, and then to share those things with others. Those are the Fruit, the very good things to have "some" of. We will only be perfected in those things when our time on Earth has come to an end and we are in Heaven.

Let's finish this first chapter with the end of this story, although it is a sad ending. Adam and Eve ate, and their eyes were opened, and they suddenly felt shame, so they had to cover themselves with fig leaves. Consequences are not easy, and we have all dealt with them. It's a part of life. "Some" of the things we choose separate us from God, even as believers. We can have the Holy Spirit living inside of us as true believers in Jesus Christ, and still…we choose poorly at times. In life, we might think a little dab will do us, but it doesn't. Later we need more, and more…and much later we can find ourselves kicked out of the place we once were…away from our family, our friends, our job, our home…to a desolate place where we feel shame and want to cover ourselves so no one will see us. We have distanced ourselves from our Father in Heaven.

The GOOD NEWS is, that's right where God finds us! When we

have moved far from Him, He has not moved. And He is most willing to rescue us. God knew right where Adam and Eve were hiding from Him. He knows right where we are, too. So, you see, this story has a sad ending, but it is filled with great hope. The Truth of the Gospel is found in this story. They tried to cover their shame with plants. God sheds the blood of an innocent animal (the first blood sacrifice) and clothes them. Jesus, the Lamb of God, was hung on a Cross, shedding His blood for us to clothe us in His righteousness.

But God did do one last thing in this story, He kicked them out of the Garden. Was He being mean? Was He being unjust? No, He was being loving. He didn't want them eating from the Tree of Life and living forever. Not now! Not here on Earth! Think about it…living here in this fallen world forever? And not being able to die? As my dad once told me, "Death is not a problem. It's an opportunity". Our loving Father didn't want us stuck on Earth with no hope for a wonderful future away from all these lies and deceptions. God has a plan to get us out of here through the death, burial, and resurrection of His Son, Jesus—Jesus is coming back for us! He has gone to prepare a place for us in the new Heaven. Death isn't a problem when we know Jesus as our Savior and Lord. Death is a Heaven full of opportunities.

Let's pray:
Thank You, Father, for making a way where there seems to be no way. Thank You for not leaving us in the fallen Garden full of deception but having a plan to bring us all the way Home to You. You will not force anyone to be with You who chooses not to be. But those who stumble and fall along the way and look up to You and ask for help and forgiveness from You will receive it freely because of what Your Son died to give us…Redemption. The greatest freedom we will ever know has come at the greatest cost of Your One and only Son, Jesus. We thank You and give You all the praise and glory You are so deserving of. We don't want just a little dab of You, we want all of You! Protect us from all the little dabs of darkness that look "beautiful" but hiss like a snake. Help us not to choose them, but to choose You, always.

In the name of Jesus Christ. Amen

Chapter One Reflections

1) If we aren't searching for complete Truth in God's Word and are willing to settle for less…then the darkness of deception can move in and overtake even the little light we have. We need to be very careful with what we listen to and believe. (Page 3)

2) Salvation is a gift, faith is a gift, but if we don't strive to walk in it fully as Scripture spells it out, then we can become weak, timid, and overwhelmed and give in to the things of this world that Satan is offering to us. (Page 4)

3) It seems when God is brought into anything it should be a very good thing. And many churches today do bring God into the discussions, the sermons, the songs…but is the true Jesus really there? Is the Good News of Jesus Christ talked about? (Page 5)

4) Why do we think we need to add to God's Word to make it more powerful? We don't! We don't need to go outside of the guidelines of the Bible to walk in the authority we have been given within those guidelines. (Page 6)

5) Just because the enemy continues to lie to us, doesn't mean we have to believe, fall for, partake in, or have anything to do with his deception. We can turn and walk away at any time…as Eve should have done. (Page 7)

6) Heresy in churches today is not being totally off the mark of Truth. It has lots of Truth in it or no one would fall for it. (Page 9)

7) "Some" of the things we choose separate us from God, even as believers. We can have the Holy Spirit living inside of us as true believers in Jesus Christ, and still…we choose poorly at times. (Page 9)

8) Our loving Father didn't want us stuck here with no hope for a wonderful future away from all these lies and deceptions. He has a plan to get us out of here through the death, burial, and resurrection of His Son, Jesus—Jesus is coming back for us! (Page 10)

NOTES

*(These Reflection/Note pages may be duplicated
and used for group discussions when needed.)*

CHAPTER TWO

LIES

Where do we look for help when it is needed? Psalm 121 talks about looking up toward the hills. Is help found there? Maybe on a nice spring hike, we can find some peace. I once went on hike up in the foothills looking for answers. I came to a sign that said, "Keep on the path". I laughed. It sounded like the perfect answer from God in that moment. Yes, God will meet us in the hills. But mostly, He will meet us in His Word.

As we continue on in Psalm 121, verse two says, *"My help comes from the Lord, the Creator of heaven and earth."* So, why would we look to the hills or anything that was made by God, the Creator, instead of looking to the One who created all things? That is when we have to ask ourselves the question found in Isaiah 44:20, *"Is this not a false god I hold in my right hand?"* It seems like a simple enough question, but it's not. It's HARD. It means taking what we hold dear, or maybe what we have worshipped, or how we have worshipped, or even what translation of the Bible we are reading, or a specific sermon, or even a pastor we have trusted, and asking, "Is this of You, Lord?" We don't want to ask that question. We want what we're used to, what we've trusted, what we're comfortable with, to be *it*. But sometimes it's not *it*. Sometimes *it* is a lie, as one translation puts it. And if *it* is a lie, then we are feeding on ashes and are a poor deluded fool/Christian. Yes, even believers can be deceived. Some may quote the verse out of Mark 13:22 (NET), *"For false messiahs and false prophets will appear and perform signs and wonders to deceive, if possible, the elect."* It seems from the way this is stated that deception is not possible for true Christians. But there is a clear warning of false messiahs and false prophets deceiving people…if not for the grace and wisdom of God.

As a Christian, have you ever been deceived? I have! In a world where rose-colored glasses could come in quite handy, they aren't the best thing to be wearing when praying for discernment. Rose-colored glasses make us unaware of the dangers and deceptions around us. Life can look grand in those glasses! We don't question people's motives, or even what they're doing when we're not with them. We don't question whether someone is telling us the truth. We just go through the world trusting and loving all people. Not a bad thing, but it's the proverbial placing-our-head-in-the-sand situation. There is no discernment in that. Only ignorance. And the Bible tells us in Hosea 4:6 (KJV), *"My people are destroyed for lack of knowledge…"* It continues on with, *"they had forgotten the law of thy God…"* If we read that in the NET Bible, it's a bit different and reads a little more succinctly; *"You have destroyed my people by failing to acknowledge me."* In the Old Testament, the priests weren't acknowledging God, and because of that, the Israelites were being destroyed. Were the people trusting the priests? I would imagine so. Were they being misled? In some ways, yes.

Let's take a few moments and think about the things we believe, and the people we believe in. This is not to make us suspicious; this is to open our eyes to what's around us. If any one of them seems out of place, so to speak, stretch out your right hand and place it/them there. Then ask yourself, "Is this a lie?" Go ahead, I'll wait….

It's uncomfortable isn't it? I know, I've done it. And there are things I want to hold onto. But trust me, it gets easier. As you take that thing, that "god," and put it down (I usually turn my hand over and sort of smack it down), it becomes less painful. These aren't always big things…I'm talking little things. Let's find an example… How about a book that you used to like, that seemed encouraging to you? But then you found out there were half-truths within the pages. That's called a "little dab". That's called heresy if it's a Christian book/author. It contains thoughts and choices that don't line up with the Word of God. And that little bit of leaven will permeate all of the dough. *"The kingdom of heaven is like leaven, which a woman took and hid in three measures of meal till it was all leavened."* Matthew 13:33 (NKJV) It doesn't take much for little things to spread through everything. Think about that little drop of food coloring when stirred into white frosting...

Now Matthew 13:33 was talking about legalism...but it still can apply in other scenarios. Think of the times when a little bit of "wrong" was mixed in with a whole lot of "right". Sort of spoils it, doesn't it? If we are holding onto something that isn't lining up with the Word of God, it can/will permeate our whole lives in time. That's why it's so important to take what we are holding in our right hand and ask ourselves that question, *"Is this not a false god I hold in my right hand?"*

"But, but...it's a very good thing," you might be saying. Yes, and Paul also thought he was doing a very good thing when he was arresting the people of the Way. He was sure he was right. He was serving God faithfully—the very same God that we are serving as believers in the Lord Jesus Christ. Paul had all the credentials to back up what he was doing. He was circumcised on the eighth day. He was of the tribe of Benjamin. He was a Hebrew of Hebrews. He was full of zeal, a Pharisee. Even as to the righteousness of the Law, he was found blameless. All this, until the day when he literally saw the Light on the road to Damascus. What else could have stopped Saul? What else could have convinced him that he was on the wrong road, headed in the wrong direction? Jesus showed up and had a question for him, *"Saul, Saul, why are you persecuting me?"* Acts 9:4 (NET) Saul/Paul had to stop. He really had no choice. He was now on the ground and blind. Maybe the three days of blindness gave him time to think it over. Maybe he decided right then and there, but Jesus gave him three days to readjust. We don't know. But we do know that when Ananias prayed for Paul and his sight was restored, Paul could clearly "see" the Truth of the Lord Jesus Christ. Paul's role had changed, his whole life had changed because a question had been asked and answered. Saul, with the new name now of Paul, was pointed in a new direction...one that shocked everyone around him. They knew Saul as the man who stood with the coats as Stephen was stoned. They knew him as the man who had believers of the Way arrested and punished. They didn't know

Saul/Paul to be a man who now, suddenly, did a complete about face and took the message of Jesus Christ to the Gentiles, and to Kings, as well as to the people of Israel. Look out you priests who were missing the mark!—Paul immediately began preaching in the synagogues saying, *"This man is the Son of God."* Acts 9:20 (NET)

Whatever we are doing on this day for God may seem to be a very good thing. But we have to ask ourselves a question, "Am I on the right road, with the right people, going the right direction, toward the right God?" If the answer is, "No," then we have to stop in our tracks, fall to our knees, ask God to remove the scales from our eyes, and begin again. It's okay, it happens to the best of us…like Paul. But when it happens, be prepared for the reaction of those around us. They said of Paul, *"Is this not the man who in Jerusalem was ravaging those who call on this name, and who had come here to bring them as prisoners to the chief priests?"* Acts 9:21 (NET)

It's okay to ask our own questions during these times. Saul did when he said, *"Who are you Lord?"* Acts 9:5 (NET). We are told to test the spirits in 1 John 4:1 (NET): *Dear friends, do not believe every spirit, but test the spirits to determine if they are from God…* It doesn't matter who we have heard it from, where we have read it, or if it seems it came straight from God. Test it! All of it!

Deception is coming! We can believe the Lord Jesus Christ who told us it is. When asked in Matthew 24:3 (NET), *"…what will be the sign of your coming and the end of the age?"* Jesus answered them in verse 4, *"Watch out that no one misleads you. For many will come in my name, saying, 'I am the Christ,' and they will mislead many."* Jesus went on to tell them a few more times, watch out! Don't be deceived! There will be false messiahs, and false prophets performing great signs and wonders. They're going to look like the real deal! But they won't be. They will be the ways that the enemy will distract us from our Lord and Savior and from doing the Kingdom work of our Father.

How do we recognize these false things that will look so real? Most say, keep looking at, reading, and feeling the real, and you will recognize the counterfeit when it comes along. I agree, but not completely. If we are not trained in something, it is not in our vision, so to speak. Think of it this way; if you're a trained gardener, what are you going to notice when you walk into church on Sunday morning? The landscape. If you are a "professional" shoe shopper, you will notice every pair of shoes that everyone is wearing. If, like me, you have done thousands of men's haircuts, you will sit in church and notice everyone who needs a haircut, if they just had a haircut, or if it's a good fade or a bad one. I can't help it. It's in my DNA! But, if we don't have an eye for deception, for New Age, Moralistic Therapeutic Deism, Mysticism, or Witchcraft, etc…we may not notice it. The wolf is not going to appear in wolf's clothing. He is going to come dressed as a sheep, and we better have the nose of a sheep dog to smell the wolves. A little dab could do us under if we don't recognize it. I know when a man has product in his hair, if it's there to give it shine, firm hold, a natural look, or whatever. Now if some guy with a terrible haircut, say in the style of Hitler (I only use him because we can all picture that in our mind.) was sitting in front of us, we'd be staring at his haircut wondering why he left the house with it looking like that. My hope in writing this book is that we will be able to pick out heresy in so-called Christianity as quickly as we could pick out Hitler's bad haircut. I hope to do this by not only encouraging you to know the Truth, the Word, and to be extremely prayerful…but to also know enough about the wolf that you will pick up on its scent immediately so as not to be deceived.

For starters, let's go to Galatians and take a look at a few things there. In Galatians 1:4, it says that Jesus Christ was given to us because of our sins, and to rescue us from this present evil age. What does that mean? It means not only were they living in an evil age back 2,000 years ago, but we're still living in it now, if not more so. And Paul was astonished how quickly they were deserting the grace of Christ. They had already started following a different Gospel, although he clarifies that by saying that there really isn't another Gospel. I mean, how could there be? Jesus Christ is the way, the truth, and the life, and no one comes to the Father except through Him. (John 14:6) So what other Gospel could there be like that? Everything else falls short. And yet, so many still seem to go after other ways…and even those going the right way can get detoured from time to time. Why? Well, Paul spells it out in Galatians 1:7 when he explains there are people disturbing us and wanting to distort the Gospel of Christ. This is tough. Are those deceiving others doing it on purpose? Or are they deceived themselves? Probably a bit of both. If they weren't deceived, they wouldn't be deceiving others…even if they think/know in their head what they are doing seems right. To do it, to deceive others on purpose, calls for deception having overtaken them already. Anybody who truly knows and understands and has accepted the true Gospel, follows it to the best of their ability. And if deception ever does come from them, and they are made aware of it, they will quickly call the thing they have been holding in their right hand a lie and repent of it. That is what a true follower of Christ would and must do! When it is brought to their attention, a change/repentance will quickly be in the works. If their hearts are callous, we have to pray harder—their deception runs very deep!

In whom do we put our stock? No one! I don't say that to be mean, I say it because that is what the Word of God says. You're reading my book, and I thank you. But please, be a Berean. Check everything I write with what Scripture says. It's imperative! Paul said in Galatians 1:8-9, *"But even if we (or an angel from heaven) should preach a gospel contrary to the one we preached to you, let him be condemned to hell! As we have said before, and now I say again, if anyone is preaching to you a gospel contrary to what you received, let him be condemned to hell!"* That's very clear! If anything that is being preached/written is contrary to the Gospel of Jesus Christ in the Word of God, discard it. It doesn't matter how good, smart, or wonderful it sounds! Throw it out with the morning trash! Paul was trying to warn people by writing this, and we should take note of it and follow his urgings. As Paul said, if we are trying to please people, we are not a slave of Christ.

Once the true Jesus was revealed to Paul, he was going to do what God told him to do, no matter how hard it was for him. And it was hard! Paul went from savagely persecuting the church and trying to destroy it, to being one of the largest contributors in the writing of the New Testament. Paul was zealous for the traditions of his ancestors. But when God called Saul and revealed Jesus to him, everything changed in Saul's/Paul's life, including his name. Even though others were suspicious of Paul, he didn't quit. Paul was now on a mission for God in the *right* direction. And when the others caught on that Paul was the real deal, that he had changed into a follower of the Way instead of opposing it, they glorified God because of him. Paul was willing to call the thing he held onto before a lie. He laid it down after God shone His light on him and literally laid him down on the road to Damascus.

How hard would this be for us? Let's take a look at how hard this was for Paul. In Acts 22:22b-24 (NET), it says, *"Away with this man from the earth! For he should not be allowed to live!"* While they were screaming and throwing off their cloaks and tossing dust in the air, the commanding officer ordered Paul to be brought back into the barracks. He told them to interrogate Paul by beating him with a lash so that he could find out the reason the crowd was shouting at Paul in this way. And we think we have it hard when we try to defend our faith? Paul was about to lose his life, as so many have around the world. In the U.S., so far, we don't have it that bad.

I hope this is making us all think…what lies are we believing? What half-truths are we willing to hold onto for comfort's sake? Jesus warned of deception…do we see it? If not, we are most assuredly missing some of the "bad haircuts" in the pews around us, in the world around us. Deception is not just found outside of the church. In these latter days, especially, it is in our churches. What better place for the enemy to hide out in sheep's clothing? So, what do we do? Do we leave our church? Do we start a home church? Even in a new church, or a home church, deception can enter in. What we do is pray and seek God's direction and help as to what we are to do, and when. This is not to make us all run for the hills. It is to make us all aware that the hills are not where our help comes from, and to recognize the difference between deception and Truth! The elect need to have discernment. We need to not only be studying the Truth but learning about deception enough that we are able to spot it quickly, pray immediately, and stand strong in the full Armor of God!

Let's pray:
Father, thank You that Your Word warns us of these things. You haven't left us in the dark. You are shining Your bright light on it all. Help us open our eyes and see clearly. We want to follow You on the right road into Your heavenly Kingdom. Thank You, Lord Jesus. Amen.

Chapter Two Reflections

1) Psalm 121, verse two says, *"My help comes from the Lord, the Creator of heaven and earth."* So, why would we look to the hills or anything that was made by God, the Creator, instead of looking to the One who created all things? (Page 15)

2) We have to ask ourselves the question found in Isaiah 44:20, *"Is this not a false god I hold in my right hand?"* It seems like a simple enough question, but it's not. It's HARD. (Page 15)

3) The Bible tells us in Hosea 4:6 (KJV), *"My people are destroyed for lack of knowledge..."* It continues on with, *"they had forgotten the law of thy God..."* (Page 16)

4) Let's take a few moments and think about the things we believe, and the people we believe in. This is not to make us suspicious; this is to open our eyes to what's around us. If anyone of them seems out of place, so to speak, stretch out your right hand and place it/them there. Then ask yourself, "Is this a lie?" (Page 16)

5) "But, but...it's a very good thing," you might be saying. Yes, and Paul also thought he was doing a very good thing when he was arresting the people of the Way. (Page 17)

6) We are told to test the spirits in 1 John 4:1 (NET): *Dear friends, do not believe every spirit, but test the spirits to determine if they are from God...* It doesn't matter who we have heard it from, where we have read it, or if it seems it came straight from God. Test it! All of it! (Page 18)

7) Deception is coming! We can believe the Lord Jesus Christ who told us it is. When asked in Matthew 24:3 (NET), *"...what will be the sign of your coming and the end of the age?"* Jesus answered them in verse 4, *"Watch out that no*

one misleads you. For many will come in my name, saying, 'I am the Christ,' and they will mislead many." (Page 18)

8) This is not to make us all run for the hills. It is to make us all aware that the hills are not where our help comes from, and to recognize the difference between deception and Truth! The elect need to have discernment. (Page 21)

<u>*NOTES*</u>

*(These Reflection/Note pages may be duplicated
and used for group discussions when needed.)*

CHAPTER THREE

WATCHMAN

When we aren't even sure which Bible translation we are to be reading, how are we to know about being a "Watchman" as it talks about in Ezekiel 33:1-9? For starters, let's take a look at that passage of Scripture. It says, *"Son of man, speak to your people, and say to them..."*

Let's stop there, even though it seems a bit too soon. When it says, *"speak to your people,"* I take notice because I speak to a lot of people...mostly one-on-one. But sometimes I speak to a small group, and sometimes larger. How would God have me/us use those moments to best glorify Him? When we are standing in line at the grocery store and striking up a conversation with someone nearby, what do we say? When we are at the doctor's office talking to the receptionist, can we be used there by God? When we are with a friend at church and someone walks up with a prayer request, will we be ready? The scenarios could go on and on. These are precious moments that we may never get again in quite the same way. How do we use them wisely? Biblically? Let's look on further in that passage:

"Son of man, speak to your people, and say to them, 'Suppose I bring a sword against the land, and the people of the land take one

man from their borders and make him their watchman...'"

Now what if we suddenly see there *is* a problem, a need, a hunger...in the person we are talking with? Perhaps a "sword" of some sort has come against them in their life. Sometimes we're put in charge of "watching" for the coming trouble. Let's look at what happens next in this part of Scripture:

"He sees the sword coming against the land, blows the trumpet, and warns the people, but there is one who hears the sound of the trumpet yet does not heed the warning."

The watchman sees a problem and knows it needs to be announced. Some will heed the warning...some won't...but that's not the watchman's responsibility. He let them know. That is his job. Theirs is to take notice. In Revelation many times it says, *"The one who has an ear* had *better hear what the Spirit says to the churches."* Some have a responsibility to give a warning. But everyone has a responsibility when given a warning to pay attention and pray about its validity. If it is from God's Word, or even a trusted "Watchman" that God has put on duty in our lives, we should give heed to it. What will be the results many times if we don't?

"Then the sword comes and sweeps him away. He will be responsible for his own death. He heard the sound of the trumpet but did not heed the warning, so he is responsible for himself. If he had heeded the warning, he would have saved his life."

I hate to say, "I told you so..." But there it is, so I don't really have to. God's Word points it out. There are times in life when we get caught off guard, when we are deceived, and we don't realize it right away...sometimes for a long time. But there are times when we have been warned of the dangers and we should pay special attention. Every day brings us closer to Jesus' imminent return, so watchmen are important. Some, like those with the gift of discernment, are placed in a "position" to see what's going on and warn others. Others, like myself, do research and share what we have learned so you can be on the lookout, too. Both can come in handy when the "sword" is headed for us and we need to be warned.

Here's another scenario in that same part of Scripture:

"But suppose the watchman sees the sword coming and does not blow the trumpet to warn the people. Then the sword comes and takes one of their lives. He is swept away for his iniquity, but I will hold the watchman accountable for that person's death."

This is a very bad situation because there could have been a warning given. There was a watchman in place, but he didn't do his job. He didn't blow the trumpet, and the sword came, and it did damage, even sometimes causing death. The person in trouble loses his life, his job, his reputation, perhaps...but the watchman is in bigger trouble. He is responsible for what has happened...the blood is now on his hands. It could possibly have been prevented. Honestly, I don't want to be either one of the people in this scene, the one swept away or the one not giving the warning.

As Christians today, there are a lot of things we need to be warned about. But we can't have our eyes looking in every direction at all times. We need each other. *Although an assailant may overpower one person, two can withstand him. Moreover, a three-stranded cord is not quickly broken.* Ecclesiastes 4:12 (NET) As a team, we can accomplish more. We need each other, to look out for one another, to help...especially when there is a "sword" coming at us.

Now, why all of this in a book on deception? Because we even need to be careful about our watchman. Perhaps we need to go back to the "drawing board" and look first at which Bible we are using? Where are we getting our information? Every "reliable" Bible comes from the Greek, Aramaic, and Hebrew writings of the Scribes. We have no original Bible, only copies, which is a very good thing. Why? Because then the original cannot be altered, and the thousands and thousands of copies we do have would be much too hard to change. Slight errors found in the copies can be checked against other copies, and the errors remedied...a very wise plan of God. But back to the reliable Bible. Not every book being called a Bible today may be just that. There is a Mormon Bible, a Jehovah's Witness Bible, and many other religions that have their own Bibles. And, in the Christian circle, we have so many English Bibles to choose from it can be completely overwhelming. Many of them are very good, but some of them are unacceptable for reasons I will go into. Let's look at a brief history of the English translation of the Bible here:

The first Bible written in English was written by Alfred the Great, who died in 901 A.D. He didn't actually get the whole Bible finished, just the Ten Commandments, parts of Exodus, Acts 15, and the Psalms. Quite an accomplishment, though. Then there was a man name Abbot Aelfic in the 10th Century who translated a large part of the Old Testament and the Gospels, including some of the other books of the New Testament. Moving forward a couple hundred years, the Psalms and New Testament were translated into middle English. They were the precursors of a version that John Wycliffe (who died in 1384) was affiliated with. Wycliffe didn't do it alone. His Bible translation was the standard Bible of the Western Church throughout the middle ages. Then the Renaissance brought about a new interest in Hebrew and Greek.

There was a huge increase in Bible production when the printing press began to be used in 1476. Martin Luther, in the early 1500's, was responsible for the Protestant Reformation. That helped advance the translation of the Bible into an everyday language. Luther's translation was from Greek into German. And then in 1525 William Tyndale translated the Bible from Greek into English. But he was executed for doing so. Quite a price to pay for putting the Bible into people's hands, as others through the ages experienced also.

For the next 100 years, Tyndale's Bible was used, and helped to bring about the King James Version of 1611. Before the King James translation, there were other lesser known versions such as the Coverdales of 1535 and the Matthews Bible of 1537. Then in 1539 the so-called "Great Bible" was used in every church in England. King Henry the VIII was responsible for that Bible.

When Elizabeth I took her reign, two more English Bibles came onto the scene. One was the Geneva Bible, which would have been used by Shakespeare. The Geneva Bible became even more popular than the Great Bible, but with its Calvinistic leaning, they needed something else to satisfy the Anglican authorities. So, the Bishop's Bible came onto the scene. With two contesting Bibles now, the Hampton Court of 1604, along with the King James' authorization, there began a new translation that became the English Bible of the day. Until 1885, when the Revised Version came out, the King James Bible was the most used Bible of the day.

In 1901, the American Standard Version of the Revised Version was published. The 20th Century saw the coming of the Revised Standard Version in 1946/1952. This was a revision of the King James Bible and the American Standard Version—this Bible was the first of the modern translations. Then came a stream of translations and paraphrases including many we know of today…the Amplified Bible, Jerusalem Bible, Living Bible, and the New International Bible to name just a few. The NIV Bible was the first to not be a revision or update of an already existing translation. Now we also have the New English Translation (NET) which is the first Bible with full computer networking support.

There are two Bibles that I haven't included in this list for good reason. One is The Message, and the other is The Passion Translation (TPT). The Message is not considered to be an actual Bible, but more like a novel written by one man. The TPT was also mainly written by one man, Brian Simmons, and is said to be a re-written and re-worded Bible. Bibles should be translated by committees. Any translation by a single person can cause us to question its accountability. Simmons did have his Bible evaluated by a small group of scholars and editors, and BroadStreet Publishing also formed a team to review it. If you have more questions about these, or any other particular translation, there are pros and cons for all of them available on the internet.

Now that we have a brief history of our English Bible, I would like to tell you a little bit about the differences we will find within them. Some Bibles are more of a word-for-word translation, while others are thought-for-thought. No Bible can be completely word-for-word since one language translated into another language would be unreadable. Not only this, taking idioms into account, it would not make much sense. <u>What's most important in any translation is the faithfulness of the Bible we are reading.</u> It is important when considering what Bible to use, that it isn't so literal that the English is difficult to read, and that the translation not be so general that it becomes an interpretation instead of a translation of what was originally intended. With the discovery of the Dead Sea Scrolls, there are as many as 5,000 hand copied documents that exist, containing 98 percent of the text. So we CAN have a well-documented, fully understandable Bible to read still today. That's exciting!

When reading our Bibles, it is always best to hold any Scripture up to the test like the Bereans would do. Today, we can easily look up two or three other translations on the Internet to check for accuracy of the thoughts and the words used. Revelation 22:18-19 (NET): *I testify to everyone who hears the words of the prophecy contained in this book: If anyone adds to them, God will add to him the plagues described in this book. And if anyone takes away from the words of this book of prophecy, God will take away his share in the tree of life and in the holy city that are described in this book.*

This comes as a warning, from the most important Watchman on the wall, our Lord. God knew that many would try to tamper with His Word through the years. He has given this warning to all of us. Some have heeded it, and some have not. Let's choose a Bible that stays within the guidelines our Father has set for us. Jesus said in Revelation 22:20 (NET): *The one who testifies to these things says, "Yes, I am coming soon!" Amen! Come, Lord Jesus!* Jesus "testifies" to these things. We can believe Him. Always! And Forever!

This book is not intended to be a witch-hunt on Bibles or anything else concerning Christianity today. But instead, it is a Truth-hunt. We will always look long and hard at Truth. But in so doing, we will be turning up many witches along the way. There is so much deception mixed in with the Truth of Christianity these days…maybe since the beginning of time…that it's not surprising our "Watchman" has warned us of all this in His Word. We will listen to our Watchman, as we proceed with caution, trusting the Holy Spirit to lead the way.

In Ezekiel 36:25-26 (NET), it says, *"I will sprinkle you with pure water, and you will be clean from all your impurities. I will purify you from all your idols. I will give you a new heart, and I will put a new spirit within you. I will remove the heart of stone from your body and give you a heart of flesh."* We don't have to worry if we notice some dirt along this Truth Journey. It is to be expected. There will be times when we realize we have been deceived. There will be times when we will see where we have been tripped up. But our loving God is always there to help us, to lift us up out of the muck and mire, to set our feet on solid ground, wash us in the blood of

Christ, and to help us learn His true way through this life. No one is going to get this journey perfect because the only perfect One is Jesus Christ. In 1 Timothy 4:1 (NET) it says, *Now the Spirit explicitly says that in the later times some will desert the faith and occupy themselves with deceiving spirits and demonic teachings...*

Some do willingly choose the deceptive path while others will be led astray onto it. Some well-meaning Christians may find themselves off God's narrow road without realizing what has even happened. There is then a choice to make when the realization comes that we've been led astray...whether it be self-study that pointed out the error of our ways, or a watchman who warned us something might be off. We have to repent and quickly turn back to the Word of God, Truth, and follow the one true Jesus when it's discovered...otherwise we will end up hanging out in the land of deception for way too long.

Sadly, some may flatly refuse to accept the Truth of God's Holy Word...occupying themselves with deceiving spirits and demonic teachings. They will hold onto the "idol" in their right hand...refusing to call it the lie that it is.

Romans 1:28-31 (NET) reads: *And just as they did not see fit to acknowledge God, God gave them over to a depraved mind, to do what should not be done. They are filled with every kind of unrighteousness, wickedness, covetousness, malice. They are rife with envy, murder, strife, deceit, hostility. They are gossips, slanderers, haters of God, insolent, arrogant, boastful, contrivers of all sorts of evil, disobedient to parents, senseless, covenant-breakers, heartless, ruthless. Although they fully know God's righteous decree that those who practice such things deserve to die, they not only do them but also approve of those who practice them.*

We must do as we are told in Hosea 6:1-3, *return to the Lord.* When God has torn us to pieces, He will then heal us. He will bandage our wounds. God will restore us so that we can live in peace with Him. Let's search for God and for His Truth as we travel along. Let's get to know the Lord and depend on Him. He will come and rescue us.

A Truth Journey like this will have many ups and downs. It will be painful at times. You may already be finding that to be true just by examining what Bible you are reading. I did. I made a change. I laid something down that I considered a "friend." It's not easy to let go of certain things and take hold of the Truth of God's Word in a more precise translation. Do we want Truth above comfort? It's imperative that we do! In 2 Timothy 3:4-5 we are warned about loving pleasure rather than being lovers of God. If we only maintain an outward appearance of religion, we will have rejected the power of God in our lives.

Daniel, chapter nine, tells us about how compassionate and forgiving our God is, even when we have rebelled against Him. God warned many through His prophets. But just as Israel did, many turn away from God and don't obey Him much of the time. God *will* get His way. His Word is Truth, and it is to be obeyed. We can ignore it for as long as we choose. But we should not then be complaining about the consequence/discipline that comes our way.

Sadly, sometimes the consequences are not even any fault of our own but have come because of the disobedience of others. Either way, we wonder why God allows these things to happen? God doesn't want any of "it" to happen. Why do bad things happen to good people? Why does anything good happen to us at all? There was only One who was ever really good/perfect, and that is Jesus.

We deserve God's wrath. Instead, the Father sent us His one and only Son, Jesus, to save us from this fallen world. All our Father asks is that we turn to Jesus, repent, and be saved. But many times, all we want is what we want, and then we want God to bless us in the process of living our own lives, doing our own thing exactly the way we choose to do it. Psalm 1 tells us our real blessings are found in obeying the Lord's commands, meditating on them day and night in the Bible. Maybe it's time to examine what translation you are reading. Do some investigation as to its origin and style. There are many search engines available for this task. Make sure your Bible is as it should be. If it is not, prayerfully lay it down.

To briefly sum up some translations:

King James Version - Finished in 1611. Written by 47 scholars. Revered for 400 years.

New International Version – Conceived in 1965. Written by 15 scholars. Known for readability.

New American Standard Bible – Evolved from ASV of 1901. Word for word translation.

New King James Version – Commissioned in 1975. Written by 130 scholars. Updates the KJV.

English Standard Version – Published in 2001. Some say it's too liberal, or too dynamic.

New Living Translation – Completed in 1996. Combined word-for-word/thought-for-thought.

21st Century King James Version – Published 1994. Easier to read than KJV.

The Message – One author. Published in segments 1993 – 2002. Contains translation errors.

The Passion Translation – 2017-2018. Re-worded and re-written Bible. Author: B. Simmons.

Modern English Version – Completed in 2013. Word-for-word. Stays close to KJV.

New English Translation – Twenty Scholars. First available online 2005. Read, studied, and checked by more people than any other Bible translation in history.

(Information gathered from gotquestions.org)

Isaiah prophesied that people will honor God with their lips, but their heart will be far from Him. It goes on to say that many will worship God in vain following the commandments of men. Sadly, in the expression of Christianity across America, and around the world, we are not hearing the Truth as it needs to be taught—not in some pulpits, not in a lot of the worship music, not even in all our Bibles, or studies, or Christian books we read...deception is everywhere and on the rise. We have been warned in Matthew 24!

Let's pay attention and keep seeking the pure Truth of the Gospel of Jesus Christ!

All scripture is inspired by God. It says so in 2 Timothy 3:16-17. The Bible has a great purpose. It is there to teach us, rebuke us, correct us, and train us in righteousness. We are to be dedicated to God and to His Word. In doing so, we will be capable and ready for everything God is calling us to do for His Kingdom until Jesus returns!

Some useful facts about the Holy Bible:

The Bible is 66 books, written in three different languages; Greek, Hebrew, Aramaic.

It was written on three different continents; Asia, Africa, and Europe.

It was penned by 40 different authors from all different walks of life from kings, to prophets, to peasants.

The Bible was written over a span of 1,500 years.

There are four different authors of the gospels from their four different perspectives. They are written for four different audiences for different purposes.

John – So that you might believe.

Matthew – Written to a Jewish audience.

Mark – Written to a Gentile audience.

Luke – Writes an orderly account as a historian.

The Bible was written by eyewitness…those who heard, saw, and touched the things written about. It was written during the lifetime of other eyewitnesses. This is important because those other eyewitnesses could hold the Biblical writers accountable. Christ appeared to over 500 people at one time after His resurrection. Over

300 eyewitnesses were still alive when 1 Corinthians was written.

Many claim the Bible has been changed many times...things were added on later. This is a multi-layered problem. There are over 6,000 Greek manuscripts alone. To change them, they would have to change all 6,000. Also, the early church fathers had a habit of writing extensive commentary of the New Testament. If all we had were their writings, we could reproduce all of the New Testament except for eleven verses...so the commentaries would also have to be changed.

Others say it's been translated so many times...it's unreliable. But the Bible was not translated from other translations. Each reliable translation goes back to Greek, Aramaic, and Hebrew manuscripts. Each translation comes from the same source.

Some complain that we don't have any of the originals. We don't. But this is a very good thing. If the original could be tampered with, instead of having to change 6,000 copies, it would be a problem.

"But men wrote the Bible." If you can't trust it or believe it because men wrote it...you would have to burn every book you own.

(These facts were gathered from Voddie Baucham's sermon on this subject.)

Let's pray:
Father in Heaven, Your Word is a gift and we treasure it. Help us to use it as You have intended, to read it regularly, to believe it, to follow it, and to share it with others. Your Truth is what we long for. In Jesus' name. Amen.

Chapter Three Reflections

1) The watchman sees a problem and knows it needs to be announced. Some will heed the warning…some won't…but that's not the watchman's responsibility. He let them know. That is his job. Theirs is to take notice. (Page 26)

2) As Christians today, there are a lot of things we need to be warned about. But we can't have our eyes looking in every direction at all times. We need each other. *Although an assailant may overpower one person, two can withstand him. Moreover, a three-stranded cord is not quickly broken.* Ecclesiastes 4:12 (NET) (Page 27)

3) Perhaps we need to go back to the "drawing board" and look first at which Bible we are using? Where are we getting our information? Yes, every "reliable" Bible comes from the Greek, Aramaic, and Hebrew writings of the Scribes. (Page 27)

4) Bibles should be translated by committees. Any translation by a single person can cause us to question its accountability. (Page 29)

5) What's most important in any translation is the faithfulness of the Bible we are reading. (Page 29)

6) When reading our Bibles, it is always best to hold any Scripture up to the test like the Bereans would do. Today, we can easily look up two or three other translations on the Internet to check for accuracy of the thoughts and the words used. (Page 30)

7) There is so much deception mixed in with the Truth of Christianity these days…maybe since the beginning of time…that it's not surprising our "Watchman" has warned us of all this in His Word. (Page 30)

8) Do we want Truth above comfort? It's imperative that we do! In 2 Timothy 3:4-5 we are warned about loving pleasure rather than being lovers of God. If we only maintain an outward appearance of religion, we will have rejected the power of God in our lives. (Page 32)

NOTES

*(These Reflection/Note pages may be duplicated
and used for group discussions when needed.)*

CHAPTER FOUR

REPENTANCE

There is a story told of a famous coach whose team had lost the playoffs the previous season. They were gathering for the first practice of the new season. Thinking they were going to be told about how to better strategize, play smarter, play better, they were surprised when their coach simply held up a football and announced to all of them, "This is a football."

I took that very simple yet astute idea and used it for my Bible study group one Wednesday morning as we entered into the subject of the week on Repentance. Since I didn't have an official football in the house, I used the official baseball that I did have which belongs to my grandson. It is a signed, official, major league ball that a friend had gifted to him.

Starting the morning with praying Psalm 25, we were all reminded that we should be asking God's Holy Spirit to help us understand His ways. We should be asking God to teach us His paths and guide us into His Truth. God is both kind and fair, and He alone teaches sinners the right way to live. When we humble ourselves, our Father will show us what is right. God will teach the humble His ways. We are to seek our Father's forgiveness for our sins, and He will show us the way to live.

2 Peter 3:9 (NET) says, *The Lord is not slow concerning his promise, as some regard slowness, but is being patient toward you,*

because he does not wish for any to perish but for all to come to repentance.

Why is repentance so important on this Truth Journey? Because without it, we can't even begin. There is no journey… Repentance is our starting point with Jesus. Picture yourself at the start of a race behind the line drawn on the track. Runners are poised and ready. The starter gun is about to be shot off…What will be the first step you take to run the race of life set before you with Jesus? Repentance! It is as fundamental to Christianity as, "This is a football" is to a team of athletes about ready to begin a new season of ball. The world would like us to be attracted to shiny objects, to new ideas, to better ways, easier ways, wider paths, broader ideas, easier routes to "victory". We will get into a lot of those as we work our way through the chapters of this book. But before we do, if we don't understand the fundamentals of Christianity, then the difference between deception and Truth won't even make sense. We won't understand how far off the path we can get. The things the world is offering to us will look very attractive most times, or perhaps even dark at other times, but we will go after them if we don't start the race as God has designed it…with repentance.

I ran across a quote by a man named Vance Havner while preparing the Bible study on repentance that blew me away. I couldn't have found it if I'd searched day and night for weeks. A quote that includes both a ball and repentance was too perfect! Mr. Havner said this: "We are trying to play ball without the ball when the church tries to evangelize before she has repented. The church can do many things after she has repented, but nothing until she first repents."

…if my people, who belong to me, humble themselves, pray, seek to please me, and repudiate their sinful practices, then I will respond from heaven, forgive their sin, and heal their land.
2 Chronicles 7:14 (NET)

The church could mean a building where we meet…and perhaps he meant it that way. But let's look at it another way. We, you and I, are the church. As believers in Jesus Christ, we are the body of Christ, with Jesus being the head of the body. Either individually, or together, we are called to evangelize, to let others know what Jesus died to give us…Salvation! Jesus and His Cross cleansed us from our sins, making a way for us to stand before our Father in Heaven one day as white as snow. That is why we must start with a repentant heart…a heart that now wants Jesus as Savior. Many think repentance is being sorry/remorseful for what we have done. And that is true, partly. But we must realize that remorse is not full repentance. Repentance includes coming into agreement with what God's Word says. It is changing our mind. It's wanting what God wants, loving what God loves, and hating what God hates. Is that the beginning of full repentance? We're almost there. At first, repentance is when we come to the point in our lives where we no longer reject Jesus as Lord. For many of us, for many years sometimes, we have rejected Jesus. We have wanted nothing to do with Jesus. Many people don't even think they need a Savior. They don't believe Jesus is the Son of God, and even if they did, they don't want Him messing in their lives. They seem to be doing just fine on their own. They think they don't need the football to play the game. They can just run around on the field, talk to the other players, and ignore the "elephant" in the room—which is they have no ball on the field!

The "football" is when we acknowledge Jesus…the Gospel Truth of His life, death, burial, resurrection, ascension, and coming back again. It's when the Coach/God sees a change in our attitude, in our heart, and He gives us the football/Holy Spirit, and we're really playing the game fully alive now. Then, suddenly, what we're doing in this life/game starts to make sense. Oh, this is why these lines are on the field! This is why there are goalposts at each end! This is how we score points for the team! We have a reason for being here on planet earth.

Repentance initially is giving God our broken heart, our shattered life, our hurting soul, our innumerable sins, and our emptiness. We hand it all over and open ourselves up to the saving work of the Lord Jesus Christ. It's coming to the end of ourselves.

Sadly, today's world looks too much like what is written about in 2 Timothy 3:1-5 (NET);

But understand this, that in the last days difficult times will come. For people will be lovers of themselves, lovers of money, boastful, arrogant, blasphemers, disobedient to parents, ungrateful, unholy, unloving, irreconcilable, slanderers, without self-control, savage, opposed to what is good, treacherous, reckless, conceited, loving pleasure rather than loving God. They will maintain the outward appearance of religion but will have repudiated its power. So avoid people like these.

Today, people are lovers of themselves. Money equates success. We are boastful, proud, ungrateful, unholy, and without self-control, to name just some of what is listed in these verses. When we come to the end of all of this, or at least recognize we need to, we can get to the place where we want something different in our lives...to a place of repentance.

Caution! When we do come to this place, there will still be many shiny objects calling themselves "Jesus." They will be waiting to swoop us up and carry us away into deception. This "Jesus" can look, sound, smell, act, and respond very much like our real Jesus. As we read in 2 Corinthians 11:3-4, just as the serpent deceived Eve, our minds can be led astray. All the while our Father in Heaven is calling us to Him, others will come proclaiming another "Jesus" different than the true Jesus of the Bible.

To illustrate this, I asked my Bible study group what they thought this other "Jesus" would look like? Then I brought out another baseball...it looked very much like the official major league baseball I had first shown them. It even had a signature on it and was made by the same company. It also belonged to my grandson...it was a game ball his coach had signed and given to him from little league. Yes, it could be used to play the game, but it did not hold the same "promise" that the major league baseball held. And if this little league ball were handed to a professional baseball player, even if they were blindfolded, they would know instantly it was not the ball they played with. My prayer, even in writing this book, is that we get better and better at detecting the deception from Truth, and the Truth from a lie. Let's dive so deep into the Truth of God's Word that nothing else will feel right...nothing else will satisfy our souls...nothing else will come close to the real Lord Jesus Christ!

Sometimes we are handed these other baseballs...another "Jesus" from the world. But sometimes we come across them even in our churches, in our worship music, and in so-called Christian books. They can sound like a good lecture or book provided in a business setting to inspire workers on the job. This is sometimes called, "Moralistic Therapeutic Deism" (MTD). It is a talk that might include an ambiguous "god," and how he would like it if we were nice to one another. We are told how we should play fair, be good, and also it's important to be happy and feel good. With MTD we are told about a loving and grace-filled god, but not the real God whose wrath would come upon us if not for the Lord Jesus Christ taking the sins of the world upon Himself on the Cross. With MTD, good people do get to go to Heaven. This is a lie.

Moralistic Therapeutic Deism is a fake baseball! It is not the real deal. It is from a little league and it is what the world/Satan would like us to believe to keep us from the real major league baseball in life, the Lord Jesus Christ. The problem is, these "lectures" sound so good, and can be so interesting, we don't even realize that the official major league baseball/the Gospel Truth is missing! Sadly, some pastors will camp in the Old Testament, too, sharing lots of Scripture, but very little if any true Gospel teaching. Then we leave church, or lay down the book, or sing the worship songs, and "feel" good! This can be MTD. We are encouraged...ready to meet whatever challenge we now have to go through. Unfortunately, we will quickly lose steam because there was so little Gospel Truth in what we have just heard. It has no power to sustain us on life's playing field. It's only a placebo, making us feel good about ourselves just long enough to make us forget that we need Jesus Christ to rescue us!

Watch out for MTD! It will even tell us that God created the world, and watches over it. But that God doesn't really need to be involved in our lives unless there is a huge problem. This message can be attractive and appealing, but also very destructive! It will make us think God is failing us, that Christianity doesn't work, and we might as well get back to doing things in our own strength...which is exactly what we will be doing after hearing a MTD message anyway.

The real Jesus has our name inscribed on the palm of His hands. (Isaiah 49:16) Just as this real official major league baseball has a golden glover's signature on it! The little league baseball is signed by my grandson's coach, which he was very excited about, by the way. But it just doesn't compare to the official baseball signed by a professional. We can get excited by some of the things we hear in the world. Of course, we should be kind, of course we should try to be good, of course it's nice to be happy...but those are not what we

43

should be focused on. Those things do come into our lives in a powerful way by first knowing Jesus and being filled with the Holy Spirit. But we need to keep things in the right order, the Biblical order.

When we give our lives, our heart, our soul to Jesus, bowing in humility before Him, our Lord hears us. (2 Chronicles 34:27.) We can be assured of this. It is what our Father is waiting for. It's why Jesus' return is taking much longer than we would like. The Lord wants that none should perish and all will come to repentance. But not all will. If you haven't as yet and would like to, there is no time like the present. Begin by laying down your life and no longer rejecting Jesus Christ as Lord. Call out to Him! Your request will be heard, and you can run the true race in life, the one that will lead you safely Home.

In Ephesians 4, starting in verse 17, we are told to no longer live in the futility of our own thinking as the Gentiles in the Bible were have said to do. With a hard heart, we are separated from God. We are told to lay aside our former way of life, which is corrupt and deceitful, and be renewed in the spirit of our mind. We can be made new! It's so refreshing to let go of the old! All those heavy coats of guilt, regret, unforgiveness, etc…can be left behind. The blood of Jesus, shed on the Cross for those who believe, will wash us clean when we stop rejecting the greatest gift known to man!

What stops people from repenting? Is it pride? Yes. But it is a lot more than that. It not only runs deeper, but also higher than we realize. Biblically, it is a spiritual battle fought in the heavenlies. Not the Heaven where we go when we die, but the space above this Earth where the spiritual forces of darkness roam about. We can read about those in Ephesians 6. In verses 12-14, it talks about our struggle not being against flesh and blood, but there are rulers, powers, world rulers, and spiritual forces of evil in the heavens. We can also read about the Armor of God shortly after that…which is much needed in the world we live in to battle against these things.

The ultimate spiritual battle, in the end times, will be between two opposing forces: The spirit that influenced Jezebel in the Old Testament, and the Holy Spirit that lived in Elijah. This makes sense because Elijah's spirit is one of repentance, the Word of God, and the voice of Heaven. The spirit that filled Jezebel was there to hinder and defeat the spirit of Elijah. Jezebel had a narcissistic spirit, an all-about-me spirit, an everyone-else-is-to-blame spirit. Before Jesus returns, the same spirit of Elijah is here to prepare hearts to meet the Lord. (Luke 1:17) The spirit Jezebel had is here to distract, distort, and cause spiritual adultery. She was worshipping other gods besides the one true God of Heaven like Elijah did.

If we wonder why there is such a struggle in this world and in our own souls, this is why! Jezebel is written about in Revelation 2:18-21. It talks about the church in Thyatira tolerating her and her teaching. She deceives God's servants. And, she is not willing to repent! If you don't think you're ready to repent, you might want to "test the spirits" as it says in 1 John 4:1 and see if you're listening to a false, lying spirit! Don't let the spirit that filled Jezebel take you down, down, down...that's where Jezebel headed when she was all done!

Repentance is not complicated. Remember, "This is a football." But the simplicity of the Gospel is sadly overlooked in today's world, and even sometimes in today's churches. The Gospel needs nothing added to it or subtracted from it. There is such Good News in Jesus Christ, and it is sufficient. But we must be willing to bend a knee to the will of God, to the reality that we are sinners who need to repent, and come into agreement with God's Word.

After our initial repentance, we should continue to repent practically every day of our life. There will be things coming against us and tempting us into all sorts of thoughts, actions, and deeds. This is normal. Life doesn't suddenly become perfect when Jesus is our Lord. Even Paul of the Bible said he did the things he didn't want to do, and the things he wanted to do he didn't do—and he wrote the majority of the New Testament. Paul needed Jesus every day, and so do we! We need Jesus to fight the good fight of faith! Yes, the Victory was won on the Cross. But the battles continue to rage on this Earth until Jesus returns. When we seek God's forgiveness daily for the things we do (1 John 1:9), it is not that we are being re-justified in the eyes of our Father. It is simply that we are showing the assurance in which we are walking because Christ has paid the ultimate price for our freedom. We continue to call out to Him, knowing He is there. Knowing we have been set free! And we can walk boldly in that freedom, proclaiming the Good News of Jesus Christ.

When God created this world, He set two large lights in the sky.

One being the sun, the other being the moon. The only problem is the moon cannot make light on its own. The moon can only reflect the sun. We are much the same. We can be a bright light in this world, as we are called to be. But only when we are reflecting the Son of God. The Holy Spirit is who shines brightly through us. Without Him, life is dark, cold, and without purpose. I heard an astronaut say that from their spacecraft, the side of it that is facing the sun is hot. The side that is facing away from the sun, is in the dark and is very cold. What a perfect illustration of what's important in this life.

In our next chapter we will talk about Salvation and Propitiation. Yes, they are large words with large meanings, but we need not fear. The Gospel is simple and true. We will talk about what we do once we have repented. After repentance/no-longer-rejecting-Jesus, what follows is another important step we will take in the race of life.

If you haven't already, get ready to push off from the starting block by repenting right now…then continue to repent so as it says in Acts 3:19-20, after turning from our sins and having them wiped out, *times of refreshing may come from the presence of the Lord…*!

Runners! On your mark! Get set! Go! And don't forget the "football".

Let's pray:
Father, You are almighty, all-knowing, all-forgiving, and we seek to know You. We want to love the things You love, and hate the things You hate. We come into agreement with You, we believe that Jesus is Lord, that He died on a Cross for us, that He was buried, and that He rose again. We will live our lives believing that Jesus is coming back again, and desiring to walk in obedience to You each day. In Jesus' name. Amen.

Chapter Four Reflections

1) We should be asking God's Holy Spirit to teach us His paths and guide us into His Truth. God is both kind and fair, and He alone teaches sinners the right way to live. (Page 39)

2) Repentance! It is as fundamental to Christianity as, "This is a football" is to a team of athletes about ready to begin a new season of ball. (Page 40)

3) "We are trying to play ball without the ball when the church tries to evangelize before she has repented. The church can do many things after she has repented but nothing until she first repents." (Page 40)

4) Many think repentance is being sorry/remorseful for what we have done. And that is true, partly. But we must realize that remorse is not full repentance. Repentance includes coming into agreement with what God's Word says. It is changing our mind. (Page 41)

5) Repentance initially is giving God our broken heart, our shattered life, our hurting soul, our innumerable sins, and our emptiness. We hand it all over and open ourselves up to the saving work of the Lord Jesus Christ. It's coming to the end of ourselves. (Page 41)

6) Caution! When we do come to this place, there will still be many shiny objects calling themselves "Jesus". They will be waiting to swoop us up and carry us away into deception. (Page 42)

7) My prayer, even in writing this book, is that we get better and better at detecting the deception from Truth, and the Truth from a lie. Let's dive so deep into the Truth of God's Word that nothing else will feel right...nothing else will satisfy our souls...nothing else will come close to the real Lord Jesus Christ! (Page 42)

8) "Moralistic Therapeutic Deism" (MTD). It is a talk that might include an ambiguous "god," and how He would like it if we were nice to one another. We are told how we should play fair, be good, and also it's important to be happy and feel good. With MTD, are told about a loving and grace-filled god, but not the real God whose wrath would come upon us if not for the Lord Jesus taking the sins of the world upon Himself on the Cross. With MTD, good people do get to go to Heaven. This is a lie. (Page 42)

NOTES

*(These Reflection/Note pages may be duplicated
and used for group discussions when needed.)*

CHAPTER FIVE

SALVATION

A great deal of this chapter was taken after hearing Paul Washer speak on the subject of Salvation. It seemed there was no need to reinvent the wheel. Washer's sermons are very Gospel-centered and encouraging for all who have the opportunity to listen to him. He is a rare gem in today's world. He is *not ashamed of the gospel, for it is God's power for salvation to everyone who believes, to the Jew first and also to the Greek. For the righteousness of God is revealed in the gospel from faith to faith, just as it is written, "The righteous by faith will live."* Romans 1:16-17 (NET)

When Kobe Bryant, his daughter, and others died tragically in a helicopter crash at the beginning of the year 2020, little did we know that the whole of the year would be a wake-up call for everyone to call on Jesus even more during such trying times in our world. Through faith in Jesus Christ alone, there can be Salvation and a growing holiness in our hearts as we turn away from the things of this world. We are to not get caught up in the chaos and confusion going on, but to continually turn toward our true hope of Heaven. How is this done?

After turning our back on sin by doing a 180-degree turn toward Jesus in repentance, we can rejoice in the very famous verse, John 3:16 (NET) that says; *For this is the way God loved the world: He gave his one and only Son, so that everyone who believes in him will not perish but have eternal life.* Our Father in Heaven (We are God's children once we have taken this step.), sent His only begotten Son to this earth, while we were still sinners, and made Jesus, who knew no, sin to be sin on our behalf. Jesus sweat great drops of blood in the Garden of Gethsemane, not because of the physical torture He was about to endure, but because of the spiritual torture that He knew awaited Him. Others went to their own cross after Jesus—they did so because they were spreading the Good News of what Jesus had already done. But they didn't sweat drops of blood even though they gave up their physical life for the Gospel. Why? Because Jesus was going to be on that Cross while His very own Father turned away from Him…placing all the sin of the whole world upon Him. That's the torture that awaited the Father's only perfect Son. That is love…on both of their parts. Why would the Father who hates not only the sin, but also the sinner (see Psalm 5:5-6) do such a thing? Because God is love. I believe the world waters down this full Truth! The world says, "God hates the sin, but loves the sinner." That is not biblical! It is heresy! And it makes it so that we don't really understand how much the Father sacrificed for us because He *is* love.

In Romans 5:6-8, it talks about how Christ died for the ungodly, demonstrating God's love for us, while we were still sinners. While we were still hated by the Father, Christ died for us. As humans, the Bible says we would possibly die for a good person…but Jesus died for us while we were not a good person. As Jesus' friends slept, He was sweating drops of blood in spiritual agony. As Judas betrayed Jesus with a kiss, He was still willing to go forward with the plan. After Peter denied Jesus three times, Jesus kept on… That's devotion. Talk about loving your enemies!! There is no *greater* love than what Christ displayed in His time here on earth.

We need to, *"Awake O sleeper! Rise from the Dead, and Christ will shine on you!"* Ephesians 5:14 (NET) This is no time to be resting on our laurels, or anything else for that matter. It's time to be fully aware, awake, and in Christ as this world draws to a close. Do we, or do we not, believe the Word of God? Romans 13:11 (NET) says, *that it is already the hour for us to awake from sleep, for our salvation is now nearer than when we became believers.* Do we believe this? One pastor said, "It's never been this late before." How true is that!! This is not "date-setting", this is Bible-believing!

Each day we live on this Earth is one day closer to living in Heaven or Hell for all of eternity for every one of us. We can stick our heads in the sand and delay our decision, but we can't delay what is coming. There is a date set that only the Father knows, and He is wanting that none perish, all the time knowing that many will. If your child had died to save others, wouldn't you want some awareness given to it? Wouldn't you want people to wake up and get the word out so that your child's death wouldn't be in vain? I know a little of that personally because my son died. He battled leukemia. I don't want any of his life/death to be in vain. If writing this book and others I have written bring a little bit of God's Truth into people's lives because of what I learned in my own son's suffering, I am thankful for how God might use it. And my son is no Savior of the world, but he is dearly loved and always will be by our family and friends.

Let's talk about Salvation in more depth now, *since all must enter by the narrow gate and broad is the way that leads to destruction.* (Matt. 7:13) We don't want anyone to go the broad way. Salvation is a gift that is given to us by faith. Before we come to believe, we are to repent. That is the first step toward the narrow gate. It doesn't mean we will no longer sin, it means we are ready to enter into a relationship with Jesus Christ and a completely different relationship with the sin in our lives. Yes, we will still sin…but we will no longer enjoy it as we once did.

After we believe on the Lord Jesus Christ, we continue in deeper repentance through the years. This builds our faith. The more we realize all of which we have been forgiven, the more our faith will be strengthened. It's a process that can continue on each day we live here on Earth through obedience in repentance. We are to grow more and more in love with our Savior by hating the things God hates and loving the things God loves. The more we do this, the more removed we are from the things of this world. In 1 John 2:15, we are told not to love the things of this world. It says if we do, the love of the Father is not in us. That seems rather harsh…I mean think of that beautiful sunset, that amazing white sandy beach, the tropical fish when snorkeling, the snowy Alps…how can we not "love" what we see? Because, the beauty of our Father so outshines what He has made. We are told to not love the creation but to love the Creator.

There is a certain well-known and entirely overrated book on the

53

Christian market today that capitalizes the word "Creation". That's another very deceptive way of taking our focus off of our God and placing it on the "gods" of this world. We have to keep our eyes and ears open for these deceptions. As it says in Revelation many times, *"The one who has an ear had better hear what the Spirit says to the churches."* We need to listen for what the Holy Spirit is doing and pointing out, otherwise we will be like those talked about in Ephesians 4:14...*we will be children tossed back and forth by waves and carried about by every wind of teaching...* There are deceitful schemes going on all around us in the expression of Christianity today, across America and beyond.

And what does all this have to do with Salvation? Let's take a longer look at Matthew 7:13-14 (NET), *"Enter through the narrow gate, because the gate is wide and the way is spacious that leads to destruction, and there are many who enter through it. How narrow is the gate and difficult the way that leads to life, and there are few who find it!"* There is a way of Salvation, but it is narrow, and few find it. Many prayed a "sinner's prayer" one Sunday morning, and now think they have a saving faith. This very well may be true...or may not be. Does praying a prayer once in our life, and then going on to live life as we've always known it constitute Salvation? I have heard it said that we are not saved this way, but we can be saved in spite of it. Even if the prayer is sincere, can we trust in a heart that is "desperately wicked"? (Jeremiah 17:9) Probably not! Does this mean there is a better formula for a prayer to save us? No. It means there is no formula, there is only the evidence of a changed heart after a person has come to the point in their life of wanting Jesus as their Savior.

How do we know we are saved for all of eternity? Do you know if you are? I had to ask myself this same question... Of course, we want to go to Heaven when we're asked about it. That's a given. We may even acknowledge that we are a sinner. And that's good...to take a look at our lives and see what's really going on. But how sad that many may be deceived thinking they are going to Heaven when they are not because they once prayed a prayer! This is not about trying to be moral, this is about what Jesus has done in our once stone-cold heart...our once very stubborn heart...our once very rebellious heart. If there has been evidence over time of some change…that is an indication that the Holy Spirit has truly come to dwell within us. The Holy Spirit lives within the heart of a true believer. The Holy Spirit is a promise from our Father in Heaven, a gift that comes when we give our heart to Him in repentance and call out to Jesus to be the Lord and Savior of our life. It's believing in Who God is and wanting what He wants instead of believing in ourselves and wanting what we want. It is being willing to bend toward God's will, resisting our own. James 4:7 (NET) says, *So submit to God. But resist the devil and he will flee from you.* There are powerful spiritual forces at work when we bend a knee to God, as all will do one day. Yes, it doesn't matter if you have Jesus as your Savior or not…there will be no choice in the end. But there will be a separation at that time…some will go to Heaven, others will go to Hell.

I would suspect if you have gotten this far into this book, you are a believer. Otherwise, these words would be too offensive to you. So thank you, and I'm glad we are in the family of God together. And as iron sharpens iron, we should help each other along the way to continue to walk in the faith we have been given…to continue to ask ourselves and one another if God is working in our life? Do we continue to see sin as God sees it? Are we desiring a closer and closer walk with Jesus, wanting to follow Him and to know Him? Do we repent often, quickly, and then receive the forgiveness we have been offered? Do we forgive others? These are signs of a genuine Christian. This is the process of sanctification, which we will talk a lot about in this book.

Let's take a look at the heart for a bit. It is the core essence of who we are. It is what will be drastically changed at Salvation and beyond. Paul writes in Romans 10:9-10 that we need to confess with our mouth that we have a saving faith in Jesus Christ. We are to believe in our heart that God raised Jesus from the dead. The heart believes, and the mouth confesses. The public confession is evidence that the heart believes. The heart believes and helps the mouth confess. They work in union with each other. Although "work" may be the wrong terminology since Salvation is by grace and grace alone. If we had 99.9 percent of Jesus working, and .1 percent of us working, we would be lost for all of eternity. We need ALL of Jesus, and none of us for this to "work".

If we take a look at the passage of Scripture in

Matthew 7:21 (NET) that says, *"Not everyone who says to me, 'Lord, Lord', will enter into the kingdom of heaven—only the one who does the will of my Father in heaven."* This is not talking about what we do, as the people stated just after this verse about how they cast out demons and did many powerful deeds. That's the .1 percent. "Hey, look what we've done. Now let us in!" That's not the way it works. To do the will of the Father in Heaven, we have to be obedient to what He asks of us, which is to believe in the One He has sent to save us. Yes, we can do many good and powerful deeds after that, but that will not save us. Only Jesus can and will save us.

How does this work? It's sort of another large word called Regeneration. This means to re-create. We are made into a new person and we are given a heart of flesh in exchange for the heart of stone that we once had. Then the changes that occur are the evidence of what has happened. Yes, the Word says we will know them by their Fruit. The Holy Spirit comes with Fruit that grows in us and allows the light of Jesus to shine through our lives. We need to ask ourselves, "Do we look any different than those in the world around us?" How's our Fruit looking? Is it ripe? Is it luscious? Is it desirable? If our answer is ambiguous, or we look more like a sour lemon, we need to repent immediately. Our Father is more than willing to clean us up and get us back on track each and every time!

In Romans, we read in 3:23-25 that all sin, all fall short, but because of the Propitiation, we are forgiven. The word Propitiation is found in those verses, but not in every translation. Your Bible may say, "Mercy Seat," or "Sacrifice." They all mean that there has been an appeasement, which means to "satisfy or relieve a demand," for the sin in our life. What we have done that is wrong has now been righted. The justification required by a just God is satisfied. And we are a changed person in God's sight.

When Paul, formally known as Saul, walked this earth, he was an enemy of the early Christians known as the Way. He thought Jesus was a terrible blasphemer and that the Christians were a sect that should be gotten rid of. He was zealous for God…the same God we as Christians worship today, minus Jesus. Saul had not yet believed that Jesus was the true Messiah. Saul was misdirected, he was wrong, and his thoughts needed to be changed. When our thoughts change about God's Truth, everything in our life will change. When Saul encountered Jesus on the road to Damascus, what he was once blinded to, he now saw clearly…Jesus. The One Saul thought was a blasphemer, was not. Jesus was exactly who He claimed to be, the Messiah the Jewish people had been waiting for. Saul's will changed…his emotions changed…and Christ was then esteemed in Paul's new life of faith. Can we say the same for our life? It's a good question to ask ourselves.

Will we still sin after Salvation? Of course. Paul did. We will, too. But now we have a new way of dealing with our sin rather than sweeping it under the rug. We have true forgiveness through the blood of Jesus Christ. Sadly, the Gospel Truth is getting watered down in these latter days, and even more sadly, we sometimes don't recognize it. Why? Because there is so much deception all around us and we start to become numb to the lies.

Think of it this way… Take a look at the lawn in your yard if you have one. Is it nice and green, mowed, and looking good? Ours is this time of year when the rains come. If you were to go out and grab a handful or two of that nice green grass, it might not be all that you were expecting. Unless you're a super-gardener and have a putting green in your yard, there are probably weeds mixed in with the grass. We don't notice them so much from a distance, or even as we hold them in our hand. It's not like the weeds feel all that much different from the true grass. But if we pick through the mixture with our fingers, really examining it, we can separate the grass from the weeds. The deception going on in the world today can be much the same. It is there, we don't see it from a distance, we don't really notice it a lot of the time when we hear it in a song, or sermon, or read it in a book, if we're not paying close attention. But if we look at it up close, and ask God to take the scales from our eyes, we are given some discernment. We will begin to listen to the words being spoken…listening for the Gospel of Jesus Christ. The one true Jesus. We will listen for a message that contains sin, repentance, the Cross, the blood, forgiveness, and the resurrection. Are they there? Even in Old Testament teachings, the message can and should point to Jesus Christ crucified. Is that what we're hearing or is it just a feel-good song, a make me rich message, a book on success or how to better live our life? Is what we're hearing there to make us happier and to help us get along with others? Is it all about signs, wonders, and emotions? Or would the sermon being preached actually have a message that would save a lost soul? Would the words in the worship music convict a heart? Could someone who doesn't know Jesus learn about Him, desire to know Him, and give their heart to Him when all is said and done? If not, why not? Are there too many weeds in the midst of a little bit of Scripture? Too many ambiguous lyrics that talk about love and not the real Source of that love? Let's start to pay more attention. Everyone's eternal lives depend on it.

The hard stuff isn't talked about as much these days. We have moved away from the "fire and brimstone" preaching of 100-150 years ago. Have we ever wondered why? Could it be because a watered-down Sunday morning sermon or worship song is the working of the antichrist? You may think I've gone too far here…and we will get into this more later. But I'm just introducing this to you here for a reason. I'm using the same tactic the antichrist is using in Christianity today. I'm getting you "used to" something that I will talk more about later so there will be less of a shock factor when it comes in full force. Ever heard of the frog in the pot that doesn't realize the heat is being turned up to boiling? Same reasoning. The expression of Christianity across the world has been changing in preparation for end-time prophecy to take place. It can't just be fire-and-brimstone sermon one day, and One World Religion the next. We would never accept it. But if Satan introduces these things to us slowly, gradually, a little dab at a time…we will barely notice that our lawn has turned to weeds. It's still green, we can still mow it…BUT it's not true lawn! It is a fake!!

Some will say, "God saved me from my sin." This is another deception, explains Paul Washer. God has saved us from so much more than that. God has saved us from His wrath! The Father sent His only Son because Jesus is the only "Thing" that stands between us and God destroying us! God used Himself, by Himself, through Himself to save us, and it is for God's Glory! We deserve to be punished. Jesus took the punishment for us. We deserve Hell for all of eternity. Jesus put a stop to the accusation of Satan by dying on the Cross as the Propitiation required. A just God can't just let us go…He would not be just, then. It would be like a judge letting us off with no punishment and no penalty after we committed a heinous crime. It would be unfair, and we would not respect/admire/trust a judge like that…especially if the crime was committed against someone we love and the criminal was set free with no consequences whatsoever. I heard it said, "Christ is the Ark that saves us from the flood of God's wrath." So true! So true!! We should marvel at what God has done. No wonder the enemy is working so God's wrath will be subdued in today's sermons...too many would see the need for Jesus if it was fully understood that we actually deserve Hell. Instead, too many churches are toning it down, telling everyone God loves the sinner, and then just encouraging us to head off to breakfast! One day that pot will come to a boil, and the frog will be doomed. Let us not be that frog...because the frog in the pot example is deception also. It is...I'll explain in a future chapter.

Christ was not only crucified, He was raised from the dead! When the Gospel is preached, it must include both of these facts! The resurrection is the proof that the wrath of our Father in Heaven was satisfied. Let's not just talk about Jesus walking around on this Earth and healing the sick, raising the dead, and going to the Cross for our sins. Let's talk about what happened on the third day and beyond when Christ returns for His bride! In 1 Corinthians 15:17-19, it talks about if Christ has not been raised, then our faith is futile. We are still in our sin, and when we die, we will have perished. It goes on to say if we only have hope in this life, then we are to be pitied. But the Truth is, Christ has been raised! Hallelujah! God has a plan, we are part of it, and it's GOOD NEWS! Our every sin was covered by the death and resurrection of Jesus Christ. God's wrath has been fully satisfied! And sadly, it was what the Father had to do to His very own Son. Yes, the Father did it. Satan didn't do it. Our enemy doesn't have that kind of power. Even Jesus said in the Garden of Gethsemane that He could appeal to His Father and He would at once send more than twelve legions of angels! Now that's power. The Father gave us the Son, and the Son laid down His life willingly.

Isaiah 53:10 (NET) is a solemn piece of Scripture. It says, *Though the Lord desired to crush him and make him ill, once restitution is made, he will see descendants and enjoy long life, and the Lord's purpose will be accomplished through him.* Can you imagine crushing your own child? Making your own child ill for someone else? But our Father did that for us. That's what should be preached from our pulpits, sung in our worship songs, written about in our books! Give us some of that fire and brimstone Gospel teaching! We need it! Help us to always remember what our freedom cost!

Ahhh, the sweet sound of Salvation. Psalm 24:3-5 (NET) says, *Who is allowed to ascend the mountain of the Lord? Who may go up to his holy dwelling place? The one whose deeds are blameless and whose motives are pure, who does not lie, or make promises with no intention of keeping them. Such godly people are rewarded by the Lord, and vindicated by the God who delivers them.*

To be godly people, we need Salvation in Jesus Christ alone! It was paid for by the only Man qualified…Jesus! With the blood of Jesus, our hands can be cleaned, our hearts can be purified! When things start going haywire in our lives, when the world looks dismal, when the news is terrifying, we can remember that God has a plan and He will see it through to the end. We can read the end of the Book already…the revealing of Jesus Christ. Jesus is the Victor! And we will march in His parade! When we hear of "peace and security" in the news, rejoice! Jesus is almost at the gate, ready to descend to this Earth once again. *While people are saying, "There is peace and security," then sudden destruction will come upon them as labor pains come upon a pregnant woman, and they will not escape.*1 Thess. 5:3 (NET) There will not be peace and security on this Earth in the last days no matter what the papers say. When "peace and security" are in the headlines, it may look that way for a short time, but we can recognize it from Scripture and know that God is at work bringing about the New Heaven and the New Earth. "Peace and security" will be yet another deception, another lie from the enemy trying to win us over to his ways—to a One World Order. But we can be one of the elect who will not be deceived by it! We can call it what it is! A WEED! And toss it out, while embracing the Truth of God's Word about the end times and rejoice. Let's remember, we cannot put a stop to what is happening, no matter how hard we try. The apostasy (2 Thess. 2:3) will come because God's Word says it will. But we can be aware, watchful, and full of Hope while we pray!

If you have prayed the sinner's prayer, that is a good start. If you continue through the years after that repenting, believing, and keeping on in your relationship with Jesus Christ of Nazareth, you are a Christian who is being regenerated. Salvation is a supernatural event that takes place in the heart of anyone who is willing to turn to Jesus as Lord, turning them into a new creature. It will be/should be transformational. We should have continual fellowship with

Christ, desire a godly life, and feed upon Jesus as our daily Bread. We are to look for these evidences in our own life, and when we see them, continue on, and give thanks for God's amazing grace.

Let's pray:
Father in Heaven, may Your will be done in our lives. We want to no longer reject Christ Jesus, but accept Him as Lord and Savior each day until we meet Him face to face when we come into Your Kingdom, witnessing Your glory forevermore. By the power of the Holy Spirit, we will continue to walk out our days in obedience to You. And when we don't, we will repent, confess, and be cleansed. In Jesus' powerful name. Amen.

Chapter Five Reflections

1) After turning our back on sin by doing a 180-degree turn toward Jesus in repentance, we can rejoice in the very famous verse, John 3:16 (NET) that says; *For this is the way God loved the world: He gave his one and only Son, so that everyone who believes in him will not perish but have eternal life.* (Page 51)

2) Each day we live on this Earth is one day closer to living in Heaven or Hell for all of eternity for every one of us. We can stick our heads in the sand and delay our decision, but we can't delay what is coming. (Page 53)

3) Salvation is a gift that is given to us by faith. Before we come to believe, we are to repent. That is the first step toward the narrow gate. It doesn't mean we will no longer sin, it means we are ready to enter into a relationship with Jesus Christ and a completely different relationship with the sin in our lives. (Page 53)

4) There is a way of Salvation, but it is narrow, and few find it. Many prayed a "sinner's prayer" one Sunday morning, and now think they have a saving faith. This very well may be true…or may not be. (Page 54)

5) Does this mean there is a better formula for a prayer to save us? No. It means there is no formula, there is only the evidence of a changed heart after a person has come to the point in their life of wanting Jesus. (Page 54)

6) Do we continue to see sin as God sees it? Are we desiring a closer and closer walk with Jesus, wanting to follow Him and to know Him? Do we repent often, quickly, and then receive the forgiveness we have been offered? Do we forgive others? These are signs of a genuine Christian. (Page 55w)

7) We are made into a new person and we are given a heart of flesh in exchange for the heart of stone that we once had. Then the changes that occur are the evidence of what has happened. (Page 56)

8) God has saved us from His wrath! The Father sent His only Son because Jesus is the only "Thing" that stands between us and God destroying us! God used Himself, by Himself, through Himself to save us, and it is for God's Glory! (Page 58)

<u>*NOTES*</u>

*(These Reflection/Note pages may be duplicated
and used for group discussions when needed.)*

CHAPTER SIX

BAPTISM

After Repentance and Salvation, Baptism is our next step. We are pouring a firm foundation in Christ Jesus so we can know the Truth from the lies around us in today's world. There are many different baptisms talked about in the New Testament, so it can get a little confusing. But it doesn't need to be.

Let's start off simply by just saying that Baptism means "to submerge or immerse." When a person is baptized, they are submerged into something new, signifying that a change has taken place. What would that be biblically?—Our heart has been changed. When we repent of our past life, turning away from what's always been into something new, we have changed. This is not just trying to be a better person or trying to be moral and good: We're talking about a supernatural change that has taken place in our heart...at the core of our being.

It is like the story of St. Augustine, one of the Latin Fathers. Before he was a "saint," he was a man who must have partaken of certain sinful activities. It is written that a prostitute called out to him one day saying, "Augustine, it is I!" After calling to him more than once in this manner, he responded with, "Yes. But it is not I. I am not the same person I was."

Can we say that about ourselves after we have repented and have been saved through the atoning blood of Jesus Christ? Are we changed? And are we continuing to change? That is what makes our Salvation visible to the world around us. We are not the same person we once were.

In Ezekiel 36:25-26 (NET) it says, *I will sprinkle you with pure water, and you will be clean from all your impurities. I will purify you from all your idols. I will give you a new heart, and I will put a new spirit within you. I will remove the heart of stone from your body and give you a heart of flesh.*

Our Father in Heaven, the Great Surgeon/Physician, has removed our heart of stone and given us a new heart. How exciting is that!? Our old heart was stiff, hard, stubborn, messy, full of corruption and sin. God replaces that heart with a heart that loves Him. This can be a painful process, as any surgery can be. There is a shattering, pulling apart, breaking down, cutting away… But in this process of coming to the end of ourselves, we find Jesus. We see Him revealed as our Rescuer and we want Him!

Micah 7:9 (NET) says, *I must endure the Lord's fury, for I have sinned against him. But then he will defend my cause and accomplish justice on my behalf. He will lead me out into the light; I will witness his deliverance.*

The Lord's fury/refining is not an easy fire to go through. But there is great purpose in it. Our changed heart is seeking His light, and we will be delivered into it when we repent and believe! It's a miracle!

So many ask why do bad things happen to good people? Well, the Bible is clear on that…*No one is good except God alone.* (Mark 10:18 NET) The good that happens, happens to very bad people. Us! We deserve God's wrath and are given His forgiveness instead. Jesus was sent to save us from what we really deserve. That's why it's such very GOOD NEWS! Jesus' death, burial, resurrection, and return should always be front and center in our minds. Then, when bad things happen, we can trust God has a way for us to go through them. And when good things happen, we can be so very thankful that anything good happens to us at all. Heaven is a place where very bad people will experience very good things for all of eternity because of the saving Grace of our Lord and King, Jesus.

Micah 7:19 (NET) says, *Who will once again have mercy on us? Who will conquer our evil deeds? Who will hurl all our sins into the depths of the sea?*

The answer to this is our Father in Heaven because of His Son, Jesus Christ. *Therefore, if anyone is in Christ, he is a new creation. The old has passed away; behold, the new has come.* 2 Corinthians 5:17 (NET) That's why we have been talking about Repentance, Salvation, and now Baptism. Each is a step on this journey of Truth. Baptism is very important in God's Word. There are actually seven different baptisms talked about in the New Testament. The Baptism of Moses (Red Sea), John (Repentance), Jesus (Begins Ministry), Fire (Judgment), Holy Spirit (Spiritual), Cross (Suffering), and Believers (Water). In this chapter we will focus mainly on two, the Baptism in the Holy Spirit, and Water. These are what are most significant for us today.

With spiritual baptism, we can read about it in Acts. In chapter one we read how Jesus told the disciples not to leave Jerusalem until they received what the Father promised. Jesus told them that John baptized with water, but soon they would be baptized with the Holy Spirit. In that baptism, they would receive power when the Holy Spirit came upon them. They would then be able to be witnesses for Jesus in Jerusalem, Judea, Samaria, and all the earth.

We should listen carefully to Jesus' words here. How many times do we leave "home" without the Holy Spirit as believers? Well, actually never because He lives in us as believers. But the better question is, do we know He is with us? Are we aware of His power in our lives? Do we listen carefully to what the Spirit is saying throughout our day? The Holy Spirit will guide, counsel, comfort, etc…us each moment of each day if we are willing to let Him do His job! That's why we need this spiritual baptism that takes place at the time of our Salvation. All true followers of Jesus Christ have the Holy Spirit dwelling within. We are sealed! Prepared! And we're now/made ready for our walk with Jesus each day just as those who believed were prepared on the day of Pentecost. All of them were filled with the Holy Spirit, and they spoke in the languages of those around them as the Spirit enabled them. What a day that was in church history! It was the beginning of all that we should be experiencing today as Christians.

After that, Christians knew their assignment if they had listened to the words of Jesus. It is written about in Matthew 28:18-19 (NET), *Then Jesus came up and said to them, "All authority in heaven and on Earth has been given to me.*

Therefore go and make disciples of all nations, baptizing them in the name of the Father and the Son and the Holy Spirit."

We can't follow through on this assignment without the Holy Spirit. If we try to, we will burn out trying to "fake" Christianity as so many do. Then it looks like there is a falling away when they never were with the *Way* in the first place.

The Baptism of John that happened in water was one of repentance. He was actually an Old Testament prophet because he continued to point the way to the coming Messiah. Jesus was baptized by John in the Jordan River. This was the beginning of the ministry of Jesus on this earth. John was a bit taken aback to think he would be baptizing the Lamb of God. But it makes sense that he did because John was a Levite. And that was the job of the Levites in the Temples. They presented the sacrifices. Jesus is the Ultimate Sacrifice. God sure has a way of working everything out.

John was talked about in Isaiah 40 as *a voice that cries out in the wilderness.* He was clearing a way for the Lord. No wonder in Matthew three John said he needed to be baptized by Jesus. But Jesus did what was proper—He wanted to fulfill all righteousness. At Jesus' baptism, we see the Trinity. They heard the Father speak from Heaven on that day about His Son, and the Holy Spirit descended upon Jesus. The word Trinity is not found in the Bible, but the concept of the Trinity is.

What is the prerequisite for water baptism? Salvation. Does water baptism save us? No. We do not need to be baptized in water to enter the gates of Heaven. Baptism in water is an act of obedience because we already have been saved. John 14:15 (NET) says, *"If you love me, you will obey my commandments."* We get baptized because we already love Jesus. There is no merit in it, no saving grace. It is merely the symbolism of the Gospel, uniting us with Christ and the rest of the body called the church. We are one in Jesus, and our baptism endorses that concept. Baptism in water shows our commitment to want to follow Jesus in our life.

When we are immersed in water, it symbolizes the burial of Jesus. When we come up out of the water, it symbolizes His resurrection. And the water itself is a portrayal of the cleansing that the blood of Jesus does in our heart. When we are buried with Jesus in baptismal waters, and then when we are raised with Him out of that water, God is pleased with our obedience. Always remember, faith is a gift. No act of obedience will change that. It's when we confess with our mouth that Jesus is Lord, and believe in our heart that God raised Him from the dead (Romans 10:9), that we are saved.

It is asked in the Bible how can a man be born again? That's a very good question. Nicodemus probably expressed in this question what many want to know. Jesus answered him in this way: *"I tell you the solemn truth, unless a person is born of water and spirit, he cannot enter the kingdom of God."* John 3:4-5 (NET) Any woman who has had a child can relate to this. Our water can break at very inopportune times. Our children are born "of water" from the womb. That is very different than being born of the Spirit, as happened at Pentecost when the Holy Spirit came to dwell within the believers. The Holy Spirit rested upon certain people in the Old Testament, but He wasn't a permanent part of their life. Now He is. And I say, "He," because the Holy Spirit is not an "it," but the third Person of the Trinity. The Holy Spirit isn't even a ghost, as some translations call Him. A ghost once had a human, fleshly body. The Holy Spirit never has. He has always been a Spirit.

When the Holy Spirit is poured out upon a person, we are changed. We have a new boldness, a new sense of what God is doing in and around us, a new way of being in this world. Just as the official church had begun at Pentecost, our walk with Jesus begins at our spiritual baptism. We are then a part of the family of God. 1 Corinthians 12:12-13 (NET) says, *For just as the body is one and yet has many members, and all the members of the body—though many—are one body, so too is Christ. For in one Spirit we were all baptized into one body. Whether Jews or Greeks or slaves or free, we were all made to drink of the one Spirit.* This is not a drinking of the "Kool-Aid". This is the real deal! This is what God designed for us even before the fall in the Garden of Eden. It might seem that we are living in a world without rhyme or reason at times. But God has a perfect plan and we can be part of it when we choose to join His family.

There are some doctrinal (interpretational) issues concerning baptism. I will spell them out here, and then move on. Otherwise, we could be here a very long time and probably not come to a resolution. We must always remember, there is the Person—Jesus Christ, and the Gospel. This is not left open to interpretation. But there are lots of things in the Bible that different denominations/people read in different ways. Spiritual Baptism is one of those. But this is not a "saved" and "not saved" issue. Let's not let the "little dabs" of different interpretations confuse us here. When Jesus is our Lord and Savior, we are saved! Sadly, the interpretations of Spiritual Baptism can be a way the enemy uses to cause division in our churches. It is not of God.

So, here we go: Some believe that what happens at Salvation with our spiritual baptism is one and the same—the Holy Spirit comes to dwell within a believer at that time. Others believe there is a filling, or shall we say more of a filling, that happens after Salvation when we open ourselves up more to the Spirit's control. When that happens, some believe there will be signs like speaking in tongues, etc... Others believe signs aren't necessarily a part of this baptism. We could stop here, but do let me add just a bit more information which could clear up some questions about receiving the Holy Spirit after Salvation that's talked about in the Bible.

There is the scripture that talks about Philip being in Samaria, and the Samaritans not receiving the Holy Spirit when they believed. Peter and John arrived later, laid hands on them, and then the Holy Spirit came upon them. With the animosity between the Samaritans and Jewish people, this was needed. The church was being built on the foundation of the apostles and prophets. Philip was only a deacon in the Jerusalem Church. There was a transition going on at this time from the Old Covenant to the New Covenant. And since Peter was at Pentecost and also at Cornelius' house in Acts 10, he was there to be used to open the door to each of these people groups. Peter needed to be there for the official start of the Samaritan Church just as he had been in Jerusalem for the Jewish Church. This kept the churches unified. Otherwise, the Samaritans might have seemed like a separate religious movement. Any animosity was being overcome by the Holy Spirit.

Also, there is the story of the disciples in Ephesus. Why did they not receive the Holy Spirit when they first believed? It was because they were disciples of John the Baptist. They took the step of repentance but had not yet taken the step of faith in Christ. They were still awaiting the Messiah. Paul shared the Gospel with them, then they became new creations in Christ and were filled with the Holy Spirit.

Whether we all agree with these explanations or not, there is one thing we must all remember and it is written in Ephesians 4:4-6 (NET): *There is one body and one Spirit, just as you too were called to the one hope of your calling, one Lord, one faith, one baptism, one God and Father of all, who is over all and through all and in all.* Regardless of how we interpret doctrine/scripture, as true followers of the Lord Jesus Christ, we all serve the same Lord. There will always be doctrinal issues to discuss. But when we are talking about the Person of Jesus Christ, we are never to argue His death, burial, resurrection, and return. These are doctrinal Truth! And with the same Holy Spirit within us, we work together to share this message of redemption to the world. That is the Great Commission!

There are some spiritual gifts that we can discuss here given to us by the Holy Spirit. These are different than the Fruit of the Spirit. The Fruit of the Spirit are *love, joy, peace, patience, kindness, goodness, faithfulness, gentleness, and self-control.* As believers, we all have this Fruit. As time goes by, our repentance deepens, and our faith grows as the needed sanctification process takes place in our lives. The Fruit of the Spirit should become more evident in our lives over time. It cannot be stolen from us, but it can be quenched when we grieve the Spirit within. When the Living Water flows, the Fruit grows. When we let anger overtake us, not forgiving as we are called to, the Fruit of peace and kindness won't be all that it can be in our lives. When we decide to steal that jewelry, or betray that friend, the Fruit of goodness and faithfulness is quenched. We can see it ripen again when we repent, seek forgiveness, and forgive.

The gifts of the Spirit are something different. To each person there is the manifestation of the Spirit. But after that there are gifts listed in three different portions of Scripture: Romans 12:6-8, 1 Corinthians 12:8-11, and Ephesians 4:11-12. I'll list them for you here as they are listed in these passages: *prophecy, service, teaching, exhortation, contributing, leadership, mercy, wisdom, knowledge, faith, healing, miracles, prophecy, discernment, tongues, interpretation of tongues, apostles, prophets, evangelists, pastors, and teachers.*

From the looks of it, God has us covered! If we all do our part in the body, the body of Christ should be working like a well-oiled machine! The timing of the giving of these gifts is not specifically mentioned in the Bible. Some probably come at salvation. Do all? That's another doctrinal issue we could debate. Timothy was given a spiritual gift at a later time when the elders laid hands on him. (1 Timothy 4:14) Solomon sought wisdom, and it was given to him. God, not us, chooses the gifts and the timing. But we can pursue gifts, like love! And seeking prophecy (edifying the church) is said to be strived for. We can be eager for spiritual gifts. But we must trust God to distribute them as He sees fit. Do *all* have *all* the gifts? 1 Corinthians 12:29-31 says of course not! Some of these things seem very clear. This is also clear, if God commands us to do something, He will equip us to do it. We shouldn't use the excuse that we aren't gifted in that way. We should seek the help and guidance of the Holy Spirit and proceed as we are asked to. Sometimes those who practice teaching, or evangelism, etc…can become better at it than those who may have the gift but never use it. So, are gifts given or fostered? Both!

Are gifts and talents the same thing? No. Talents are more genetic and trained in us. They can be used for very non-spiritual endeavors. Gifts/fillings are of the Holy Spirit and should be used for God's glory. Talents can also be used for God's glory, but unbelievers do not use them that way.

When Jesus ascended back into Heaven, and the Holy Spirit came to indwell all believers, our heart of flesh was filled and is now more willing to bend to the will of the Father. We are a new creation in Christ, regenerated. We are no longer called "sinners" in the New Testament. We are called by many names like elect, beloved, children of God, and saints. Yes. We are saints who now sometimes sin still, but we know we are forgiven by the blood of Jesus. When we understand this, we understand how much it cost the Father to send His only Son. While we were still "hated" by God, (Psalm 5:5-6), He is also Love. And to water down this amazing miracle is deceptive. To say, "God hates the sin. But He loves the sinner," makes it seem like God will go easy on us. He won't. He never will. But the Father did send His Son so it can be just as if we never sinned—Justified. That is a much greater miracle than just looking past the wrongs we have done and saying we are loved. NO! God is so LOVE that even while we were still sinners, He sent His Son to die for us.

Our Spiritual Baptism comes at the time of Salvation. It can seem complicated, but it doesn't need to be. The Holy Spirit comes to dwell within us, and there are spiritual gifts that come with Him and are given to us by God as He deems the time and need is right.

Our Water Baptism is a demonstration of what God has done in our lives. We are saved before we ever climb into that tank of water. We know the change has already taken place when our heart of stone was replaced with a heart of flesh. But we now should want to make a public profession of what it is we believe. It can feel like we are going from being engaged to Jesus, to being married to our Groom.

In all this, I'd like to finish with the prayer that Paul prayed in Ephesians 3. (NET)

For this reason I kneel before the Father, from whom every family in Heaven and on Earth is named. I pray that according to the wealth of his glory he will grant you to be strengthened with power through his Spirit in the inner person, that Christ will dwell in your hearts through faith, so that, because you have been rooted and grounded in love, you will be able to comprehend with all the saints what is the breadth and length and height and depth, and thus to know the love of Christ that surpasses knowledge, so that you will be filled up to all the fullness of God.

Now to him who by the power that is working within us is able to do far beyond all that we ask or think, to him be the glory in the church and in Christ Jesus to all generations, forever and ever. Amen.

Chapter Six Reflections

1) After Repentance and Salvation, Baptism is our next step. We are pouring a firm foundation in Christ Jesus so we can know the Truth from the lies around us in today's world. (Page 65)

2) Let's start off simply by just saying that Baptism means "to submerge or immerse." When a person is baptized, they are submerged into something new signifying that a change has taken place. What would that be biblically?—Our heart has been changed. (Page 65)

3) Our Father in Heaven, the Great Surgeon, has removed our heart of stone and given us a new heart. How exciting is that!? Our old heart was stiff, hard, stubborn, messy, full of corruption and sin. God replaces that heart with a heart that loves Him. (Page 66)

4) With spiritual baptism, we can read about it in Acts. In chapter one we read how Jesus told the disciples not to leave Jerusalem until they received what the Father promised. Jesus told them that John baptized with water, but soon they would be baptized with the Holy Spirit. (Page 67)

5) What is the prerequisite for water baptism? Salvation. Does water baptism save us? No. We do not need to be baptized in water to enter the gates of Heaven. Baptism in water is an act of obedience because we already have been saved. (Page 68)

6) When we are immersed in water, it symbolizes the burial of Jesus. When we come up out of the water, it symbolizes His resurrection. And the water itself is a portrayal of the cleansing that the blood of Jesus does in our heart. (Page 68)

7) But there are lots of things in the Bible that different denominations/people read in different ways. Spiritual Baptism is one of those. But this is not a "saved" and "not

saved" discussion. When Jesus is our Lord and Savior, we are saved! (Page 70)

8) Whether we all agree with these explanations or not, there is one thing we must all remember and it is written in Ephesians 4:4-6 (NET): *There is one body and one Spirit, just as you too were called to the one hope of your calling, one Lord, one faith, one baptism, one God and Father of all, who is over all and through all and in all.* Regardless of how we interpret doctrine, as true followers of the Lord Jesus Christ, we all serve the same Lord. (Page 71)

NOTES

(These Reflection/Note pages may be duplicated and used for group discussions when needed.)

CHAPTER SEVEN

PRAYER

Most of us have heard about the frog in the pot. How about the lobster that screams when dropped into boiling hot water? Both of these, I will come back to in just a bit…

You may be wondering how these two subjects are tied to prayer? What we will be looking at today concerning prayer seems a daunting task, so I think the easiest route there is to give an illustration of where we're going with it, and then read the "last page" of the book/Bible first so we can know the importance of the subject at hand. We can then work our way back to prayer with a greater knowledge of Why this? Why now? Why at all? Since we are going to be considering deception concerning prayer, as well as biblical prayer, I hope to give us some perspective before diving in.

So, let's go to the end of the story in Revelation 13:11-14 (NET) where it talks about a One-World Religion in the Tribulation. Who will be worshipped in those days? What will the deception look like? And who will believe it?

Then I saw another beast coming up from the earth. He had two horns like a lamb, but was speaking like a dragon. He exercised all the ruling authority of the first beast on his behalf, and made the Earth and those who inhabit it worship the first beast, the one whose lethal wound had been healed. He performed momentous signs, even making fire come down from heaven to Earth in front of people and, by the signs he was permitted to perform on behalf of the beast, he deceived those who live on the earth. He told those who live on the Earth to make an image to the beast who had been wounded by the sword, but still lived.

Revelation 17 also talks about the Great Harlot/Prostitute, which is a metaphor for a false religion that will exist during the Tribulation. This will be an inclusive religion, one focused on "unity" and in the end willing to worship the antichrist—he will be very busy in the later days. The antichrist will demand that people worship him, and he will be opposed to Christians and Jews. At the three-and-a-half-year mark when he takes a place in the Temple there will be an "abomination that causes desolation." (Matthew 24:15) An abomination is a great sin—this one in Revelation is involving major covenant violations, including idolatry. The antichrist will profane the Temple and take away the regular burnt offerings. This will cause desolation. (Destruction) Again, what does this have to do with prayer? Stick with me...

Usually when we have something in this world like the poor, we also have the rich. When we have a cold day, we also have hot days. There are usually opposites to most things. With Christ, we have the antichrist. What I'm seeing with "prayer" is that we have the opposite in "anti-prayer," if we can call it that. Jesus taught His disciples how to truly pray using the Lord's Prayer (Matthew 6 & Luke 11) as an example of how to talk to our Father. Jesus teaches the disciples about honoring the Father, acknowledging Who He is, and where He is. It talks about the Kingdom, God's will, our sustenance, forgiveness, temptation, evil, deliverance, and many times ends with the doxology of "For Thine is the Kingdom, and the power, and the glory forever. Amen," when we pray it out loud. It is a well-rounded, direct, purposeful, powerful, and clear prayer. With prayers being taught today across America and throughout the world, anti-prayer, as I'm calling it, is creeping in—which is prayer designed by man, and when prayed by man, is deceiving man. Which brings us back to the frog in the pot now.

If I share the frog in the pot story with you, most Americans recognize the saying with no explanation needed. We can just say,

"It's like the frog in the pot," and others will nod in understanding... If explained, it is that the frog, put in a tepid pot of water, with the heat slowly rising, will not realize the trouble it is in, and will sit there until the water comes to a boil and it dies. I use this illustration many times when talking about the world we live in today and what is happening in Christianity. Things are creeping in, lots of little dabs, and we don't realize the temperature is being turned up bit by bit, and true Christianity is dying a slow death. We are being deceived, many times, even as mature Christians who are in the Word. How is this happening? Well, let me first tell you about the lobster and the pot part of this... The lobster is alive when it's thrown into an already boiling pot of water. We sometimes hear it scream. It is not known for sure if lobsters feel pain in that moment, but perhaps. Regardless, the scream can be a bit-unnerving...so can deception.

Now to the truth, because I just lied to you, twice...

Upon doing some research, I came upon some interesting information about what many of us take for granted about the frog-in-the-pot story, and the lobster-may-scream experience. The frog story is a myth...a lie. But we don't even research it before passing it on to someone else as truth. I'm guilty of that! Also, the lobster doesn't scream...it can't. It doesn't have any vocal cords! What we hear with the lobsters are probably just expanding air bubbles trapped in the shells finding a way of escape as their bodies boil. The frog, if given a way of escape out of the pot, will do so, and probably even before the water warms up, if not before. For certain, as discomfort does set in, the frog will get out of there! It's not waiting around to boil to death.

The reason I'm sharing all this is because not only are the frog and lobster stories untrue, we believe them without doing our own research! I'm thinking the frog has more sense by quickly exiting the pot than some of us do today in following God's Word by choosing not to exit a church that doesn't teach the true Gospel. Many times, we are following myths, lies, teachings, and techniques that might even be giving us a check in our spirit...but we still sit there a bit too long, perhaps not searching the Scriptures when that check comes. Are we going to end up boiling alive because we're not heeding God's warnings about deception in the end times? It is time to be a Berean more than ever before. These untruths in our churches are ultimately leading us to a place where many people will be soaking in the lies and dying in that boiling pot called a One World Religion. We need to realize that this is the goal of the antichrist. He will be the one worshipped by so many, and they won't recognize it's not God they are worshipping until the abomination of desolation takes place. Then some, not all, will see him clearly.

All this does not happen overnight. (A watched pot never boils, it is said... Another lie!) But it does take decades, centuries, perhaps since the beginning of time for the antichrist to set the stage for this. What we do know is that the foundation being poured as we "speak" is going to set and be ready for the congregation of a universal religion to build upon…also known as the false world church talked about in Revelation 13. This is a time when the antichrist *deceived those who live on the earth.* The things going on right now have huge spiritual ramifications. A false Christianity is being prepared, and this form of Christianity will play a part in end times prophecy being fulfilled. How is this happening? Because of what it says in 2 Timothy 4:3-4 (NET), *For there will be a time when people will not tolerate sound teaching. Instead, following their own desires, they will accumulate teachers for themselves, because they have an insatiable curiosity to hear new things. And they will turn away from hearing the truth, but on the other hand they will turn aside to myths.* That's why it's so important to pay attention to these things now before the lies invading our churches are turned up so hot, and we are so deep into them, that the way of escape becomes extremely difficult.

Now, let's get back to what prayer and anti-prayer look like for us today. First of all, there is no exact way to pray. We can pray the Lord's prayer, which is always powerful, or we can choose our own words, pray out loud or silently, read the Bible and pray God's Word, etc… We have been given great freedom in prayer. But there are certain things we should <u>not do</u> when praying, and one of them is an ever-increasing way of praying called "Contemplative prayer." It is a very popular prayer "technique" encouraged in many Christian circles today. What is contemplative prayer? I'll give you a brief overview of it…see if you recognize anything you have been taught, or the wording being used. (This is to open our eyes, not scare us to death. God always gives us a way of escape when we

80

recognize what is happening. We stop, we repent, we receive forgiveness, and we move forward in greater Truth.)

Contemplative prayer comes from the Desert Fathers who lived in the 3rd and 4th century. If we are using this form of prayer, we are turning to Catholic mystics for their prayer technique. This occult technique opens the person up to demonic manifestations, thus opening the mind to truth as our imagination defines it. Jesus never encouraged this. It's not about imagination in prayer, it's about Truth.

Jeremiah 9:24 (NET): *"If people want to boast, they should boast about this: They should boast that they understand and know me. They should boast that they know and understand that I, the Lord, act out of faithfulness, fairness, and justice in the Earth and that I desire people to do these things," says the Lord.*

When we "try" to go deeper spiritually in ways that are not biblical, we sometimes end up being led astray and will eventually lead others astray.

Jeremiah 13:10a (NET): *These wicked people refuse to obey what I have said. They follow the stubborn inclinations of their own hearts and pay allegiance to other gods by worshiping and serving them.*

John 8:31-32 (NET): *"If you continue to follow my teaching, you are really my disciples and you will know the truth, and the truth will set you free."*

The Desert Fathers (Contemplative Monks) were teaching a different form of consciousness. Their goal was not just saying prayers but living in constant union with God. That is biblical, since Paul told us we are to pray without ceasing. (1 Thess. 5:17) But the rest of what I learned from a Catholic priest who was explaining contemplative prayer was that they are assuming Jesus hadn't taught the disciples about verbal prayers because the disciples asked Jesus to teach them how to pray. (Luke 11:1) "Assuming" things is not good/truth. This priest, who practices this kind of prayer and was encouraging others to do it in the video, said that, "When Jesus went into the wilderness, we can assume He used contemplative prayer"—another dangerous assumption. He went on to teach us that this kind of prayer is a rewiring of your mind so that everything you do is in loving union with the "moment…with whatever is right in front of you." That sounds like it could be dangerous also. Not focusing on Christ, but whatever is in front of you? He then said we are to rediscover the mystical, contemplative, non-dual mind (having to make a decision between two separate things) so we can have an alternative to western civilization—we are to take a long, loving look at the "Real" with an emphasis on the capital "R" there. He explained when we look at something long enough, we can love it and let it be reality for us. He said that this is the "first door" of contemplative prayer…teaching contemplative minds to be change agents…our truth being held within us…the secret is to stay in the flow.

Can we say, NOT BIBLICAL?! Does this line up with 2 Corinthians 10:5b (NET), *...we take every thought captive to make it obey Christ.* And shouldn't our churches/pastors be warning us against this type of prayer technique before we get sucked into practicing this? The Bible encourages us to put ourselves to the test and see if we are in the faith. (2 Corinthians 13:5)

I'm going to give you a bit more information about contemplative prayer from another source, "gotquestions.org," and then we'll talk about what REAL biblical prayer is.

"Contemplative" comes from the Latin word, "contemplar," which means "in the temple." Various professional mystics or seers would go into temples and commune with the god of that temple. Today, "contemplation" just means to ponder things. But contemplative prayer has nothing to do with using your intellect, instead it is switching off your mind. The first step in contemplative prayer is to stop thinking about God when praying. The goal is an altered state of consciousness, where you are in a kind of trance. It also can include using a mantra, a word or phrase, and repeating it over and over for 20 minutes. This is done so the person can be liberated from thought. Nowhere in Scripture are mantras used.

Matthew 6:7 (NET): *When you pray, do not babble repetitiously like the Gentiles, because they think that by their many words they will be heard.*

Some translations use "vain repetitions," instead of "babble repetitiously…as the heathens do." The actual meaning of these repetitions become void after a certain period of time in contemplative prayer, although it is meant to try and lead us into a "deeper level" of our encounter with God. Is this powerful? Yes, it is! But that's because it is opening us up to evil…other gods/spirits. This is powerful but also dangerous! It is not only unbiblical, it is antibiblical.

How do some arrive here? Why are some praying this way after learning the Lord's way of praying in the Bible? Well, many are on their way to buying into a One World Religion, a merging with all other forms of prayer, worship, and religions...that wide road that will encompass so much of the world and lead to destruction. Remember our pot with the frog/lobster? Picture us in that pot and these things are being introduced to us in the world, in our churches, and seminars, etc...the water is heating up. Are we paying attention? What are we going to do? Are we willing to bail out from all that is false when we notice what is anti-biblical entering into our walk with God? Are we willing to call what we hold in our right hand a lie/idol? (Isaiah 44:20) We need to be, as hard as it is sometimes.

A bit more history on all this before we turn to the real prayers that God hears and answers. The early desert fathers were Catholic monks. They started doing contemplative prayer in the desert isolation they lived in. In some ways it is similar to Hindus and also what is experienced in yoga. A man named John Cassian traveled around the areas where the desert fathers were, and he eventually took their prayer method back to Europe. It then became part of what the monks and nuns were doing in Europe for centuries—they all thought they were doing something very spiritual as they entered into altered states of consciousness. Fast forward to our day...in 2004 contemplative prayer ended up in *Charisma* magazine in an article by James Goll. He said, "God is restoring (this) as a means to develop intimacy with Him." He laid out the particulars in an article saying, "First you practice centering." (This is also called "Centering Prayer.") He went on to say, "The ultimate goal is spiritual ecstasy." This is man's opinion. There is not a biblical basis for this. It is subjective and experiential. Also, remember the old game of telephone?...the idea being passed from one person to the next. We need to know how corrupted all this has become through the years.

Some will say just because contemplative prayer isn't biblical doesn't mean it's not good. But it's not only not good, remember it's anti-biblical! When a person experiences god in everything and everybody, this nullifies the Gospel. That's called "pantheism," meaning tolerating all gods. There is no preaching of the Cross in this type of belief.

Paul also talks about "seducing/deceiving spirits" in 1 Timothy 4:1 (NET): *Now the Spirit explicitly says that in the later times some will desert the faith and occupy themselves with deceiving spirits and demonic teachings.* We don't know we're being seduced because it's seduction. When people occupy themselves with these things, being trained in extrabiblical ideas, concepts, and methods, which are not in Scripture, it leads to another spirituality…it's spiritually demonic.

In 1 Corinthians 4:6 (NET), Paul says, *I have applied these things to myself and Apollos because of you, brothers and sisters, so that through us you may learn "not to go beyond what is written," so that none of you will be puffed up in favor of the one against the other.* To not go beyond what is written, isn't easy these days with so much being offered to us from every direction! This is where we can really start arguing doctrine, ideas, concepts, etc…causing division instead of unity in the body of Jesus Christ. But Jesus did say in Matthew 10:34 (NET), *"Do not think that I have come to bring peace to the earth. I have not come to bring peace, but a sword."*

We are on the verge of the Great Tribulation, so we need to look at what is really going on in the world and in our churches. We always need to weigh what is being said and done with the Truth of the Gospel. It may seem good, it may feel "heavenly," but is it the Word of God?

1 Corinthians 5:8 (NET): *So then, let us celebrate the festival, not with the old yeast, the yeast of vice and evil, but with the bread without yeast, the bread of sincerity and truth.*

1 Corinthians 6:11 (NET): *Some of you once lived this way. But you were washed, you were sanctified, you were justified in the name of the Lord Jesus Christ and by the Spirit of our God.*

As believers, we need to study the Truth and live by the Truth in the Bible so as to avoid the false teachings of the times we live in. Leviticus 20:8 (NET) says, *You must be sure to obey my statutes. I am the Lord who sanctifies you.* As believers, we are all in the sanctification process until we meet Jesus face to face.

Now that we've talked about the "pot" of anti-prayer that's boiling, let's take the jump out of it and look at what true biblical prayer can look like from one of the masters. Charles H. Spurgeon wrote, "As in proportion as you feed on the Word and are filled with the Word and retain the Word in your faith, and obey the Word in your life, in that same proportion you will be a master in the art of prayer."

Spurgeon, when preaching on prayer, used the words "abide/remain" in one sermon more times than I could keep count. He said we have to live with Christ to know Him…that we learn Truth by remaining in Jesus. He went on to say that "those who stay away from Jesus, don't pray….that prayer buds, blossoms, and fruits come out of souls remaining in Jesus."

Isn't this refreshing already?... as compared to the talk of being "change agents," and staying in the "flow," previously talked about? We have to be aware of this type of terminology and know where it's coming from. The Word of God is of utmost importance in all things. As I sat looking at the Bible on my lap this morning, I thought of all that it contains…so much in one small book, really. But each word it contains is so vitally important in our lives…to feed, be filled, retain, and obey the Word as Spurgeon urges us. This is how we learn to pray, by using the Word as our guide.

2 Corinthians 2:14 (NET): *But thanks be to God who always leads us in triumphal procession in Christ and who makes known through us the fragrance that consists of the knowledge of him in every place.*

Praying does not need to be long and arduous. Spurgeon said that true prayer is measured by weight and not by length. Sometimes it's a groan as the Holy Spirit prays through us when we don't have the words. When abiding, it's about being attached to the Vine, remaining in Christ (praying without ceasing). This is Biblical. John 15:7 (NET): *"If you remain in me and my words remain in you, ask whatever you want, and it will be done for you."* And quoting John 8:31 (NET), *"If you continue to follow my teaching, you are really my disciples."*

This is not encouraging us to do our own thing, but only what Jesus has taught in the words of Scripture. Spurgeon said we are "never to go an inch farther…we must remain in Jesus or we will be cut off and become withered…and if Christ's word doesn't remain in us in both belief and practice, then we are not in Christ." That's quite the warning! You would think that Spurgeon was living in this day and age by saying that…but maybe there were the same things going on in the 1800's as there are today! Charles Spurgeon lived from 1834 to 1892. He was known as the "Prince of Preachers."

In teaching on the liberty in power and prayer, Spurgeon said we "get liberty because of the fullness of Christ which includes grace, holiness, pardon, etc…" Also, because of the richness of the Word of God, he said, "The best praying Christian is the one who knows and believes the promises of God…the renewed heart echoes the mind of the Lord." Regeneration is part of the sanctification process. We will know it when we see it because we will see a person being re-created in Christ Jesus…becoming more Christlike.

One last thing included in this sermon that Spurgeon preached can give us some excellent steps in prayer. He said: First, pray specific requests that are simple and direct. Second, be earnest in what you are asking by comprehending the greatness of God. Third, have a firm faith in prayer being the greatest power in the entire universe while having real expectations when making your needs known to God.

Praying isn't complicated. It's not mumbo jumbo or mystical. It's talking to our Father, in our own words, or in using His own Words, and being honest, open, humble, and trusting. It's not emptying our minds but instead filling our minds with the Lord Jesus Christ and His sacrifice for us on the Cross. When we read the Word of God often, it will be the real nourishment our souls need, and we will grow in our prayer life. We can stop while we are reading, sit quiet with Him, or speak to God about what He is saying to us through His Word. We can tell our Father what we think, how we feel, what we're struggling with, what we're sorry for. Being in God's Word and praying to our Father in Heaven is having a real relationship with a real God who loves us and sent His Son as a sacrifice for us while we were still sinners. It's knowing that the wrath of God is what we are deserving of, but the forgiveness of God is His gift to us instead.

If we never hear about counterfeits, will we even be looking for them? Will they pass through our lives as easily as the real thing if we are unaware? Probably so! If we never hear about counterfeit prayer, will we even know there is such a thing? Had you heard about Contemplative Prayer before? Exposing this deception isn't easy, or fun, but it is needed. Jesus said in Matthew 7:14 (NET), *"How narrow is the gate and difficult the way that leads to life, and there are few who find it!"* It's not just that the gate is narrow, but the way/path after that is difficult. So if the road we are on seems wide, very spacious, oh so comfortable, perhaps even "mystical," we need to check our surroundings and our footing against Scripture because we may have gotten lost down a side road. We might discover it's time to turn around, repent/change our mind, and begin again on the way that leads to life. When we read the following passage in Galatians, that even Barnabas was led astray, we can know we are in good company when we find ourselves down a road we shouldn't be on.

Galatians 2:11-14 (NET):

But when Cephas came to Antioch, <u>I opposed him to his face,</u> because he had clearly done wrong. Until certain people came from James, he had been eating with the Gentiles. But when they arrived, he stopped doing this and separated himself because he was afraid of those who were pro-circumcision. And the rest of the Jews also joined with him in this hypocrisy, <u>so that even Barnabas was led astray with them by their hypocrisy.</u> But when I saw that they were <u>not behaving consistently with the truth of the gospel,</u> I said to Cephas in front of them all, "If you, although you are a Jew, live like a Gentile and not like a Jew, how can you try to force the Gentiles to live like Jews?" (Underlines are mine.)

We are to live consistently in the full truth of the Gospel and stop the lies from being a part of our own "deceptive truth." The frog in the pot is a lie many of us believe because we don't research its origins. It is even known in many languages, in different ways. We are not isolated in the deception we deal with on a daily basis here in the United States. One friend told me the same thought is expressed this way in Spanish, "es como el sapo en la olla." Let this not be said about us in any language! We need to be like the Bereans and search the Scriptures daily to see if we are hearing the Truth of the Gospel.

So then, have I become your enemy by telling you the truth?
Galatians 4:16 (NET)

On Sunday morning, it's easier for pastors to tell us how wonderful life will be once we become a Christian…just give your heart to Jesus and all will be well. I heard it preached, if they're only telling us how much God loves us, we will readily agree because we love us, too. If they're telling us that God has a wonderful plan for our lives, we'll readily agree since we have a wonderful plan for our lives, too. It's not easy to tell those interested in Christianity that being a Christian is also a road that can be difficult…this is especially so as they join the family of God in these last days. But we all need to heed this Scripture: *Do not be deceived. God will not be made a fool.* Galatians 6:7 (NET)

The enemy would like God to be made a fool, and you and me also. But we can be wise to Satan's ways, and we should be. We can spot his little dabs of lies before they mushroom. We should also warn one another there may be a pot we're going to soon be boiling in if we don't take a true leap of faith and escape the One World Religion that's surely coming! Let's read the Truth, learn the Truth, live the Truth, and pray the Truth! Amen. (Let it be so!)

Therefore consider carefully how you live—not as unwise but as wise, taking advantage of every opportunity, because the days are evil. For this reason do not be foolish, but be wise by understanding what the Lord's will is.
Ephesians 5:15-17 (NET)

I constantly trust in the Lord; because he is at my right hand, I will not be shaken.
Psalm 16:8 (NET)

Let me leave you with this biblical prayer:

And it is my prayer that your love may abound more and more, with knowledge and all discernment, so that you may approve what is excellent, and so be pure and blameless for the day of Christ, filled with the fruit of righteousness that comes through Jesus Christ, to the glory and praise of God.
Philippians 1:9-11 (NET)

Chapter Seven Reflections

1) Many times, we are following myths, lies, teachings, and techniques that might even be giving us a check in our spirit...but we still sit there a bit too long, perhaps not searching the Scriptures when that check comes. (Page 79)

2) It is time to be a Berean more than ever before. These untruths in our churches are ultimately leading us is to a place where many people will be soaking in the lies and dying in that boiling pot called a One World Religion. We need to realize that this is the goal of the antichrist. (Page 79)

3) We can pray the Lord's prayer, which is always powerful, or we can choose our own words, pray out loud or silently, read the Bible and pray God's Word, etc... We have been given great freedom in prayer. But there are certain things we should <u>not do</u> when praying, and one of them is an ever-increasing way of praying called "Contemplative prayer." (Page 80)

4) Contemplative prayer comes from the Desert Fathers who lived in the 3rd and 4th century. If we are using this form of prayer, we are turning to Catholic mystics for their prayer technique. This occult technique opens the person up to demonic manifestations, thus opening the mind to truth as our imagination defines it. Jesus never encouraged this. (Page 81)

5) The first step in contemplative prayer is to stop thinking about God when praying. The goal is an altered state of consciousness, where you are in a kind of trance. It also can include using a mantra, a word or phrase, and repeating it over and over for 20 minutes. This is done so the person can be liberated from thought. Nowhere in Scripture are mantras used. (Page 82)

6) To "not go beyond what is written" isn't easy these days with so much being offered to us from every direction! This is where we can really start arguing doctrine, ideas, concepts, etc…causing division instead of unity in the body of Jesus Christ. But Jesus did say in Matthew 10:34 (NET), *"Do not think that I have come to bring peace to the earth. I have not come to bring peace, but a sword."* (Page 84)

7) Spurgeon said we are "never to go an inch farther…we must remain in Jesus or we will be cut off and become withered…and if Christ's word doesn't remain in us in both belief and practice, then we are not in Christ." That's quite the warning! (Page 85)

8) First, pray specific requests that are simple and direct. Second, be earnest in what you are asking by comprehending the greatness of God. Third, have a firm faith in prayer being the greatest power in the entire universe while having real expectations when making your needs known to God. (Page 86)

NOTES

*(These Reflection/Note pages may be duplicated
and used for group discussions when needed.)*

CHAPTER EIGHT

TRUST

Since this chapter will be focused on trust, let's take a look at the definition of the word first. Trust is having a firm belief in the reliability of something or someone. To me, it sounds very much like faith, so I also want to define faith here. Faith is a complete trust in someone or something. As far as faith concerning religion, it's a strong belief in God. It's not based on proof, but spiritually understanding it. Faith and Trust are not all that different. We trust something or someone, or we have faith in someone or something, and that is the basis for a lot of the ways we act, respond, understand, feel, etc...to things in life. To have confidence is a bit more emphatic. It's having a firm trust...to feel or believe we can rely on something or someone.

What is the something or someone we are to trust in? Well, since we are talking about Christianity in this book, God will be our focus here. Trusting in, having faith in, our God. How do we trust our God? First, we have to be introduced to Him, get to know Him. That can happen in a variety of ways. Some "find" God in church, some in nature, in tragedy, in joy, and a variety of other ways. We, then, as disciples of Jesus Christ, are commissioned to go out into the world and make other disciples, baptizing and teaching them all that He taught us. Basically, we are to share the Good News of Jesus

Christ with others…introducing them to our God. How are we doing in this department? Most times, not all that great. And why would that be? It could be because our trust in God and believing in all that He offers us through His Son, Jesus Christ, isn't all it should be. That makes it extremely difficult to share confidently, with a "firm trust," all that we understand about our God. And why would that be? It could be deception. I chuckle as you might be thinking to yourself, not again. But, yes. Again. We're back to the frog in the pot, now that I've introduced that lie. Our understanding in the Almighty God of the Universe gets totally out of whack with what we are being exposed to in this world as we head toward a One World Religion. There are so many lies going on. This can deeply and profoundly affect our trust in the one true God. I'll explain…you knew I would!

Recently I was handed a paper. On it were the core beliefs of a present-day church. I was given the paper to look over and see if they were "up to snuff" we might say. At first glance, I smelled a "wolf". I couldn't really tell you why. But it seemed "off". Oh, it talked about God, the Bible, Humanity, Jesus Christ, and the Church. But it also seemed…well, vague. Almost like they wanted to mention the appropriate subjects a Christian would be looking for when searching for a church to attend…but it seemed like there were many core issues not being addressed. Perhaps their "Christian" description of what they believe is a good way to woo someone into the church, and then they could take them from there into their deceptive doctrines. Not good! Let's go back a bit and see what's going on here and where this might be coming from.

In listening to a talk by R.C. Sproul (An apologist and Presbyterian pastor), he was explaining how, in 19th Century Europe, there was a growing awareness of a shrinking globe. People were able to travel and be exposed to many more things—things which included Islam, Buddhism, Hinduism, Deism, and such… He said there is an essential core in all religions, a concern for ethics and values. (Deism is a belief in a supreme being that's not God.)

Let me say upfront, true salvation is not part of this. Salvation in Jesus Christ stands alone. There is no other religion that has a Savior like Jesus. Christ came to this Earth to save us, to redeem us, and having our faith in Him is what it costs us. We do not work our way to Heaven as these other religions attempt to do. Sproul said the world will talk about the *Fatherhood* and *Brotherhood* of God. This *hood* is reserved for those in God's family through Jesus Christ, alone. Outside of the Church of Jesus Christ, it doesn't exist. We have been adopted into this family *hood*. Others not in the body of Christ are known as our neighbors, and we are to love them, and treat everyone with dignity. But there are non-negotiables in Christianity that are not in any other religion or the world—the Incarnation of Christ (living in a human body), the Atonement of Christ (Reconciliation of God and humankind through Jesus Christ), a need for the Savior (Jesus Christ) because of sin, and the Resurrection of Christ (Rising on the third day after crucifixion). In Christianity there are other important matters like "predestination" which might put us into the camp of either Calvinism or Arminianism, but these are not hills to die on.

What is happening in today's world concerning all of this is an outward hostility toward true Christianity…the non-negotiables. R.C. Sproul said it could be summed up in one word: UNBELIEF. He also exclaimed, "Why not have the integrity and honesty to say so." That is the same reaction I had in reading the "beliefs" on the paper I was handed about this church. Why are they skirting around the most important issues? They are acting like they believe what a Christian would want them to believe just to get us into their church. Then they teach something different about the core values that make up a true, authentic Christian who follows the Lord Jesus Christ of the Bible when we get there. In investigating this, I learned a bit more from R.C. Sproul about this. He said that a crisis came, and as ministers were educated, some of them didn't believe what they were learning, so they tried to substitute a social agenda in place of it…ethical issues that weren't personal to redemption. He said churches became museums in Europe in the 20th Century. I lived in Europe for eight years in the 1990's. I saw that long before I understood it as I do today. I thought it was great that the churches weren't locked. We could go into them, walk around, take pictures…unlike our churches in America that are locked during the week. But come Sunday in Europe, from the way R.C. Sproul was talking about it, the churches were practically empty. I didn't personally know because their sermons were in German, so we didn't attend. We wouldn't have understood the message anyway.

In all this, when looking for a church to attend today in America, we have to look past a well-composed statement of faith that flashes words we are familiar with but aren't supported by the core truth of Christianity. We have to find out if their fundamental beliefs are aligned with the Word of God. Also, are such things as Heaven and Hell, adultery, homosexuality, and abortion even on the table for discussion? We have to find out who Jesus Christ really is to them. Was Jesus fully human and fully man when He walked on this earth? He was, although some deny this. But in Colossians 2:9 it says, *For in him all the fullness of the deity lives in bodily form, and you have been filled in him, who is the head over every ruler and authority.* This Truth is not being taught in some very large, influential churches today. They are claiming Jesus laid down His deity, using Philippians 2:7 which says he *"emptied himself."* They claim Jesus was only fully human on earth, performing miracles as purely human, and as such, we should all be able to do everything Jesus did. This is being hostile to the Word of God, causing so-called Christians to actually be in conflict over this! Absurd! We need to hold tight to the Truth God has given us, and not be deceived *through arguments that sound reasonable* (Col. 2:4)...because they will!

The paper I read about that church sounded very reasonable. But as I said, it smelled of "wolf". After some investigation, I was seeing more and more wolf than I was sheep. We cannot let this world take the true Christ out of our Christianity! One movement doing this has a name. It's called Progressive Christianity. It is similar to the New Age/New Thought movements of the past. Some think those are long over. They are not! New Age is more about atheists looking to be spiritual. Progressive Christianity is more about evangelicals wanting to hang onto Jesus but omit certain parts of God's Word that they don't agree with. The One World Religion is on the rise, even as I write this. In the last chapter we took a look at Contemplative Prayer. Now we will go this step farther and look at the dabs of the Progressive Christianity movement since it is dividing many churches/Christians today. Sometimes it takes a while to recognize them, but we should always be Bereans and keep a watchful eye.

R.C. Sproul said when the fundamentals of Christianity started disappearing in the lives of some of those studying for the pastorate in the 19th and 20th century, this type of deception was then brought into the pulpits by those more trying to disprove the Bible than teach it. This is passed onto the congregations under the disguise of Progressive Christianity.

Paganism is less of a threat than this type of "Christianity" because at least it claims to be what it is—it's out front and obvious. Progressive Christianity is a lot more devious. This type of thing is what we have been warned about in the Word of God. To have pastors preaching heresy from the pulpit is so deceptive. Many think the pastors "know" and can be trusted. But are we putting our trust in something or someone that we should be? We all need to be careful. Some pastors don't believe the Word of God fully, so they will taper it, conforming it to the world. We are in a battle for Biblical Christianity, not outside our churches, but many times within the walls of the very places we think we are safe. Let me give you more insight into what Progressive Christianity is, and then we will spend time in the Word, touching, feeling, seeing, reading, and believing the Truth of the Gospel of Jesus Christ.

Like you just read, with Progressive Christianity coming out of the evangelical churches, it's more a changing of the Gospel rather than outright paganism. No wonder Colossians 1:23 (NET) tells us to *remain in the faith…without shifting from the hope of the gospel that you heard.* This type of false teaching walks away from a lot of the Bible. It rejects the view of the Bible's authority, and even redefines the terms used. That's why we can read a description of a church and see the words Jesus, God, Bible, Creator, etc…and "conveniently" miss that the words prayer, repentance, one and only Son, Holy Spirit, Baptism, Gospel, Sacrifice, Grace, Forgiveness, Redemption, Faith…need I go on, are missing? Some of these terms may even be included, but don't mean the same thing. That's why it's so deceptive. It's like they want to identify with Jesus but want to change the core of His teaching. Their view of the Bible, the Cross, the Gospel, the Atonement is radically different. I have heard they will even say that the Father is a "Cosmic Child Abuser," because of how He treated His Son. They think that those of us who believe the theology of the Cross should repent for presenting the Gospel like we do. Some even go so far as denying original sin/the fall and that we have a sin nature. They say it was more the shame than the sin that separated Adam and Eve from the Father.

Progressive Christianity could be more out to change the world through Social Justice than share the Gospel. I recently heard it preached that throwing a net into the water in an attempt to change the water instead of attempting to capture fish is not what we are to be doing as Christians. We are fishers of men. We are not here to change the water. Helping people and taking care of our environment is Biblical. It is good. (Col. 1:10 and Col. 3:17) But it's not the way to Heaven. Good works are what Christians do on Earth because we are going to Heaven…not in hopes to earn our way there. Colossians 1:5 says, *Your faith and love have arisen from the hope laid up for you in heaven, which you have heard about in the message of truth, the gospel that has come to you.*

We have hope because we have heard the Truth of the GOSPEL: God's Only Son Provides Eternal Life.

The world's thinking is not so much about eternity, but the here and now. Many don't believe in a place of eternal torment, and many do believe all paths lead to heaven. With a belief that Christ is redeeming everyone, they can quote John 14:6 (NET); *"I am the way and the truth and the life. No one comes to the Father except through me"* claiming that Jesus accomplished this for everyone. Many believe it's not necessary to put your trust in Jesus alone. Do you see how they can say, "Jesus", but mean someone entirely different? Some even think the resurrection is just symbolism. Many prefer just posing questions, but don't necessarily want to come to a conclusive answer about anything. They feel the question is where the enlightenment is—no real concrete answer is needed. Progressive Christianity also includes some mystical practices and even some contemplative prayer. It seems so much of this today is a mixture of all that has come down through the ages. It can get confusing. But what we can find is that the Bible is not confusing. When we listen to someone preach the true Word of God, it is clear, concise, and practical. This is a good way to measure what we are hearing/reading. If things seem "off", they probably are.

I heard an interview which contained a lot of the information I'm sharing here. It was broken down in a simple way by Alisa Childers and at the end of the interview she said to look for these signs with Progressive Christianity: They will have a lower view of the Bible. Feelings will be emphasized over facts. There is no absolute Truth. Doctrines are open for interpretation with terms being redefined.

The Bible is put on the same level with perhaps a Tozer or C.S. Lewis. Sin and redemption usually shift to a social justice focus. Without thinking you're a sinner, there is not much need for a blood sacrifice. None of this is to be trusted! With no moral accountability, it's not Christianity. (Like I said, a great deal of this information was acquired from Alisa Childers during an interview.)

Much of Progressive Christianity is creating a god they can understand, and then worshipping him. But as Alisa Childers said, "If my god looks like me when I look in the mirror, chances are I'm just worshipping myself. That's idolatry."

Now that we know what a false god/idolatry looks like in today's world, let's dive deep into God's Word and see what the Truth we can trust looks like. First of all, how do we trust if we don't know we have something concrete to stand on? That's why Paul was working so hard at *instructing and teaching all people with all wisdom so that we may present every person mature in Christ.* Colossians 1:28 (NET) True followers of the Lord Jesus Christ need to know the foundation we stand on and always be growing and maturing in our Faith. God wants us to understand the Gospel and be confident in it! Ephesians 6:10-14 urges us to "stand" four times! It tells us to *"stand against the schemes of the devil," "stand your ground," "having done everything, to stand,"* and then in verse 14, *"Stand firm."* If all we have are questions with no concrete answers, as in Progressive Christianity, it can feel like very shaky/unsure ground, although they aren't going to admit that. The Word of God gives us no place for such shaky insecurity! Our true God is firm, secure, and trustworthy. (Colossians 2:5)

Paul Washer said, "A true believer will doubt their salvation, but never doubt that Christ is their only hope."

Jesus Christ is the same yesterday, today, and forever. (Hebrews 13:8) We don't have to wonder if we are righteous enough to be saved. That has been settled when we believe the promises of God.

Let's think of what we are like when we place our trust in the one true God. It can be like having a plumb line in our life. A plumb line hangs straight down to a datum mark (fixed starting point) toward the nadir (in the direction of the force of gravity) as the builder gets ready to begin construction to insure the structure will be straight. The plumb line is a *vertical reference* line. It has been used in construction as far back as ancient Egypt. We, too, need this vertical reference line in our life when we start to lean one way or another.

It is said, "If you don't believe in something, you'll fall for anything." (Eric Davis)

Trust in the Lord with all your heart, and do not rely on your own understanding. Acknowledge him in all your ways, and he will make your paths straight.
Proverbs 3:5-6 (NET)

Trust seems a very good "plumb line" as God makes our paths straight when we don't rely on our own understanding. We shouldn't try to design a god we can understand and then worship him. We should give the one true God our full attention, give Him all of our heart in everything we do, and trust Him as our Plumb Line. That is true wisdom!

The word "Pisteuo" in the New Testament Greek means to have faith, to believe, which is equal to trust. Our Pisteuo/Trust is not only in a fact, it's about believing in a real Person. When we believe God to be our absolute Plumb Line in life, we can be assured we are on the right path, moving in the right direction, toward the right Person of Jesus Christ. We have the Vertical Reference that is most needed in life when Jesus Christ is our Savior, and the Holy Spirit lives within us. Anything less than this type of Plumb Line focus will throw everything in our life off kilter. It can seem we are doing okay for a bit, maybe even years, but after enough time has passed, it will become more noticeable that we are leaning in ways we shouldn't be. Acknowledging God in all our ways is so important. We cannot rely on our own understanding. Being focused on our Plumb Line, although our lives will have many trials and tribulations, we can still have an assurance that what is happening is the cause of living in a fallen world and not because we have strayed away from Truth.

If we think about Paul, formerly known as Saul, he understood this. Although his life was far from perfect—he persecuted the followers of the Way, before he put his trust in Jesus. Paul endured beatings, imprisonment, shipwrecks, etc…even having a thorn in his side that he prayed would be removed but wasn't…he wasn't confused. Paul accepted when God said His grace was sufficient to endure it, and Paul continued to trust God. How do we know this?

Because Paul wrote most of the New Testament instructing all of us to follow his example of following Jesus. It's not an easy life that will build our trust most times, but a difficult one that has seen the hand of God working as He brings us through the hard times. When a construction project gets higher and higher, the plumb line is moved up along with it to assure everything is lined up correctly. How do we test whether our Plumb Line is actively working as we move up through the years of our life growing in our faith? We, too, can ask ourselves some questions. When we do this, we are truly searching and wanting answers as followers of Christ.

Some questions to consider are: Do we truly desire to know Jesus? Is the Holy Spirit alive and active in our days? Are we drawn to the Word of God and prayer? Is worshipping our Lord important to us? Do we rejoice in the God of the Bible? Does our relationship with Jesus motivate us in ways this world cannot? Has sin lost its appeal? Is our confidence in the flesh or in the Lord Jesus Christ? (These questions were mostly adapted from Paul Washer.)

As we grow older, we need to always be aware of whether we are leaning *away from* instead of *into* a closer walk with Jesus. We have to examine ourselves and get back to our God if we are drifting. In Colossians, Paul is writing to the faithful brothers and sisters in Colossae. He tells them that he heard about their faith in Jesus Christ and the love they have for all the saints. Their faith and love are rising up because of the hope they have of Heaven. They heard the Truth, the gospel that came to them, and they believed it. The Colossians found their Plumb Line in life, they were trusting in God, and it was showing! Paul says since hearing it, he is asking God to fill them *with the knowledge of his will in all spiritual wisdom and understanding, so that you may live worthily of the Lord and please him in all respects.* Colossians 1:9-10a (NET)

We can't have trust in something/someone we don't believe in. We also have to be careful to not trust in something that shouldn't be believed in. If there are no concrete answers to questions, what do we stand on? No wonder Christianity is about having a relationship with our Savior. God's Word IS to be believed, and trusted. It is a firm foundation. How do we learn/know this? Many times, by making mistakes along the way, by not trusting, by going it on our own...then we might notice that God is not working as He should. We notice things getting messed up. At first, we might try to blame God. How could He do this to me? How could He let this happen? When we finally come to our senses, thankfully, we have a redemptive God and a forgiving God. The minute we notice that what has happened could be because we have gotten off track, because we have made some bad choices, etc…and we then repent, we can be right back as good as new in God's eyes! Our sins are forgivable…all except blaspheming the Holy Spirit. (Matthew 12:31)

He delivered us from the power of darkness and transferred us to the kingdom of the Son he loves, in whom we have redemption, the forgiveness of sins.
Colossians 1:13-14 (NET)

This is where a lot of us get tripped up…because we don't really believe this verse. We think after we sin, we have to punish ourselves…maybe just long enough to make it painful enough so we don't do it again. This is NOT the way God works. This is of our own thinking, and it doesn't work. We'd be following the wrong plumb line if we think punishing ourselves has some merit. That's not going "vertical" for help; that's going horizontally into the world, taking on the world's thinking, and designing our own way of redemption.

Here is God's Plumb Line in Colossians that will show us the way of renewal:

And you were at one time strangers and enemies in your minds as expressed through your evil deeds, but now he has reconciled you by his physical body through death to present you holy, without blemish, and blameless before him— if indeed you remain in the faith, established and firm, without shifting from the hope of the gospel that you heard.
Colossians 1:21-23a (NET)

Most of us have heard it's not good to build our house on shifting sand. It would be very hard to keep that plumb line working when the ground underneath is constantly changing. That's what happens when man designs a religion instead of its being God's creation—it shifts, changes, evolves, etc…over the years. Those in Progressive

Christianity have that name for a reason…they think Christianity is still progressing today, still shifting… But since Jesus is the same yesterday, today, and forever, Progressive Christianity is NOT the right vertical reference we are to be using! We are to remain in the faith we have been given from day one in God's Word. Period!

I was pondering over an acronym for TRUST, and nothing was coming to me. Then just tonight driving along in the car, barely thinking about it, this is what came. Trust is:

To
Really
Understand
Salvation
Thoroughly

I was blown away by our God once again! As I thought about this, it seemed SO RIGHT! If we don't understand our salvation, really, thoroughly, then there is no way we can trust God. We will always be questioning not only Who He is? and What His plan is? but whether or not we are part of it? Do we qualify? And just by asking whether we qualify shows we don't understand. There is no qualifying. We don't have to try out for the team. We don't have to be good enough to make it. All we have to do is open our heart to the saving grace of the Lord Jesus Christ, repent by coming into agreement with God's way of how this all works, and accept the gift of salvation that is being given to us through the atoning blood of Jesus Christ on the Cross at Calvary. We have to believe that the Gospel is not only true, it is true for us. *Christ in you, the hope of glory!* Colossians 1:27 (NET)

Here's the catch! The enemy is out to steal, kill and destroy any ounce of faith we have been given. And he's very good at it. Satan has so many ways of working against us we could never count them all. And he knows us so well, he knows every button to push, and just when to push them. Is this discouraging? It could be, if we didn't TRUST what Jesus has already done! The victory is ours! We aren't fighting for it. We already have it because Jesus defeated Satan on the Cross. The only problem is we still live in this world until Jesus comes again. So, we have to "stand" firmly, confidently, and courageously in our faith until that Day comes! Thankfully, *He who*

103

is in you is greater than he who is in the world. 1 John 4:4 (NET)

We have to trust what we have learned in the Word of God and keep on learning. Faith is shown to be true in our lives if we see evidence of our maturity. It helps to repent, often. This keeps the walls down between us and our God. Paul explains the reason why he is writing to those in Colossae about all this. He explains in Colossians 2:4 (NET), *I say this so that no one will deceive you through arguments that sound reasonable.* Both he, and the Holy Spirit who is inspiring Paul to write this, know what the battle looks like. We know the Holy Spirit does, and I believe Paul shares enough of his life struggles with us to know he has "heard and seen it all". Paul was one of the ones who was going after and killing the Christians to begin with. Now Paul's fighting from the other side. No wonder he is rejoicing to see the morale and firmness of faith in Christ the people living in Colossae have!

Paul encourages them in Colossians 2:6-7 (NET), *Therefore, just as you received Christ Jesus as Lord, continue to live your lives in him, rooted and built up in him and firm in your faith just as you were taught, and overflowing with thankfulness.*

Let's always keep an eye on how the "building" is going in our lives. If things are off-kilter, we should read on to what Paul says next in verse 8: *Be careful not to allow anyone to captivate you an empty, deceitful philosophy that is according to human traditions and the elemental spirits of the world, and not according to Christ.*

What might this look like? For one, what does Progressive Christianity contain?

Deceitful philosophy? It's there. Doctrines are open for interpretation, terms are redefined.

It is written: *If anyone adds to them, God will add to him the plagues described in this book. And if anyone takes away from the words of this book of prophecy, God will take away his share in the tree of life.*
Revelation 22:18b-19 (NET)

Human traditions? There also. Let's work on social justice and forget that this world is really coming to an end.

It is written: *"...we are waiting for new heavens and a new earth..."*
2 Peter 3:13 (NET)

Elemental spirits of the world...not according to Christ? There again. Saying Jesus was not fully God!

It is written: *For in him all the fullness of deity lives in bodily form.* Colossians 2:9 (NET)

No wonder Paul warns us to not allow anyone, and he means ANYONE, to captivate us through these things. We are to trust in Christ, and Christ alone! We are to *hold fast to the head from whom the whole body, supported and knit together through its ligaments and sinews grows with a growth that is from God.* Colossians 2:19 (NET)

Paul goes on to ask a good question in Colossians 2:20-21 (NET): *If you have died with Christ to the elemental spirits of the world, why do you submit to them as though you lived in the world? "Do not handle! Do not taste! Do not touch!"* This goes on to talk about things destined to perish although they have the appearance of wisdom. It seems to be talking about what we might eat, drink, partake in... But what if this also includes false religions? False teachings? False Christs? Why are we submitting to them? Why are we losing our trust in Jesus? Why is our faith wavering? If we are dead to the things of this world, and I mean really dead, these false things should not concern us. We should not touch them, taste them, handle them...this IS Biblical!

As Bible-believing Christians, we are covered by the blood of Jesus, washed clean, forgiven, and forever sealed with the Holy Spirit. We believe the Gospel Truth. Paul goes on to say in Colossians 3:1-3 (NET), *Therefore, if you have been raised with Christ, keep seeking the things above, where Christ is, seated at the right hand of God. Keep thinking about things above, not things on the earth, for you have died and your life is hidden with Christ in God.* Maybe we are spending way too much time thinking about the things here on earth, and neglect putting our nose in the Good Book and staying there so we can not only grow in knowledge and wisdom from God, but also help others when they have questions. So many of us avid readers love to pore over books that take us into a different world, a different time, a different life… But we can sometimes use those books as an escape from the harsh reality we might live in. And yet at the same time, our Bible might be collecting dust there on the shelf. Are we spending enough time soaking in the hope-filled reality inside the pages of Scripture….in words that will feed our starving souls? No wonder we have a hard time trusting! Many times, it's because we don't really understand our salvation fully. We haven't taken enough time to study it! We turn to other comforts first. We all do it… But hopefully, less and less as we build our lives on the firm foundation of Jesus Christ. Old age doesn't have many benefits. But one of them can be, "Just a closer walk with Thee!"

Let the peace of Christ be in control in your heart…Let the word of Christ dwell in you richly…and whatever you do in word and deed, do it all in the name of the Lord Jesus, giving thanks to God the Father through him.
Colossians 3:15-18 (NET)

With our Plumb Line of Truth in the Word of God being used daily, we are building a straight life on the firm *foundation of the apostles and prophets with Christ Jesus as the Cornerstone.* We won't be leaning to the right or to the left as we grow vertically toward our heavenly home. Our TRUST in God will grow as it was meant to when we thoroughly understand the salvation we have been called to. Then…*We will become a holy temple in the Lord…a dwelling place of God in the Spirit.* (Eph. 2:19-22)

I'll leave you with two different translations of the same verse about a plumb line as we continue to trust in the One who constructed us all!

Thus He showed me: Behold, the Lord stood on a wall made with a plumb line, with a plumb line in His hand. And the Lord said to me, "Amos, what do you see?" And I said, "A plumb line." Then the Lord said: "Behold, I am setting a plumb line in the midst of My people Israel; I will not pass by them anymore."
Amos 7:7-8 (NKJV)

Then he showed me another vision. I saw the Lord standing

beside a wall that had been built using a plumb line. He was using a plumb line to see if it was still straight. And the Lord said to me, "Amos, what do you see?" I answered, "A plumb line." And the Lord replied, "I will test my people with this plumb line. I will no longer ignore all their sins."

Amos 7:7-8 (NLT)

Let's pray:

Father, we want to be perfectly lined up with Your Truth. We want to know You to the depths of our being, and follow You on the narrow, straight path toward our heavenly home. Grow our trust in You along the way, and help us share You with others we meet on the journey. In Jesus' name. Amen.

Chapter Eight Reflections

1) We trust something or someone, or we have faith in someone or something, and that is the basis for a lot of the ways we act, respond, understand, feel, etc…to things in life. (Page 93)

2) How do we trust our God? First, we have to be introduced to Him, get to know Him. That can happen in a variety of ways. Some "find" God in church, some in nature, in tragedy, in joy, and a variety of other ways. (Page 93)

3) In all this, when looking for a church to attend today in America, we have to look past a well-composed statement of faith that flashes words we are familiar with but aren't supported by the core truth of Christianity. We have to find out if their fundamental beliefs are aligned with the Word of God. (Page 95)

4) In the last chapter we took a look at Contemplative Prayer. Now we will go this step farther and look at this Progressive Christianity movement since it is dividing many churches/Christians today. Sometimes it takes a while to recognize it, but we should always be Bereans and keep a watchful eye. (Page 96)

5) With Progressive Christianity coming out of the evangelical churches, it's more a changing of the Gospel rather than outright paganism. No wonder Colossians 1:23 (NET) tells us to *remain in the faith…without shifting from the hope of the gospel that you heard.* This type of false teaching walks away from a lot of the Bible. It rejects the view of the Bible's authority, and even redefines the terms used. (Page 97)

6) Progressive Christianity could be more out to change the world through Social Justice than share the Gospel. I recently heard it preached that throwing a net into the water in an attempt to change the water instead of attempting to

capture fish is not what we are to be doing as Christians. We are fishers of men. We are not here to change the water. Helping people and taking care of our environment is Biblical. It is good. (Col. 1:10 and Col. 3:17) But it's not the way to Heaven. (Page 97)

7) Much of Progressive Christianity is creating a god they can understand, and then worshipping him. But as Alisa Childers said, "If my god looks like me when I look in the mirror, chances are I'm just worshipping myself. That's idolatry." (Page 99)

8) Trust seems a very good "plumb line" as God makes our paths straight when we don't rely on our own understanding. We shouldn't try to design a god we can understand and then worship him. We should give the one true God our full attention, give Him all of our heart in everything we do, and trust Him as our Plumb Line. That is true wisdom! (Page 100)

NOTES

*(These Reflection/Note pages may be duplicated
and used for group discussions when needed.)*

CHAPTER NINE

THANKSGIVING

We're going to talk about thanksgiving, but not the "turkey" kind...this is about the Gospel of Jesus Christ. I just listened to a song that I knew from years ago by Walt Mills. It talks about not being able to even come close to paying for a splinter of the tree that Jesus died on...or a single drop of blood that was shed for my salvation. The gift of salvation is so priceless that we can't even comprehend it. And when Thanksgiving does roll around this year, I hope this chapter gives us more of an urgency to give our thanks to God above for the gift of His beloved Son first and foremost.

As talked about in the last chapter, GOSPEL in an acronym could look like this:

God's
Only
Son
Provides
Eternal
Life

If asked about our Hope, and why it is in Jesus, this is a simple way to explain what is not only simple but also extremely deep and complex. I love the mixture of the two... We can never get to the depths of all the promises that God's Word contains. But we can share our Hope in six words when needed! How amazing is our God? We have SO much to be thankful for. But we also have so much we should be watching out for as we walk along the narrow path that leads us through the gates of Heaven.

God's Word and plan is perfect for our lives. It may not seem to be at times, and it may be hard to be thankful at times. But as we talked about in the last chapter, Trust is needed. God knows what He is doing. As an example of the extent and detail that God goes to in His planning, God placed fourteen generations from Abraham to David, fourteen from David to the departure to Babylon, and then fourteen generations from that departure to Christ. Everything God does, He does with perfection and accuracy.

As Christians, we should be soaking in the Word of God and the Good News of Jesus Christ every day of our believing lives. This will give us a heart of thanksgiving because no matter what happens, or what we have done, God's mercy is new every morning. We can have our sins washed as clean as the freshly driven snow with the shed blood of Jesus Christ on the Cross. And not just that Jesus shed His blood, but that the wrath of God was put upon Jesus and not us. Our heavenly Father chose to crush His only begotten Son instead of us. He did that while we were still sinners, because of His amazing love. And the same amazing love shown on the Cross will continue on for all of eternity for those who will believe in the death, burial, and resurrection of the Lord Jesus Christ for salvation.

Our pride is one of the hardest things to give to God to attain this eternal life. But it is the one thing that MUST go to receive the gift of Jesus Christ! We must have a repentant heart, a humbled heart, because that is the sacrifice that God requires of us—not hopes for, not wishes for, but REQUIRES. (Psalm 51:17) Our flesh will fight this until we come to the end of us...and God will wait. He will not rush us. It will be our decision to make, when we decide to make it. But it must be done before we meet Jesus face to face. There will be no mercy at that meeting. We will either be one of the wheat or one of the tares—also known as darnels. What is a darnel? I'm about to tell you.

Darnel is weedy rye grass found in grain fields. It is intoxicating to humans and animals. That's why the enemy sneaks into God's fields and plants those poisonous tares among His children. Darnels are wheat's evil twin, and they are difficult to recognize if one is not trained in spotting them. A big enough dose of darnel, the "evil twin," can kill a person. The farmers do their best to separate them out of the true harvest of wheat unless they are planning their wheat to be used for beer and bread. Then they are left on purpose in order to get a high. Darnel seeds are stowaways. They need human assistance to grow amongst the wheat. They get stored and replanted next season if not found and separated out. They are so similar to true wheat that they are called a "false wheat".

Let's bring this into the realm of our churches/Christianity today. It can be found in Matthew 13:25, which tells us how the enemy came and sowed darnel... How does the enemy infiltrate Christianity so deceptively? By looking just like the real deal. A darnel/deception is hard to spot if we're not a professional farmer/truly devoted, Bible-believing Christian who is in the Word of God a lot. Darnels can sneak in and infiltrate the body of Christ right before our very eyes and ears if we are not aware of them. We are warned of this! We will take a longer look at that in a bit, but first let's focus on the Truth of the Gospel so we will be more equipped to spot the counterfeits when they appear. When focusing on Truth, we will gain the wisdom and knowledge needed to walk the path of Christianity that few find...sadly.

Let's start the Truth Journey in Matthew today, focusing on the life of Jesus. Much of this will be a review, but let's get to really know our Savior. We will take a look as Jesus walks on this earth, and what He was doing while He was here. We can start with Jesus' Mom, who was a noble young woman. She was chosen out of all the women who ever lived on planet Earth to give birth to the Christ child. Can you imagine such a privilege? And such a difficult assignment? Then Jesus' father on this earth, Joseph, was another person of noble character. So noble in fact that even when he thought his soon to be wife had cheated on him, he was going to "divorce" her privately so as not to bring shame to her or her family. Matthew 1:19 said Joseph was a righteous man...one who did exactly as he was told. Well, who else would a young woman like Mary want to marry? Jesus was getting some awesome parents on this earth. Of course, we know that Joseph did not "divorce" Mary (in our day and age, it would be more like an engagement), but married her and waited for the Son of God to be born to them.

When Jesus was born, God the Father placed a new star in the sky to announce the birth of His only Son. Talk about a birth announcement! Astronomers are still trying to figure out how all this worked. With today's technology they can run the stars back in time and see what the night sky looked like. But there are still different thoughts about all of this. Was it a Super Nova? A planet? Maybe we will get that answer in Heaven, because, for us, stars are fixed and unchanging. But God can do what He wants with the stars He places in the sky.

Who, besides all of Jerusalem and the Wise Men, was paying attention to this star? Herod was. He assembled the chief priests and experts in the law and asked them where the Christ child was to be born? They knew it was Bethlehem because it was recorded in Micah 5:2. Herod wasted no time in calling the Wise Men and asking them about when the star first appeared. He then sent them to Bethlehem and awaited the news they would bring back about Jesus. But they never return to Herod with the information. They were "wiser" than Herod thought!

By the time the Wise Men arrived in Bethlehem, Jesus was no longer in a stable, and He was no longer a brand-new baby. He was somewhere under the age of two. He was in a house by then as it is written in Matthew 2:11. And we are not exactly sure how many wise men actually visited Jesus. We know it's at least three because there were three gifts given: Gold for a King, Frankincense representing prayers, and Myrrh, which is a fragrant perfume used in embalming bodies prophesying Jesus' death. We know Jesus was under two because when the Wise Men did not return to Herod, he sent men to kill all the children in Bethlehem from the age of two and under. (Matthew 2:16) Herod's monarchy was threatened since he had been considered to be the King of the Jews. Herod was Jewish by choice, not descent. He was an Edomite, and a man full of selfish pride and ambition. Herod's kingship was because of Caesar's appointment, not by birth. He realized a new King had been born and he wanted Him gone! (Herod was the one who built the Second Temple.)

Now the shepherds in the field tending the sheep arrived right after Jesus was born. They weren't as far away as the Wise Men...and think about it...an angel came and gave them the announcement! (Luke 2:10) So who of us wouldn't have RUN to see the Christ child immediately?

Do you ever wonder about Jesus as a child? We don't have much information about Him as a young boy, but one thing we do know, angels were protecting Him. (Matthew 2:13, 2:19-20) Joseph took his family to Egypt to protect little Jesus, and then later after Herod died, they moved to Nazareth where Jesus spent His boyhood years. When Jesus was twelve, His parents made their yearly trek to Jerusalem for the Feast of the Passover. This is when Jesus got left behind. Yes, His parents lost our Savior for a bit. But they went back and found Jesus after three days...in the temple courts. Was He in big trouble! Mary asked Him, *"Child, why have you treated us like this? Look, your father and I have been looking for you anxiously."* Luke 2:48 (NET) Sound familiar? Ever lose a child? We have! Jesus, being God, had a good answer. He said, *"Why were you looking for me? Didn't you know that I must be in my Father's house?"* Luke 2:49 (NET) It's said His parents didn't understand the remark He made to them. But after returning to Nazareth, He was obedient to them. (Matthew 2) Good boy!

Meanwhile John the Baptist, Jesus' cousin, was growing up and paving the way for Jesus' earthly ministry. John was baptizing people in water as they repented of their sins. When the right time came, grown-up Jesus met John down by the river. He was around 30 at this point. Jesus wanted to be baptized by John, but John tried to prevent this by saying, *"I need to be baptized by you, and you come to me?"* Matthew 3:14 (NET) But John eventually yielded to Jesus. When Jesus came up out of the water, they got to hear our Father in Heaven speak as He said, *"This is my one dear Son; in him I take great delight."* Matthew 3:17 (NET)

Jesus was then led into the wilderness by the Spirit to be tempted by the devil. Ever feel like you gave your life to Jesus in faith and, soon after, your own wilderness experience began? It was a 40-day trial for Jesus as He was tempted greatly by the devil...three distinct times that we know of which you can read about in Matthew 4. Jesus not only used Scripture to battle the enemy, He obeyed the very Scripture He was quoting. That's where we can get power to battle the enemy...in obedience. After those forty days, Jesus went from Nazareth to Capernaum and He lived by the sea. I have been there and it's a beautiful place! Jesus began to preach there, and guess what His first sermon was? *"Repent, for the kingdom of heaven is near!"* Matthew 4:17 (NET) Such an important sermon to give—and one that is being sorely neglected in our churches today.

We don't know how many times Jesus walked along the Sea of Galilee before He came to the day when Simon (Peter) and Andrew were casting out their nets. He told them, *"Follow me, and I will make you fishers of men."* Matthew 4:19 (NKJV) They followed Jesus immediately, as did the other disciples that He chose. Jesus was gathering 12 men to be with Him during His time on this earth. They went around teaching in the synagogues, healing diseases and sickness, and casting out demons. It was during this time in Capernaum that we were given the gift of the sermon of the Beatitudes. (Matthew 5) Jesus preached and spoke through parables, while also healing many people. Those who rejected His message were left in spiritual blindness. Jesus warned if righteousness doesn't go beyond the experts in the law and those of the Pharisees, the people would never enter the kingdom of Heaven.

Let's take a break here in the life of Jesus and look at some things we also have been warned about in the Word since that time. Taking a look into 2 Peter now, we can listen in on the same Simon/Peter who was first called to follow Jesus by the Sea of Galilee. This is the same man who denied Jesus three times before Jesus' crucifixion. When Peter writes 2 Peter, he is walking the Earth without his Friend, Jesus. But Peter had matured in his faith, with the Holy Spirit living inside of him, he is aware that he will probably soon be martyred. Peter was not afraid but was faithful in serving Jesus with the time he had left. Sadly, Peter saw that heresy was already entering into the church through false teachers (2 Peter 2:1-3). He left many warnings in his writings, as well as encouragement for the faithful. They apply to us still today. During the end times, which we are probably in, the true Christians will be labeled as ignorant fundamentalists. We will be accused of, and rightly so, taking a literal interpretation of the Bible. We will look like the hate mongers instead of loving people. We have to remember our goal is fishing for souls, not changing the world that God will soon destroy before creating a New Heaven and a New earth.

When we talked about the darnels/false wheat earlier, Peter was warning the believers about all of this. Satan is a counterfeiter who will bring in a false gospel, preached by false pastors, and this will produce false believers. This can have many names, but in this chapter we're taking a look at what is sometimes called "Pop-Theology." This type of "Sunday morning message" will contain dabs of what people want to hear instead of what they need to hear in the Truth of the Gospel. Instead of Truth, what is "preached" will be very superficial stories using superficial illustrations, cute anecdotes, and entertainment for the "audience." 2 Peter 2:1b (NET) says, *"These false teachers will infiltrate your midst with destructive heresies, even to the point of denying the Master who bought them."* These words were written over 2,000 years ago and are even now ramping up stronger and stronger in our world, in our churches. Look at 2 Peter 2:18 (NET), *"For by speaking high-sounding but empty words they are able to entice, with fleshly desires and with debauchery, people who have just escaped from those who reside in error."* New believers are the most easily fooled, although even mature believers need to be very aware of all that is being preached.

What is debauchery? The definition is "excessive indulgence in sensual pleasures". Does this sound like our world today? Our TV today? Our music today? So many lifestyles today? What if Peter was here to see what is happening? He would probably say, "I tried to warn you." Are we listening to his warnings in the Words of Scripture? We need to be! When high-sounding sermons filled with empty words are being preached from the pulpit, we have to stand up and take notice! Pop-Theology will make people feel good. It can be encouraging. It can even make sense and give us some good insight into how to live life. But it's not the Gospel. When Jesus is left out, or just appears on the fringes of a sermon, it's not the Gospel message we need to hear! It will not save souls!

Peter tells us in 2 Peter 2:17 (NET) that, *"These men are waterless springs and mists driven by a storm, for whom the utter depths of darkness have been reserved."* Now, this not only warns us how useless their words are, how empty, but it also warns them to not be speaking such heresy. Our Father in Heaven is not going to go lightly on this!

Peter lists in 2 Peter 1:5-7 (NET) what is available to true believers…true followers of Jesus Christ. With faith, excellence can be added, then knowledge, self-control, perseverance, godliness, brotherly affection, and unselfish love. This is what a true Christian possesses. If we lack these things, it says in 1:9, we are blind, and we have forgotten about the cleansing of our past sins. We have so much to be thankful for, we must never forget! And when we hear Pop-Theology put in place of the Gospel, we need to pay attention and reject it. If we are hearing "cleverly concocted fables" (2 Peter 1:16), meaning stories that have nothing to do with Jesus Christ and are not even being connected with His atonement for our sins, it is wrong. There is nothing to be thankful for in heresy. Hopefully, we do not come to church to be entertained by a pastor who can weave a good tale. We come to find medicine for our hurting souls that only comes from the Word of God.

My son had a t-shirt with a Cross on it that said, "It's not medicine. It's the cure." He would wear that shirt almost every time he went to the clinic for chemotherapy. He knew where his Hope came from, and it wasn't in the chemo. It was in what Jesus promised him about eternal life. I hope many doctors and nurses took note, because when Phil did go Home to Heaven at the age of 16, he was cured!

2 Peter 2:3 (NET) says, *"And in their greed they will exploit you with deceptive words."* What is this greed? Money? Perhaps, the paycheck given by the church to pay their bills. But also, the approval of men over the approval of God…tickling the ears of the churchgoers, instead of speaking hard Truth that is needed. My son didn't need his ears tickled when he attended church each Sunday. He needed to hear that Jesus was his Savior, and that Jesus died on a Cross, was buried, and rose again on the third day, confirming that Satan had been defeated, sin and death had been defeated, and no matter what happened in the clinic, it could be well with my son's soul. If false preachers leave Jesus out, or push Him to the outskirts of their message so as not to offend anyone, then they are exploiting those who have come to hear the Truth. My son didn't, and all of us really don't, need to hear how to live a more prosperous, happier life. What we need to hear is how to live eternally with Jesus in Heaven. How many, sadly, sit in church on Sunday morning and leave with less than this? Far too many! What is needed is in 2 Peter 1:11 (NET), *For thus an entrance into the eternal kingdom of our Lord and Savior, Jesus Christ, will be richly provided for you.*

Jesus said on the last day many will call Him *"Lord, Lord,"* but He will tell them to depart from Him. Those preaching Pop-Theology may have a happy Sunday, and a good breakfast afterward, but it will not be a good day when they are face to face with Jesus. If they left Jesus out on earth, He will leave them out of Heaven. Matthew 10:33 (NET), *"But whoever denies me before people, I will deny him also before my Father in heaven."*

The darnels/tares (dabs of lies and deception) are in the midst of the wheat fields/churches. We should not be surprised by this. Peter warned us, as did many others in the Bible. There are counterfeits all around us. They look like wheat, but they are poison.

Today I was in a restaurant with a friend. A young boy was there, and I asked him if he was home-schooled. He said, "No." Then his mother told us he was out of school sick. He looked right at me, and with the cutest little voice said, "I ate a flower." His mother said they had called poison control, but he seems fine. He ate a flower...an innocent looking little plant on the playground, I suppose. And it could have harmed him greatly. No matter how innocent the darnels look, let's not "eat them"! I write this book to protect you as I also learn this myself. Pastors and elders are there in our churches to protect the flock. If they aren't doing their job as shepherds, or are part of the problem, let's wake up to it ourselves and call it what it is! A flower by any other name may still be poison!

The book of 2 Peter is Peter's last letter to the church. He wanted to get the word of warning out. He said in 2 Peter 1:12-15 (NET), *Therefore, I intend to remind you constantly of these things even though you know them and are well established in the truth that you now have. Indeed, as long as I am in this tabernacle, I consider it right to stir you up by way of a reminder, since I know that my tabernacle will soon be removed, because our Lord Jesus Christ revealed this to me. Indeed, I will also make every effort that, after my departure, you have a testimony of these things.*

Peter knew there was no time to waste, as should we. Peter's tabernacle/body was soon to be buried in the ground. His spirit and soul would ascend to Heaven and he would see his Friend, Jesus. What a glorious day that must have been for Peter. I'm sure Jesus said, *"Well done, good and faithful servant."* This is the same Peter who denied Jesus three times. What great hope this gives us all!

Always remember what Peter wrote in 2 Peter 3:9 (NET), *"The Lord is not slow concerning his promise, as some regard slowness, but is being patient toward you, because he does not wish for any to perish but for all to come to repentance."* Peter repented and became the Rock Jesus built His church on. We need to repent, every day, and encourage all those inside and outside of the church to do the same...even the darnels (false believers/unsaved/deceivers) need Jesus! They will be in our churches, so let's identify them and love them into the family of God. I've heard it said that this is not dividing the body of Christ, it is helping us identify the body of Christ.

Pop-Theology, which is so prevalent today, makes us all feel good when we hear it. But it will only get us so far...only the Truth of Jesus Christ will get us all the way through the narrow gate into Heaven. Only the Jesus that Matthew wrote about as Jesus walked this Earth and went to the Cross on our behalf will bring us safely Home for all of eternity. Jesus' life was difficult those last three and a half years after He started His earthly ministry. Interestingly enough, the last three and half years of the Tribulation time will be a very, very difficult time for those still left on this earth. Should there be a pre-tribulation rapture (this is debatable), the believers will not have to endure such trials. It is called the time of Jacob's trouble, which is in reference to the Jewish people, so it will be a time of their discovery of the Messiah since they missed who Jesus was the first time He came to this earth.

At the end of Jesus' life on earth, He had to return to Jerusalem to suffer many things. Jesus told His disciples exactly what was going to happen in Matthew 16:21—the elders and experts in religious law were going to have Him killed. But He told His disciples He would be raised on the third day. Peter, yes Peter, said, *"God forbid."* What if God had forbid it? But Jesus was always Plan A, never Plan B. Sometimes it doesn't make sense to us. But how else would we know the grace and mercy of God if God had not planned it this way? Sometimes Pop-Theology makes more sense in our every day. But this isn't our every day, this is our eternal day. We have to trust God's Word at all times. We don't need stories and anecdotes when lives are on the line. Yes, those things can be used for brief illustrations, but Jesus MUST BE of utmost importance in any message. I have learned that even the physical suffering of Jesus on the Cross, although important in the message, must be moved beyond into how we were really saved. It wasn't merely Jesus' physical suffering inflicted by the Romans that saved us. It was the wrath of the Father poured out on His Son that did. That's what paid for our sins. Because Christ lived a perfect life, He was the only Perfect Sacrifice that qualified. God, being a just Judge, had to punish the wicked. The wicked is what we are. But we were spared because Jesus took our punishment in full…all the sin that God hates was placed on Jesus. The only way God could forgive our sins was to do it Himself, to Himself, through Himself. (Isaiah 53:10) God had to come down and pay the penalty through Jesus Christ alone. God hates sin, and sinners. (Psalm 5:5-6) But He also loves us so much that Christ died for us while we were still sinners. Now we are saints who sometimes sin.

When Jesus told His disciples that they would need to take up their cross and follow Him, He had not yet hung upon it. In Matthew 16:27, Jesus also told them that the Son of Man will return with His angels, and there will be rewards according to what has been done. Did you ever think about the fact that angels have no redemption? This was preached in a strong sermon I heard recently, and I had never thought about it. We have no concrete answer for the angels' plight, but we can be very thankful that we have redemption! The one-third of the angels who fell had seen the face of God, and they still rejected Him and will not be redeemed. We know that to be true. When we meet Jesus face to face, our trials and temptations will be over. We will never reject Him. This will not happen again once there is a New Heaven and a New Earth. What a relief that will be.

When Jesus asked the cup to pass Him by if possible, He was talking about the cup of wrath, not the cup of physical suffering. When they had that last supper together, Jesus Himself broke the bread and handed it to them. Jesus Himself took the cup and gave it to them. Jesus did it willingly, all of it. He could have called on more than twelve legions of angels to save Himself, but He didn't. When Jesus hung on the Cross, the Father turned His face from all the detestable sin that we had ever and would ever commit—past, present, and future. Jesus hung there alone, not only abandoned by His friends, but by His Father as the sky turned dark and the Earth shook. What an amazing last statement He made when He said, *"Into Your hands I commit my spirit."* There may have been no sweeter words that passed His lips on Earth because it was finished. He could go Home and see His Father once again after saving those He loves.

Now we must come to Jesus with thankful hearts as little

children. Our thankfulness must go beyond what our minds can even comprehend. We don't feel what Jesus felt. When we do feel the weight of our own sins, it can seem unbearable at times. But Jesus took all of our sins and everyone else's on at one time. And because of the Cross and the wrath of the Father being satisfied upon it, upon His Son, we are washed clean. We can now daily bring our repentant heart, our sins, to the foot of the Cross and leave all that weight there. Our thankfulness first and foremost should be because of who God is and what He has done. The truth is, if God's mercy and grace were not available, we would be going nowhere but straight to Hell. It has been said, "The Christian should meet every adverse circumstance of life not with a spirit of stoic resignation but with a spirit of unfailing gratitude."

Even if life is dark, hard, and extremely painful, we can look to James 1:2-4 (NET) which says, *"...consider it nothing but joy when you fall into all sorts of trials, because you know that the testing of your faith produces endurance. And let endurance have its perfect effect, so that you will be perfect and complete not deficient in anything."*

In 1 Thessalonians 5:18 it says, *In everything, give thanks!* Is it hard? Yes! Impossible? Yes...without Jesus. We need the power of the Holy Spirit <u>within</u> to have thankful hearts when we are <u>without</u>. Sometimes it is a little easier when we have lived long enough to look back on God's faithfulness—our thanksgiving has had time to grow. We can begin to see, if we haven't already in the midst of hardship, how God has been molding and shaping us our whole lives—how He's orchestrated things just so. Paul Washer said, "The weakest person can believe, if they have a high view of God." We have to trust that God is God and we are not.

This is why we can't let the enemy plant darnels/tares amidst the wheat in our lives. They have the possibility of weakening our faith. Nothing but the full Truth of the Gospel of Christ can be victorious over the schemes of the enemy. We can't settle for Pop-Theology in a world that is moving closer and closer to the time when things written about in Revelation are becoming a reality in our world. God's goal is conforming us to His Son until Jesus returns for His bride, the church/us. This "conforming" only happens when Truth is what we are soaking in. As Peter wrote, we have to strive to be found at peace, without spot or blemish, when we come into His presence. (2 Peter 3:14) If we don't talk the hard stuff…about man's sinful state and being totally lost without God, and how repentance and Jesus are the only way to salvation, then many will be eternally lost. "Preaching only part of the Gospel will send people to Hell as much as none of the Gospel." (Okie Rambler) It's either the whole of the Gospel, or it's the hole that will lead people to Hell.

At the end of Jesus' earthly life, He told His disciples He would be handed over to the chief priests and experts of the law, that He would be condemned to death, mocked by the Jews and Gentiles, flogged severely, crucified and then raised on the third day. Jesus spelled it out for them, clearly. He spells our destination out for us today, clearly. Were they listening? Are we? I think not, a lot of the time. After Jesus told His disciples this, one of their moms even dared to ask Jesus for a favor? Hello?!! The timing seems off to me! In Matthew 20:21 she wants to know if her two sons can sit one at His right hand, and one at His left in His Kingdom? Wow! That's bold! Jesus told her she didn't know what she was asking…Jesus was talking about the cup He was about to drink. The wrath He was about to endure. We can be so self-centered. But the Son of Man came to serve, not to be served. Jesus modeled that for us!

When our eyes are focused on ourselves and this world, we won't get to know the Word of God or our Savior. From beginning to end, God's Word is focused on Jesus Christ. We know this because there are over 300 prophecies in the Old Testament that point to Jesus, and He fulfilled them all in the New Testament. Let me list just a few here:

Jesus was born in Bethlehem, born of a virgin, tempted by Satan, entered Jerusalem, rejected by His own people, betrayed by one of His followers for 30 pieces of silver, tried and condemned, silent before His accusers, spit upon, crucified, garments divided by casting lots, bones not broken, sin offering, buried in rich man's tomb, raised from the dead, now sits at God's right hand…

It is said that in terms of historical reliability, the Bible is superior to any other ancient writing. Why do so many trust other writings, other history books, and not the Bible? As we read through Matthew, we will see Jesus used an expression quite often. He says, in Matthew 5:18, *"I tell you the truth."* Different translations will use different wording meaning the same thing. Jesus was emphatic! He wanted His followers to know that He wasn't messing around, and we shouldn't be either. When asked multiple questions about things in this life, I like Jesus' answer in Matthew 22:29 (NET), *"You are deceived, because you don't know the scriptures or the power of God..."* He is talking about marriage here, but how many times could this be applied to our own lives? Are we being deceived because we aren't in the Word like we should be? And by not being in the Word, we really don't understand the power of God in our lives. When Jesus was questioned by the Pharisees and the Sadducees, He gave such simple yet powerful answers. When asked about paying taxes, He asked whose image was on the coin? He told them to give to Caesar what belonged to Caesar. Then Jesus turns the question on them asking them (the Jewish leaders) what they think about the Christ? (Matthew 22:42) They couldn't answer Him, and after that day they stopped asking Him questions. He told the people they were to pay attention to these teachers, but they were not to do what they do because they didn't practice what they taught. (Matthew 23:3) Such wise advice for us still today. If we don't see Fruit in someone's life, even if their words are right, their actions are not to be followed. How can we not be thankful for such a clear Gospel, for such Truth to follow, for such a Savior as Jesus Christ our Lord? This isn't tough, or hard to understand. Even a child can understand this message if we will take the time to teach it to them. But we must watch out, as Jesus warns us, so that no one misleads us. (Matthew 24:4) Those who mislead children are held very accountable for their actions. (Matthew 18:6)

Why would the enemy not want to counterfeit what is so powerful in this world—the Truth of the Gospel. Why would the enemy not want to steal, kill, and destroy all that God is doing in our lives? False messiahs and false prophets...little dabs here and there, are to be expected. Jesus told us so. (Matthew 24:24) They will perform great signs and wonders to deceive all they can. Let it not be said of us! Let's stay faithful to the Truth. Let's, *"Awake, oh sleeper!"* Unlike the disciples who could not stay awake in the Garden of Gethsemane with Jesus. Jesus knows that the spirit is willing, but the flesh is weak. When Jesus said this in Matthew 26:41, I wonder if He was also speaking of Himself? He was at that time fully man and fully God. His flesh was just like ours. He had a heart beating in His chest that was breaking. He had the enemy coming at his flesh just like the enemy does to ours. It was hard! He understands weakness. We know that, because an angel came and strengthened Him. (Luke 22:43) But Jesus' Spirit was willing to do His Father's will. *"My Father, if this cup cannot be taken away unless I drink it, your will must be done."* Matthew 26:42 (NET) The Father can't simply forgive our sins, the law demands punishment/payment. If God simply let us go free, He would be wicked Himself in the same way a judge in court can't just let a criminal go free. The judge must punish the perpetrator. God remedied this by coming down Himself to pay the penalty. He died so the law could be satisfied. God is both just and the Justifier.

While Jesus was still talking about His betrayer coming, Judas showed up with a large crowd ready to arrest Jesus. They took Jesus into Jerusalem and found people who would testify falsely against Him. Jesus remained silent. He didn't answer even one accusation when standing before Pilate, another fulfillment of Scripture. (Matthew 27:14) Isn't it interesting that after Pilate said in verse 24, *"I am innocent of this man's blood. You take care of it yourselves!"*, the Jews replied in Matthew 27:25, *"Let his blood be on us and on our children!"* Jesus' forgiving blood on them/us is the only thing that can save our souls. A crown of thorns was braided and placed on Jesus' head. I wonder who it was that did that? Can you imagine being given such an assignment? After Jesus was flogged, mocked, spat upon, and hung on a Cross, it is written that they kept guard over Him there. Really? Like He was going anywhere? Maybe it was because they were taunting Him, saying, *"If he comes down now from the cross, we will believe in him."* Matthew 27:42 (NET) When Jesus cried out, *"My God, my God, why have you forsaken me?"* one of the bystanders immediately tried to give him a drink. Matthew 27:47-48 (NET) What must the Son of God thought in that moment of compassion from someone who moved so quickly to help in His time of need? Jesus asked His Father to forgive them because they didn't know what they were doing—such love! Then He cried out saying *"It is finished,"* and gave up His Spirit. The Temple curtain tore, the Earth shook, the rocks split, and the Son of God's work on the Cross was finished. *"Truly this one was God's Son,"* it was said. But others still threatened by Jesus said, *"...we remember that while that deceiver was still alive he said, 'After three days I will rise again.' So give orders to secure the tomb..."* Matthew 27:63-64 (NET) They were still on guard not knowing what to expect. But on the third day our Father in Heaven confirmed that His wrath was satisfied when the Earth shook again, an angel descended from Heaven, and the stone was rolled away to reveal that truly the Son of God had risen from the dead. The angel said, *"He is not here, for he has been raised, just as he said. Come and see the place where he was lying."* Matthew 28:6 (NET)

We can visit that place today—His empty tomb is just outside the walls of the city of Jerusalem. It's not 100 percent sure that it is the exact tomb, but all the facts that need to back it up seem to indicate that it is. After Jesus' death when the soldiers were given a large sum of money (Matthew 28:12) to conceal the truth of the Resurrection, it began a lie that Jesus' body was stolen. That lie continues to this day amongst the Jewish people. But we know that Jesus came and appeared to the twelve and then to more than 500 others to prove that it was no lie. Jesus is alive! This is the absolute Truth of all that Jesus said was going to happen and did happen. Jesus promised us saying, *"I am with you always, to the end of the age."* Matthew 28:20 (NET)

We very well could be at the *end of* the end of the age and we are being warned of what is happening. We need to take heed! A pastor said, "You are the house the thief is trying to break into." The thief is coming in all different ways, but there is one way to discern if he is amongst us…it's when the focus is not on Jesus, but on self. When the preaching is not on the Gospel of Jesus Christ, but on Pop-Theology that makes us feel good and laugh for a few moments, it is dangerous. It might even pique our interest or bring on a tear. But when the message is not about Jesus and all He died to give us…we are not being taught to be thankful, we are being taught to be selfish. Could it be Satan? That is why in this chapter we have spent a great deal of time learning about Jesus Christ…who He is, what He did, why He came, what happened, and where it took Him, and will take us. We need to know our Savior up close and personal.

In Isaiah 14:13 (NET), it is written; *You said to yourself, "I will climb up to the sky. Above the stars of El I will set up my throne. I will rule on the mountain of assembly on the remote slopes of Zaphon."* When there is a whole lot of "I" going on in a Sunday morning message, and very little "I AM," then it is self-focused theology. It is not for us!

In a hungry, thirsty, lonely, naked, sick, imprisoned world, let's bring God's Hope of eternity to satisfy the hunger, God's Son to quench the thirst, a warm invitation into God's family to comfort the lonely, God's love to clothe the naked, a new life to heal the sick, and Christ's freedom to release those in captivity. When we do this for the least, we are doing the most for the greatest, our Jesus.

It is said things in this world have gone from Tolerance, to Intolerance, to Violence. There is an attack on true Christianity that will continue to increase until the return of our Lord. The love of Jesus is not only sadly missing in our world, He is more and more going missing in our churches that claim to preach in His name. Is this the end of the age? Yes, it is happening. But we live with great Hope! Let's remember, when we deserved nothing but judgment, our Father in Heaven made us sons and daughters through the sacrifice of His dearly loved Son. Thank You, Lord Jesus! *Always rejoice, constantly pray, in everything give thanks. For this is God's will for you in Christ Jesus.* 1 Thessalonians 5:16-18 (NET)

Let's pray:

Father, we want to know Your Son, personally. We want our hearts' desire to be to serve Jesus only, to follow Him closely, and to know Him intimately. Thank You for making a way for us to come Home to You when this Earth comes to its last day. In Jesus' name. Amen.

1) How amazing is our God? We have SO much to be thankful for. But we also have so much we should be watching out for as we walk along the narrow path that leads us through the gates of Heaven. (Page 112)

2) Darnel is weedy rye grass found in grain fields. It is intoxicating to humans and animals. That's why the enemy sneaks into God's fields and plants those poisonous tares among His children. Darnels are wheat's evil twin, and they are difficult to recognize if one is not trained in spotting them. (Page 112)

3) Satan is a counterfeiter who will bring in a false gospel, preached by false pastors, and this will produce false believers. This can have many names, but in this chapter we're taking a look at what is sometimes called "Pop-Theology." This type of "Sunday morning message" will contain what people want to hear instead of what they need to hear in the Truth of the Gospel. (Page 116)

4) Pop-Theology will make people feel good. It can be encouraging. It can even make sense and give us some good insight into how to live life. But it's not the Gospel. When Jesus is left out, or just appears on the fringes of a sermon, it's not the Gospel message we need to hear! It will not save souls! (Page 117)

5) Jesus said on the last day many will call Him *"Lord, Lord,"* but He will tell them to depart from Him. Those preaching Pop-Theology may have a happy Sunday, and a good breakfast afterward, but it will not be a good day when they are face to face with Jesus. If they left Jesus out on earth, He will leave them out of Heaven. Matthew 10:33 (NET), *"But whoever denies me before people, I will deny him also before my Father in heaven."* (Page 118)

6) We don't need stories and anecdotes when lives are on the line. Yes, those things can be used for brief illustrations, but Jesus MUST BE of utmost importance in any message. (Page 120)

7) This is why we can't let the enemy plant darnels/tares amidst the wheat in our lives. They have the possibility of weakening our faith. Nothing but the full Truth of the Gospel of Christ can be victorious over the schemes of the enemy. We can't settle for Pop-Theology in a world that is moving closer and closer to the time when things written about in Revelation are becoming a reality in our world. (Page 122)

8) If we don't talk the hard stuff…about man's sinful state and being totally lost without God, and how repentance and Jesus are the only way to salvation, then many will be eternally lost. "Preaching only part of the Gospel will send people to Hell as much as none of the Gospel." (Okie Rambler) (Page 122)

<u>NOTES</u>

*(These Reflection/Note pages may be duplicated
and used for group discussions when needed.)*

CHAPTER TEN

CONFESSION

We have already spent time on repentance in this book, and we have talked a lot about its importance. Now as we continue to look at what John the Baptist was doing in preparing the way for Jesus, we also need to look at confession and the difference between it and repentance.

Repentance is a turning, a change. The first repentance we experience is when we no longer reject Christ—it is a changing of our mind. Then, we continue to repent throughout our life as we hate the things that God hates and love the things that God loves. It is a continual growing in faith, holiness, and the desire to not want to be like the world. As a true Christian, we begin to identify our sin and confess that we agree with God that sin is wrong. We come into agreement with the Word and all that it contains as it corrects, rebukes, and encourages us in season and out. (2 Timothy 4:2)

It is one thing to know that Jesus lived on this Earth. It's another to believe He died on the Cross and rose again as an act of propitiation for our sins as well as the sins of the whole world. (Propitiation: A sacrifice that satisfies the demands of God's justice.) We have to understand our personal need for the forgiveness Jesus offers us. When the story of Jesus' death on the Cross becomes our story of being born again by the blood of Jesus and we have been redeemed, that's when the Bible becomes more than just a book on our nightstand—it becomes our life, containing our new identity in Christ Jesus. This is salvation…God's saving grace. This is how we will live eternally with our Father in Heaven. We will still sin in the meantime, of course. But we will now recognize it and confess it.

Confession is not just asking God to forgive us, it is agreeing with the Holy Spirit when He convicts us of something we have done—then repenting/changing our mind and turning away from it. There is great joy in this response to sin. It is a great relief when we know that there is nothing we can do to merit God's gift of salvation other than to believe in His one and only Son, Jesus. How does all this happen?

In Mark 1:2 (NET) we read, *"Look, I am sending my messenger ahead of you, who will prepare your way."* He was a *"voice shouting."* Wouldn't it be nice if we had a messenger sent to us, preparing us for what is ahead? We actually do… John was telling everyone to *"Prepare the way for the Lord."* What if this is exactly what the corona virus is doing right now around the world? What if it is preparing the way for the Lord Jesus to return? It could be! For the young people, all this might not have as big an impact. They haven't lived long enough to know that this is SO not the norm. Maybe for some, it has happened in the past, but not to this extent. When has something ever been worldwide? When has it ever closed schools? Churches? Restaurants? Brought "Shelter in Place" to our homes? What is happening? Let's look to the Word and find our answers. Maybe not the ones we want, but the ones we need.

John was preaching repentance and baptism for the forgiveness of sins, and people were flocking to him. It says the people came from the whole Judean countryside and all of Jerusalem. (Mark 1:5) They confessed, they were baptized, they were having their hearts made ready for the Savior of the world. Did they know that? Perhaps not. Maybe they were doing the next thing that God placed before them, not knowing that Jesus was soon to be revealed in their midst. What if Jesus is soon to be revealed in our midst? What if our hearts are being prepared for His return?

As we think about these things as true believers in the Lord Jesus Christ, should our hearts be filled with excitement? Yes! And what is set before us to do in preparation? 2 Peter 3:11-12a (NET) says, *Since all these things are to melt away in this manner, what sort of people must you be, conducting your lives in holiness and godliness, while waiting for and hastening the coming of the day of God?* Holiness and godliness are so important right now. What is happening could be the very thing we have read about, looked forward to, and wanted to hasten...the return of our Savior! If this is the ultimate answer we are all looking for, what an amazing time to be alive. But if it's not? Well then, we keep on with the assignment we have before us right now because *the person who endures to the end will be saved.* Matthew 24:13 (NET)

John the Baptist knew his assignment. He knew why he walked on this planet. He leapt in his mother's womb when Jesus came near in Mary's womb. (Luke 1:41) John was humble. We know that because of the way he dressed in camel's hair and a belt of leather. Nothing fancy about him. He also said about Jesus that he was, *"not worthy to bend down and untie the strap of his sandal."* (Mark 1:7) And when Jesus came to him to be baptized, John didn't feel qualified for such a privilege. He knew Jesus was more powerful than he could ever hope or want to be. When Jesus entered the world's scene, John stepped aside. He was then imprisoned for his ministry of talking to Herod about the sin in his life, concerning his brother's wife to whom he was now married. John knew about repentance, he preached about repentance, and then when Jesus came to be baptized, John knew his job was just about finished. Jesus would take over from there, preaching His very first sermon. We talked about it before but it is stated just a bit differently in the book of Mark 1:15 (NET): *"The time is fulfilled and the kingdom of God is near. Repent and believe the gospel."*

Jesus preached the Gospel. But what was the Gospel before Jesus died, was buried, and rose again? What was Jesus preaching exactly? The same thing that was preached in the twenty-seven books of the Old Testament, starting in Genesis 3:15 where we "hear" for the first time about salvation through Jesus Christ. What? you may say, I don't remember that... We can take a look in Genesis 2:16-17 where Adam and Eve broke their relationship with God by their sin. Then when we turn to Genesis 3:15, where it speaks of someone who will "crush the head of the serpent". This is our Hope of the Gospel. This is our Jesus...right there! Thousands of years before John the Baptist announced Jesus' arrival...thousands of years before we read of Jesus dying for our sins on the Cross...and in all those years, God never veered from this path. Our Father stayed true to His promise, showing us His love and mercy as the story of salvation wove a path through all of the Old Testament. In Isaiah 53, Jesus is perfectly described. And then Jesus does just that, crushing the head of the serpent on the Cross at Calvary.

What did that crushing look like? It started with the crushing of the Father's only begotten Son on the Cross. It looked like pain, torment, and crucifixion of One so innocent that there was no sin in Him and yet He became sin for us. (2 Cor. 5:21) It looked like defeat instead of triumph. It looked wrong…so very wrong. And yet it was so very right because it was and is the perfect plan of our Father in Heaven to save us from His wrath and an eternity in Hell. On the Cross, Jesus took on the sin of the world and crushed Satan's power over sin and death. (Hebrews 2:14) It has been said, "Christ delivered us from the fear of death. Not death itself." Most of us will still die a physical death. But Satan's final defeat will come at the end of time, as stated in Revelation 20:10 when Satan is cast into Hell and we live eternally in the New Heaven and the New Earth.

And now, what do we do in the meantime? We accept this most precious gift of salvation. We don't just read about it and talk about it…we embrace it and live it. And we confess! The Greek word for confess is "homologeo". It means to "Say the same thing," and then to "Agree." This is what we must do! Walk in obedience and agreement with God. It's not easy. The bar is high!

Let's take a look at what Paul is telling young Titus in the book of Titus. It's not a long book, but it's a powerful one when we read it in the light of confession—in agreeing with God. The book of Titus was written after Paul was released from prison in Rome about AD 63. As Paul and Titus travelled together, they spent time in Crete. There were problems in Crete with the believers that needed to be given instructions, and there were elders that needed to be appointed. Paul laid it out to Titus, how the believers were to live, and what the qualifications of the elders were. In reading this, we may want to say, "Well, I'm not an elder. This doesn't apply to me." But as I read through it, it seemed it could speak to each one of us who call Jesus Lord. And if we would take the time to really examine ourselves, we would find ourselves needing to confess many things that need to be "set in order" in our own lives, whether we are an elder or not.

Let's list them and see how we match up. It says we are not to be arrogant, not prone to anger, not a drunkard, not violent, not greedy for gain. We are to be hospitable, devoted to what is good, sensible, upright, devout, and self-controlled. How are we doing so far? Let's continue…we are to hold firmly to God's faithful message, and give exhortation (communicate it), and correct those who speak against it. Paul goes on and tells Titus even more…talking about those who are rebellious, idle talkers, deceivers, and even Jewish people who are teaching what should not be taught for dishonest gain. It was said that Cretans were liars, evil beasts, and lazy gluttons.

As I read through this, personally, I had many things to confess/agree with God about. I could see myself in this list in more ways than I would want to count. It made me pause, and confess, and repent, and receive forgiveness…and be so thankful for the blood of Jesus Christ. Without the Restrainer, the Holy Spirit in our lives, these things grow like mushrooms in the dark…just take a look at our world. But this is exactly what Jesus died for…these very things that we can get caught up in and need forgiveness for. This is us, this is the world, without Jesus. When we examine ourselves and understand this personally and worldwide, it can break our heart…it should break our heart—to see so many lost without their Savior. But these can also be the very things that get our attention and lead us to our Savior. When we hit rock bottom, we can find the secure Rock to stand on.

Paul wrote: *Now I rejoice, not because you were made sad, but because you were made sad to the point of repentance. For you were made sad as God intended so that you were not harmed in any way by us. For sadness as intended by God produces a repentance that leads to salvation, leaving no regret, but worldly sadness brings about death.* 2 Corinthians 7:9-10 (NET)

Sadness seems…well…so sad. But what Paul is telling us here is that the sadness that God brings into our lives is not to harm us, but to bring us to repentance that leads to our being saved by the blood of Jesus. It brings joy to our soul when we understand all that Jesus died to give us. Many times, we can't see our own sin. But when the Holy Spirit shows us our sin, then our only course of action should be repenting, confessing, and being set free with Christ's forgiveness. That's saving grace!

Paul begins the book of Titus by writing that this letter is, *to further the faith of God's chosen ones and the knowledge of the truth that is in keeping with godliness, in hope of eternal life, which God, who does not lie, promised before time began.* Titus 1:1-2 (NET) We have to be reminded of these things because keeping with godliness isn't easy in this fallen world. We are surrounded by so much that isn't of God, even in the expression of Christianity across America, even in our churches with those we fellowship with, even by pastors and worship leaders we love and want to trust. Sometimes we don't see it! We can be blinded to things that we should be doing, or shouldn't be doing, how we are supposed to be reacting, behaving, and also Who we are to be following.

Let's think of it this way…your young son comes home from his baseball game. It had started to rain, so the game was shortened, and now his cleats are filled with muck and mire. What is muck and mire? Muck is a slimy mud, and mire is a deep mud. In Psalm 40:1-2 (NET) it is written: *"I waited patiently for the LORD, he turned to me and heard my cry. He lifted me out of the slimy pit, out of the mud and mire; he set my feet on a rock and gave me a firm place to stand."* When we walk into church, we usually have a lot of mud on our "cleats". We are looking for a firm place to stand, but we are walking in with all sorts of slimy things from the world to which we have been exposed. We bring it inside our church, many times unknowingly. Everyone, from the pastor, to the worship team, to the congregants have been exposed to such things. We come together to hear the Word of God, to pray together, to worship together, and wash some of that muck out of our lives by soaking in the Word of Truth.

We actually need to be doing this every day of our lives by reading the Word and praying. Otherwise, we can be leaving tracks of the world's slimy mud everywhere we go. As Christians, we can stop, scrape it off, and walk free of it through being made aware, confessing, repenting, and being washed clean by the blood of Jesus. If we don't do this, we will be leaving bits of mud and mire in our homes, in our places of work, and even in our churches. It's happening more and more in the day and age we live in because too many are not soaking in the Truth of the Gospel.

Before I share a situation with you along these lines, I want to share one more verse out of Philippians. It's in 1:8-11. *For God is my witness that I long for all of you with the affection of Christ Jesus.*

And I pray this, that your love may abound even more and more in <u>knowledge and every kind of insight</u> so that <u>you can decide what is best</u>, and thus be sincere and <u>blameless</u> for the day of Christ, <u>filled with the fruit of righteousness</u> that comes through Jesus Christ to the glory and praise of God. (Underlines mine)

Please note where I have underlined in the passage. I long for you to have knowledge and insight so you can decide what is best, to be blameless and filled with the fruit of righteousness. I don't write this book because it's fun. I write it because I believe these truths and deceptions need to be addressed. By bringing things into the light, then we all can decide what is best with the knowledge we have gained. You may disagree with me, and that is your right. But I can rest knowing that I have told you what I have discovered and be at peace. So here we go...

There are situations in some churches that have come to my attention...things being done by amazingly talented worship leaders. But something seemed off to me. Was it just because I had not seen these things done before in a church setting? Or is it just because I could be considered old now? I began to wonder what was acceptable to God as worship. These are questions that we all must ask. We are to be Bereans, even in worship. This is not really about the people; this is about the source behind their behavior. Titus 3:2 (NET) says, *They must not slander anyone, but be peaceable, gentle, showing complete courtesy to all people.* This was my goal in this.

I decided to look up some more information about what was happening. Because of that, I did have some knowledge about it while being present at a conversation concerning similar things. I was a bit surprised and said to God on my way home, "So many are lapping this up." I heard a gentle voice within say, "Instead of looking it up." That set me on a course of even more research. Since this book is about being on a Truth Journey and discovering the ways we may be deceived on that journey, I knew what I had to do...dissect the dabs!

1 Corinthians 14:20 (NET) says, *Brothers and sisters, do not be children in your thinking. Instead, be infants in evil, but in your thinking be mature.*

Many of us are infants in evil, which is good. But at the same time, when we become mature in our thinking, we begin to see the evil, the muck and mire, that we are not to be a part of. So, let me tell you what was going on, and then we will "investigate" this from here. What was being introduced was spinning while worshipping on stage. This is not like spinning class on a bicycle. It was spinning the body rapidly while the worship music was playing. It was actually impressive. But I had to ask, was it *going beyond what is written*? (1 Cor. 4:6) Are worshippers supposed to dance undignified in worship, especially on the stage? Did David? I needed to do more investigation.

As we read on in Titus, we come to Titus 2:6-8 (NET) where it says, *Encourage younger men likewise to be self-controlled, showing yourself to be an example of good works in every way. In your teaching show integrity, dignity, and a sound message that cannot be criticized, so that any opponent will be at a loss, because he has nothing evil to say about us.* These are Paul's instructions to young Titus for the young men in Crete. This is what caught my attention and why we are in Titus for what might be deception/the enemy invading Christian worship time.

Not only did I see many of my own sins listed while in the book of Titus, I knew that there needed to be a humbling of my own heart before tackling this difficult subject. I needed the log to be removed from my own eye before I talked about the speck in someone else's. (Matthew 7:3) This is not a battle of flesh and blood, this is not to speak badly about those doing their best to worship God as they think it should be done...this is about what Satan could be doing in our churches when we aren't looking, aren't paying attention, or don't even have a clue that we should be. We don't want muddy cleats in our churches! This is what this book is dealing with, as painful as it might be.

Why would spinning/whirling be a problem in Christian worship? Many will say, *"David danced before the Lord."* How many times have we heard that? I've said it myself. (2 Samuel 6:14) Now we're going to really get into it here...and it may be a bit more uncomfortable. But it does say in Titus 2:3-5 what older women, such as myself, are to be doing—I am to be teaching what is good. Sometimes that involves pointing out some muddy cleats...

David danced, yes, he did. David also was not in a Tabernacle at the time he danced before the Lord as they moved the Ark of the Covenant. (Just to be noted.) Also, why was David wearing a

Levitical priestly item like an ephod when he was from the tribe of Judah and not a Levite? Just some things to think about. We are not told in Scripture that it was right of him to be wearing this or dancing like this. It just says this is what was happening. Was it prescriptive or descriptive? Michal, his wife, was upset about his display. She said he was, *"...in full view of the slave girls of his servants as any vulgar fellow would."* (2 Samuel 6:20) David thought he was worshipping the Lord, but was he? Properly? David was drawing attention to himself. Worship of any kind should bring glory to God alone and edify others in that process. Worship should not distract others from focusing on Christ.

Michal was not David's only wife. He had multiple wives, and concubines. This was not God's idea for marriage. Deuteronomy 17:17 says, *Furthermore, he must not marry many wives lest his affections turn aside, and he must not accumulate much silver and gold.* David was not being obedient to God in many ways that we can read about. David was a human being who made many mistakes. That's why Uzzah died the first time they tried moving the Ark disobediently. It is good to read that David was a man after God's own heart (Acts 13:22) because we all make mistakes. We can all be forgiven through the sacrifice of Jesus Christ. But all this is just to bring into question whether we can use the *David danced* excuse card when certain types of dance during worship could actually be considered ungodly. We all worship in different ways. David might have had a full heart for God that day. But was it what God wanted in the form of worship before the Ark? I have never heard these questions asked or answered before I spent time doing this research.

Sometimes we feel the need to worship God with everything we have, we love Him so very much…but we are told to worship God in both spirit and truth. Recently I witnessed a young woman at church step out into the aisle and dance before the Lord during worship. It was quite beautiful. Even Miriam, in Exodus 15:20, danced and sang with a drum while praising God. I know many churches incorporate dancing into their worship. But I believe we need to be careful when and how that is done. I'm not saying it's all wrong, or all right. I'm just bringing this into the light so we can take a look at it, pray about it, and seek God in our own walk and worship of Him. As one pastor put it, "The church that can't worship must be entertained. And men who can't lead a church to worship must provide that entertainment." Let that never be said about us! Worship is not about entertainment…it is about drawing near to God, focusing on who He is, what His Word teaches us, and learning and growing in that environment. If those in church are not interested in true worship, but merely entertainment, and are, therefore, bored, they need to go to a play on Broadway, or a concert. Church is where God is worshipped. It is a place where the leader/pastor of the church is to be protective of the flock, keeping the ways of this world from entering in.

Romans 14 talks about not putting any stumbling block or obstacle in your brother's way. Spinning/whirling in church as a worship leader could cause some to question what godly worship is to look like, especially for new people who come in seeking a relationship with Jesus Christ. There is also more involved in this, which I will address in a bit. But let's go back to the book of Titus now, and soak in more of the Truth that is needed for balance in all of this. The Truth in God's holy Word is mainly what we want to soak in as we travel on this journey.

Paul instructed Titus what to do with those in Crete who needed to be set on the right path. Titus 2 talks about God's grace, and how it brings salvation and *trains us to reject godless ways and worldly desires.* (v. 11) We are *to live self-controlled, upright and godly lives in the present age.* (v. 12) How much harder is that for us today? It tells us we are to do this *as we wait for the happy fulfillment of our hope in the glorious appearing of our great God and Savior Jesus Christ.* (v. 13) It is written that Jesus *gave Himself for us* to set us free and to *purify* us for Himself. (v. 14) Paul told Titus he was to *communicate these things* with the authority that he had. (v. 15) Titus was to remind the Cretans many things, one of which was to be obedient. (3:1) Paul tells him they, too, were once *foolish, disobedient, and misled,* and the list goes on… No one is exempt from what is being written to Titus. And that's exactly the point…we all need to repent. We all need to confess. We all need cleansing from muddy things we are exposed to every day.

Some may want to quote Titus 3:10 to me right now. I get it! It says, *Reject a divisive person after one or two warnings…* But what am I to do when I see things that need to be looked at a little more, talked about, and written about? I want us all to be "Bereans". To pray, to seek God, and to discover for ourselves what it is we believe about David dancing, worshipful dancing, or any kind of dancing. What about hula dancing? Salsa dancing? Belly dancing? Are we to dance for rain as the Indians do? The list could go on… All these should be prayed about and see how they line up with Scripture. As I wrote previously, "We are not dividing the body of Christ. We are trying to identify the body." That is my heart's desire. Let's find out what is of God, and what is not.

I said, "I will confess my rebellious acts to the Lord." And then you forgave my sins. For this reason every one of your faithful followers should pray to you while there is a window of opportunity.
Psalm 32:5b-6a (NET)

Here's our confession! And it is powerful! Right now, with the corona virus putting many of us in a position of having more time to spend in the Word, we should be using this window of opportunity wisely. Being in the Word, we can uncover what the enemy would like to keep hidden. It's not an easy thing in today's world, to uncover the muck and mire, but it is so needed.

John the Baptist had a hard job. He was in prison for preaching the truth to Herod. Mark 6:18-20 (NET) says, *For John had repeatedly told Herod, "It is not lawful for you to have your brother's wife." And yet, Herod stood in awe of John and protected him, since he knew that John was a righteous and holy man. When Herold heard him, he was thoroughly baffled, and yet he liked to listen to John.* This did not end well for John the Baptist. During a banquet, Herodias, Herod's wife's daughter, came in and danced. Herod was so pleased, he told her he would give her anything, even up to half of his kingdom. She went to talk with her mother, and since her mother had a grudge against John for disapproving of their marriage, she had her daughter ask for the head of John the Baptist on a platter immediately. The King didn't want to, but he sent an executioner at once to bring John's head to the girl. She gave it to her mother.

It just came to me, isn't it interesting that this part of Scripture comes up about what happened as the result of someone dancing…while we are looking at the "David danced" idea? Believe me, I am not against dancing, and this was not planned by me. I wonder if God is confirming for me that I am to be addressing this.

I surely hope so. Because I feel more like John must have felt as he talked to Herod about his marriage. It's not comfortable.

After his beheading, John's disciples came and took his body away and placed it in a tomb. (Mark 6:29) When Jesus was told of John's fate, they tried to go away to a remote place for a while. (Mark 6:32). But Jesus was given little time to rest as many saw them leaving and followed them. Time alone with His Father was probably so needed. Still, Jesus had compassion on the people. (Mark 6:34)

As I studied Titus, I wondered why such a book would be included in Scripture? I then came across a sermon about worship. The pastor was talking about the church as the bride of Christ. And how the Bridegroom has gone away and left the bride with the world. We are to take good care of the bride until Christ returns. But are we? The pastor said so many are trying to change the bride into something she is not…holiness is disappearing in so many ways in our churches. It was said if we decide to renovate the bride, change the worship by "raising the hem of her skirt," it will be better for a hostile atheist on the day of Christ's return. This makes me realize what Paul was instructing Titus to do…to watch over the bride in Crete. Paul gave Titus instructions, and then one day Paul would return and see how he had done in putting God's house in order there in Crete. Putting elders in place and communicating the behavior that goes with sound teaching. (Titus 2:1) Would there be a lot of "mud" around the place when Paul got there? Honestly, I have been to Crete, and some of it didn't feel very clean. I remember men standing in the doorways of their shops and trying to lure us women to enter in and buy their gold.

All of this to say, we are to steward well what we have been given. Titus was doing his best in this because he understood our salvation has been bought with the precious blood of Jesus Christ. *We proclaim him by instructing and teaching all people with all wisdom so that we may present every person mature in Christ.* Colossians 1:28 (NET) It's not easy to point out ungodliness, even when it is going against the core fundamentals of our Christian belief. But we are called to when it truly violates God's holiness.

What is happening in so many ways within Christianity today is of Satan and not our Savior. Some are mimicking pagan rituals in worship and they don't even know it. But we should be watching and be wary when what we see and hear is something different than what was written in the Bible thousands of years ago. Ephesians 5:11 says, *Do not participate in the unfruitful deeds of darkness, but rather expose them.* Perhaps it is now time to expose where some of this spinning/whirling might have originated since 2 John 9-11 (NET) tells us that *Everyone who goes on ahead and does not remain in the teaching of Christ does not have God. The one who remains in this teaching has both the Father and the Son. If anyone comes to you and does not bring this teaching, do not receive him into your house and do not give him any greeting, because the person who gives him a greeting shares in his evil deeds.*

We do not want to participate in any of Satan's evil deeds of darkness. Sometimes we have no idea even where they originated. But with some investigation, we can find the answers, as I did. There is an 800-year-old tradition which developed in the city of Konya. It is called Sufi dancing and it can be seen when watching the Whirling Dervishes in Turkey. Whirling is a form of physically active meditation. It is steered by rhythmic breathing and chants of "Allah," emphasizing introspection and spiritual closeness with god. This style of worship can transcend sects. It has become a popular cultural attraction in Turkey. Konya, Turkey is the center of Rumi's teaching. Rumi is a 13th Century Persian Poet, Islamic scholar and theologian. He was a Sufi master, mystic, and one of Iran's leading psychiatrists. One woman commented on this type of dancing saying the next time she watched the Whirling Dervishes, "…it will be …with greater openness to suspend my restless mind and lose myself within the divine."

Sufism is a form of mysticism…knowing god through experience rather than studying Scripture. In my research, I have now found that many churches openly practice this form of spinning/whirling type of dancing during worship. It is common in many religions. A leader at a very large church took the stage and explained what they were doing as the worship team were finishing up this type of dancing. He is quoted here:

"What looks like chaos is what God put in order. This is what is going to hold your world together…in spinning…I spin over you…the planets spin around…the galaxy spins around. So, when your world is chaotic, get chaotic with your body. That is God's version of finding stability. That is God's version of putting you on track. That is God's version of finding your path because it's the rotation that keeps Earth on a steady path. Find your steady path, get wild, start spinning. Start spinning with God. See His spinning over you."

Zephaniah 3:17 says God does rejoice over us with singing…but spinning? Let me quote God's Word here: *There must never be found among you anyone who sacrifices his son or daughter in the fire, anyone who practices divination, an omen reader, a soothsayer, a sorcerer, one who casts spells, one who conjures up spirits, a practitioner of the occult, or a necromancer.* Deuteronomy 18:10 (NET)

The Bible says we can lose our heads over things like this! When Herodias danced for King Herod, he was so taken with her he lost his mind and offered Herodias up to half the kingdom as a gift. Because of the dance that was performed, John the Baptist **literally** lost his head. What was the powerful spirit that was *conjured* up when Herodias danced?

Not all spinning around is evil, obviously. But when it is associated with Eastern mysticism, it is not to be played with. When in doubt…don't! Otherwise we may be tracking slimy worldly mud into our places of worship instead of honoring our One True God. Sometimes, unbeknownst to us, we may be practicing divination (To be inspired by a god). We are not to *participate in the unfruitful deeds of darkness, but rather expose them.* (Eph. 5:11) Let's check our shoes for mud before we dance!

I wish that you would be patient with me in a little foolishness, but indeed you are being patient with me! For I am jealous for you with godly jealousy, because I promised you in marriage to one husband, to present you as a pure virgin to Christ. But I am afraid that just as the serpent deceived Eve by his treachery, your minds may be led astray from a sincere and pure devotion to Christ.
2 Corinthians 11:1-3 (NET)

In worship, are we trying to appease God and/or manipulate Him when we should be communing with Him? Let's take a look now at what might be the result of spinning and such? This is going to be a bit much, but hang with me…

Being spiritual doesn't mean turning off our minds and spinning in an undignified manner. This can bring an emotional cathartic experience similar to hypnotism. Some worship music can be designed in such a way that the congregation lets their guard down as certain words are repeated over and over. (Mantras) Then the music may be brought to a crescendo, working the worshipers into a frenzy. The crowd can become so pulled into the music at this point that they become helpless, sometimes even being brought into a trancelike state. At this point, it's not about the message in the music, it's more the feeling and/or the experience. This is not worshipping *in spirit and in truth*…it is merely in spirit. (John 4:24) This type of worshipping has been known to even cause Kriya manifestations, which is an energy force moving through the body causing involuntary reactions. This is found in Eastern mysticism involving a Kundalini spirit. Why would we want anything to do with this?

The arrival of the lawless one will be by Satan's working with all kinds of miracles and signs and false wonders, and with every kind of evil deception directed against those who are perishing, because they found no place in their hearts for the truth so as to be saved. Consequently God sends on them a deluding influence so that they will believe what is false.
2 Thessalonians 2:9-11 (NET)

This is a lot. And I understand that it isn't possible for all of us to take the time to research many of these things to this depth. But for those of us who do have this call on our lives, it is our responsibility to share what we have discovered, and then allow others to pray about it and decide for themselves. For me, not sharing this now, would be for me not to be a watchman, and then the blood would be on my hands.

It is said, "If the Bible is unread and unknown it is nothing but dead cows, dead trees, and soot. The Bible is not holy in its presence. It's holy in its message." The Bible is divinely inspired and that is why we must read it—not just let it sit there gathering dust while we get lost in experiences instead of gaining wisdom and knowledge about the Truth of our Lord Jesus Christ from the very Word of God. There was a time when my Bible was nothing but a "dead cow and trees and soot." Not now, and that is why I write this book. I know many are still there with their Bible gathering dust. I understand. But the world is changing, and the Kingdom of Heaven is drawing ever near so these things need to be exposed!

Some may say I'm being a Pharisee by writing about these things—that in pointing out false prophets, false teachers, and a false Gospel, I'm the one in error…that I'm being divisive. I get it. I really do. *So then, have I become your enemy by telling you the truth?* Galatians 4:16 (NET*)* I still must do it.

For false messiahs and false prophets will appear and perform signs and wonders to deceive, if possible, the elect.
Mark 13:22 (NET)

They will maintain the outward appearance of religion but will have repudiated its power. So avoid people like these.
2 Timothy 3:5 (NET)

Titus is a small but important book. It is filled with instructions on how we are to be as men and women of God. It tells us how older men and older women can encourage the younger generations. It warns us what not to do, and how not to be. It also tells us what to do and how to be. We are not to be like the world, we are to be set apart. Like it's written, Titus was to *communicate the behavior that goes with sound teaching.* If it was needed then, how much more is it needed today!

Paul goes on to tell Titus in 2:11-12, that the grace of God has appeared bringing salvation to all people. It is there to train us to reject godless ways and worldly desires, to live self-controlled, upright and godly lives in the present age. Why should we do this? We are told in Titus 2:13, because we are waiting for the happy fulfillment of our hope in the glorious appearing of our great God and Savior Jesus Christ. Who is to be trained to reject these things? All of us who call ourselves Christ followers!

He gave himself for us to set us free from every kind of lawlessness and to purify for himself a people who are truly his, who are eager to do good.
Titus 2:14 (NET)

When I asked a young man in a store the other day if he had an Eternal Hope, he had no answer for me. He asked me what I meant. Thankfully, I was able to give him a direct, clear, answer about the Hope we have in Jesus, just as it says in Titus 2:15 about communicating these things with exhortation (advice/counsel) that carries with it a full authority. In all of this, we are not to *slander anyone* as it says in Titus 3:2. We are to be *peaceable, gentle, and courteous*. But we are to *be*...we are to have an answer, speaking the Truth in love. We are to warn, or even rebuke if necessary. As I heard one pastor answer when he was told that someone didn't like his translation of a certain verse—he said, "I didn't translate it. I just read it." God's Word can be offensive, but it shouldn't be avoided.

My purpose in writing this is not to point a finger at anyone. This is not a struggle against flesh and blood, but against spiritual forces of evil. (Eph. 6:12) My purpose is to point a finger at God's Word and ask us all to read it, believe it, and follow it. Many people who are acting in ways that aren't godly don't even realize it. They haven't been taught correctly. It is loving to let others know about the mud we might all be tracking around and Who washes it away. We all have these things in our lives that are muddy, and hopefully they will make us hunger for our Savior. Little by little, from glory to glory, and strength to strength, God will help us sort these things out when we follow Jesus. When the darnels/tares are spotted, we need to not allow them to continue on as we learn to communicate the Truth in peaceful, gentle, and courteous ways.

...he saved us not by works of righteousness that we have done but on the basis of his mercy, through the washing of the new birth and the renewing of the Holy Spirit, whom he poured out on us in full measure through Jesus Christ our Savior.
Titus 3:5-6 (NET)

Confession/agreeing with God is so important. We are to confess that Jesus is Lord and agree that we are saved by grace through faith alone. We are to confess our sins and to hate sin the way that God hates sin. We are to repent...to change our mind about something in our lives when the Holy Spirit convicts us that it is not in alignment with God's Word. This is more than remorse and then not changing anything. This is coming into an agreement with our Father in

Heaven and allowing Him to do His work in our heart. This is regeneration…being made new by the power of the Holy Spirit who dwells within. This is being washed clean of all the muck and mire.

We all want our prayers heard, and one very powerful verse in the Bible tells us how our prayers can be very effective. It is found in James 5:16 (NET): *So confess your sins to one another and pray for one another so that you may be healed. The prayer of a righteous person has great effectiveness.*

But if we confess our sins, he is faithful and righteous, forgiving us our sins and cleansing us from all unrighteousness.
1 John 1:9 (NET)

Paul tells Titus in 3:8, that he is to *insist on such truths* that Paul has been instructing him in. *Why?* Because *these things are good and beneficial for all people.* They are still good and beneficial for all of us today, over 2,000 years later. We must insist!

Let's pray:
Father in Heaven, we can be so easily entertained and distracted by the things of this world. Help us always look to You first and foremost. We want to worship You in Spirit and in Truth the way Your Word tells us to. Wash us clean as we confess to You the things we have stepped into. Help us follow You more closely today and each day forward. In Jesus' name. Amen.

Chapter Ten Reflections

1) Confession is not just asking God to forgive us, it is agreeing with the Holy Spirit when He convicts us of something we have done—then repenting/changing our mind and turning away from it. There is great joy in this response to sin. (Page 132)

2) And now, what do we do in the meantime? We accept this most precious gift of salvation. We don't just read about it and talk about it…we embrace it and live it. And we confess! The Greek word for confess is "homologeo". It means to "Say the same thing," and then to "Agree." This is what we must do! Walk in obedience and agreement with God. It's not easy. The bar is high! (Page 134)

3) Let's take a look at what Paul is telling young Titus in the book of Titus. It's not a long book, but it's a powerful one when we read it in the light of confession—in agreeing with God… It says we are not to be arrogant, not prone to anger, not a drunkard, not violent, not greedy for gain. We are to be hospitable, devoted to what is good, sensible, upright, devout, and self-controlled. How are we doing so far? (Page 134)

4) Right now, with the corona virus putting many of us in a position of having more time to spend in the Word, we should be using this window of opportunity wisely. Being in the Word, we can uncover what the enemy would like to keep hidden. It's not an easy thing in today's world, to uncover the muck and mire, but it is so needed. (Page 141)

5) We are to take good care of the bride until Christ returns. But are we? The pastor said so many are trying to change the bride into something she is not…holiness is disappearing in so many ways in our churches. It was said if we decide to renovate the bride, change the worship by "raising the hem of her skirt," it will be better for a hostile atheist on the day of Christ's return. (Page 142)

6) What is happening in so many ways within Christianity today is of Satan and not our Savior. Some are mimicking pagan rituals in worship and they don't even know it. But we should be watching and be wary when what we see and hear is something different than what was written in the Bible thousands of years ago. (Page 142)

7) Titus is a small but important book. It is filled with instructions on how we are to be as men and women of God. It tells us how older men and older women can encourage the younger generations. It warns us what not to do, and how not to be. It also tells us what to do and how to be. We are not to be like the world, we are to be set apart. (Page 146)

8) It is loving to let others know about the mud we might all be tracking around and Who washes it away...God will help us sort these things out when we follow Jesus. When the darnels/tares are spotted, we need to not allow them to continue on as we learn to communicate the Truth in peaceful, gentle, and courteous ways. (Page 147)

NOTES

*(These Reflection/Note pages may be duplicated
and used for group discussions when needed.)*

CHAPTER ELEVEN

JUDGMENT

Each chapter is titled with one word. I don't choose the word. I wait...and when I believe it is what God wants, I begin. Believe me, I would not have chosen many of these subjects, especially this one. It seems like such a huge, scary word...but here we go!

You may be reading this book long past the corona virus situation faced in the year 2020. But even if it is now 2030, and Jesus hasn't returned yet, we can still keep on this Truth Journey until He does come back for those who believe in Jesus Christ as our Lord and Savior. If you're part of this journey during the "Shelter in Place" pandemic, we have to ask ourselves, "What is this all about?" What if I told you it's all about Judgment Day? You might say I have gone way overboard. And perhaps I have. But...what if this "storm" does have to do with going overboard for Jesus, so to speak? It just might!

If Jesus hadn't been in the boat the night of the storm, they might have all gone overboard and drowned. If Jesus hadn't been there to be awakened, and calm the storm...then what? (Mark 4:35-41) If we don't have Jesus to call on when Judgment Day comes, we are really in a storm without the Eternal Life Preserver. We HAVE TO KNOW that Jesus is with us, sleeping in the stern of our boat, ready and willing to come to our aid each day, and especially on the final day. There will be no escape on that day. There will be no extra life preservers if we aren't already clothed with our Life

Preserver/Christ. There will be no extra oil for our lamps on that day. If we have not taken the time before then to examine our lives, to come into a saving grace relationship with the true Jesus of Nazareth before then, it will be over. There will be no "better late than never" when we stand before our Father in Heaven. There will be no excuses accepted. We will either be all in, or all out. No gray areas, no middle ground, no purgatory, no nothing. It will be Heaven or Hell. And it will have already been decided.

This is what the corona virus pandemic may be here to teach all of us. But whether or not this is the end of life on Earth as we know it…it can still help us all think about the book of Revelation, because the end of God's Book IS COMING one day. Perhaps that little microscopic corona/crown germ cell carries with it what we all need. Buried deep within it could be the very question Jesus asked the disciples in the boat that day in the storm when He said to them, *"Where is your faith?"* That is how it is written in Luke 8:25 (NET). There is no more important question to ask ourselves, right here, right now. "Where is my faith?" What is happening can bring that question into full view.

Let's take a look… If our faith is in toilet paper, canned goods, a facemask, hand sanitizer, or even the shelter of our home, we're in trouble. If our faith is in a religion, a government, or a false savior, we're in trouble. Even before the pandemic, if our faith in Jesus was missing because we were depending on our family to satisfy us, or our job, or the latest video game, or book, we were in trouble. When the rubber meets the road, where will our faith be found? That's what we need to sort out now. I don't care if we have been a Christian for 50 years, or three months, we can, and should, all examine ourselves and find out exactly where our faith is. Is the one true Jesus reigning in our lives? The answer to that question will show each one of us if we are prepared for Judgment Day. That's the bottom line. Now let's work back up through this and sort it out.

If our faith is failing us right now during the pandemic, it can be a very good thing in many instances. Why? Because it may show us that we don't have a true faith to begin with, and we need to know it. I know that's hard, but it's also loving. Remember, it's so important to get this figured out now rather than on Judgment Day. God loves us so much that He wants us to know Him, the One true God.

Jesus will never leave us nor forsake us. He will always be faithful, even when we are not faithful. (2 Timothy 2:13) If anyone is distanced from Jesus, it's we who have left or moved, not Jesus. And many times, it can be because we have our faith in the wrong place, and sometimes even the wrong Jesus. Sadly, this may be because of what's being preached today from many pulpits. Jesus said it Himself in Matthew 24:5, "...for many will come in my name, claiming, 'I am the Messiah'. They will deceive many". It is better to get rid of the fake messiahs right now and find the real one while there is still time. Oh, how gracious our God is being toward us!

The Cross of Jesus Christ is what's most important at all times and on every occasion. It is good to be thankful to our God for all that He provides; homes, food, clothing, health, etc... But if we don't thank our Father in Heaven for Christ crucified first and foremost, then we have things out of order. Why? Because the Cross is the only thing that can't be taken from us. The Holy Spirit living within each believer is there to stay. No shelter in place, no closed churches, no closed parks, hair salons, restaurants, or anything that is happening in this world should shake us to the core when Jesus is at the core of who we are. He is our only firm foundation. Yes, things will shake us some, but that is when we call on the name of Jesus to steady us like the disciples did in the boat that night. Our Lord is there to rescue us. We have the Holy Spirit to strengthen us. That is what Christians should do in a crisis. Let's take a look at the storm on the Sea of Galilee again before we move more deeply into judgment.

Isn't it interesting that the disciples were upset because Jesus was sleeping, and they thought they were about to die? What could that bring to mind? The Garden of Gethsemane perhaps? Jesus knew He was about to die then, and not one of them stayed awake with Him. His soul was deeply grieved, even to the point of death. (Matthew 26:38) He asked the disciples to remain where they were and to stay awake. Jesus was throwing Himself down with His face to the ground and praying, "My God, if possible, let this cup pass from me! Yet not what I will, but what you will". He came back from that time in prayer and found the disciples sleeping. I wonder if they thought about all of that years later as they spread the Gospel message? Jesus knew their spirit was willing, but their flesh was weak. (Matt. 26:41) Three times Jesus went a stone's throw away to pray in the garden, and three times He returned to find them sleeping. He eventually told them to, *"Get up"* because His betrayer was approaching. Perhaps now Jesus is saying the same thing, "Awake, oh sleeper, the betrayer is approaching." Are we buried in fear in our homes? Or are we buried in the Word and fearing God as we should during these times of quarantine? This is a time for believers as much as unbelievers. Some will come to know Jesus for the first time, and some will come to know Him better.

Oh, what a Savior we have! We don't deserve all Jesus died to give us. There in the boat, Jesus just needed a little rest. It's not that the storm wasn't a big one, it was. But think about the timing…when Jesus was in the wilderness for 40 days, Satan tempted Him, and then Satan left Jesus for a time. (Luke 4:13) Satan was only leaving for a bit. In the boat, when Jesus just needed some shut eye, the enemy sent some gale-force winds! We know they weren't from God because Jesus *rebuked the wind and the raging waves; they died down, and it was calm.* Luke 8:24 (NET) The disciples didn't die, but the enemy's force against them did. Jesus was in complete control, and He always will be. Mark 4:36 talks about other boats that night. To be in Jesus' boat was the place to be!

As I studied this part of Scripture, and how it's being shared in different sermons during the corona virus…it is mainly being used as an encouragement. Many pastors are telling their congregations that we will come through this time and not to worry because Jesus is with us. This is very true. God brings us through, and out of, so many storms in our lives. But when I read it over and over and prayed, I saw something very different. It was more about who we believe Jesus is, rather than what He is doing with the storm. When they woke Jesus, He said to them, *"Where is your faith?"* In some of the gospels, because it is shared in Matthew, Mark, and Luke, it is written in a slightly different way. Some think this "proves" the Bible contradicts itself. It doesn't…if any three reporters write a story for three different newspapers, they will vary slightly. This actually proves the reality of the Bible. But in Luke where it says, not asks, *"Where is your faith,"* I paused. In posing it that way, could it be Jesus wasn't questioning whether they had faith, but what their faith was in, exactly? Maybe it wasn't condemnation, but consideration. Was Jesus giving the men an opportunity to see in whom or what their faith was in? Like saying, "Examine yourself, guys, what are you thinking? What are you depending on in life?" So, when they then asked, *"Who then is this…?"* (Luke 8:25 NET), that is the perfect question for them to ask in response. If they could answer their own question by exclaiming, "This is truly the Lord, the One we have seen heal the sick, raise the dead, and cure lepers," then they would know they had their faith in the right Lord. They would validate that Jesus had proved Himself to them over and over. He must be their Messiah. They would know that is where their faith should be. We can know the same… They could be confident that all would be well, then, and so could we.

We have to understand, these guys weren't wimps in the water. At least four of them were fishermen. They had seen their share of storms, so this must have been quite some storm to frighten them. What if this storm, like many storms in our lives, isn't just to rock our boat but to build our faith? To help us know we have placed our trust in the right Person of Jesus Christ? And why is this so very important? Because as it says in 2 Corinthians 6:2 (NET), *Look, now is the acceptable time; look, now is the day of salvation.* There will come a time when it will not be an acceptable time; it won't be the day of salvation. There will come a day of judgment separating those who believed here and now, and those who didn't. That is why our Father is calling us all to repentance NOW! Not later! (2 Peter 3:9) We need to know Jesus now, not later. They learned a lot in the boat that day. We can learn a lot in this pandemic today.

Let's take an even closer look at that one line, *"Where is your faith?"* Try reading it out loud in four different ways: WHERE is your faith? Where IS your faith? Where is YOUR faith? Where is your FAITH? We don't know where Jesus put the emphasis in that question, but it can cause us to think more deeply about it when we say it in these four different ways. The first one with WHERE, seems faith has gone missing. With the IS emphasized, it makes us ponder what has happened to their faith. When the YOUR is emphasized, it makes it seem very personal. And with FAITH being stronger than the rest of the words, it shifts the focus to what they have their faith in. You may even come up with different ways of looking at these than I have. But one thing is for sure, it can mean many things when said differently.

Again, I like that Jesus "said" this. He didn't "ask" it. It's like Jesus letting them ponder things a bit… "Come on guys, what have we been doing together all this time?" We do see that their faith was in Jesus, to some extent. After all, they did wake Him up when things got bad. They knew Jesus had powers that none of them had because they already witnessed it many times.

This is a time in our world when the wheat and tares are being separated...perhaps the goats and the sheep are becoming obvious. The darnels may be showing up a bit more if we're watching and aware of them. If our repentance/confession deepens and our faith grows strong in the Jesus of the Bible, we can know that we are depending on the right Jesus during difficult times. If our repentance/confession goes missing and/or turns into anger, and our faith wanes or completely gets shoved aside, or we go looking for messiahs/gods elsewhere, we have to ask ourselves what have we been believing in all along? What have we been taught? What have we held onto that now seems to be failing us when the storm beats against us? All this is what prepares us for Judgment Day!

Why would God be preparing us? Because, unlike in the world today, not everyone gets a trophy as many in the younger generations have been taught. There are those who will be given the Crown of Life for persevering under trials, and those who will be sent straight to Hell. (James 1:12 and Revelation 2:10) Jesus tells the church in Smyrna to *"not be afraid of what you are about to suffer...Be faithful even to the point of death, and I will give you the crown of life."* Christianity is the only religion that levels out the playing field on Judgment Day. There will be no favorites, no star athletes, and no special exceptions made. The only tears that will be wiped away will be wiped away in Heaven. It's all about Jesus on that day, plain and simple.

Let's take a look at Luke 3:4-6 (NET).

"The voice of one shouting in the wilderness: 'Prepare the way for the Lord, make his paths straight. Every valley will be filled, and every mountain and hill will be brought low, and the crooked will be made straight, and the rough ways will be made smooth, and all humanity will see the salvation of God.' "

With every valley filled in, and every mountain and hill brought low, there is nothing more we need to do to be welcomed into Heaven except to know Jesus as our Lord and Savior before meeting

Him face to face. We know it says in Romans 3:23 that all have fallen short. We are all sinners. That's why God's wrath is what we are all being saved from. We all deserve the same judgment…Hell. But all those who belong to the family of God will be ushered into Heaven. Works will not count on that day, Salvation is a free gift as we read in Romans 3:24 (NET), *But they are justified freely by his grace through the redemption that is in Christ Jesus.* We don't deserve any of Heaven, nor could we have obtained it on our own. God's love and forgiveness are offered to us by our Father through His Son, Jesus Christ. *For while we were still helpless, at the right time Christ died for the ungodly.* Romans 5:6 (NET) When we begin to understand that without the cleansing blood of Jesus we will be condemned as the worst of all sinners…although I know Paul has already claimed that position…we can begin to see the reason for the Cross, the power of the Cross, and the blessing in the Cross. It doesn't matter when we occupied space on planet Earth. It is the same for everyone. Pride is a big thing that will keep us from the Cross. Those in the Old Testament were believing forward for this, those in the New Testament were believing in this, and we, to this day, look back at the Cross and believe upon it for our Salvation. Each individual is provided for equally. Our world doesn't work this way, but God's Kingdom surely does! There is an absolute equality before God on Judgment Day. We can rest assured in that.

If this is the Jesus we are believing in during difficult times, we are to run to Him! If it's anything or anyone different than Jesus Christ of Nazareth, we are to get out of there! God has waited thousands of years, and utilized millions of lives, getting people ready for the day of judgment where the harvest is great, and the workers are few. (Matt. 9:37) Our Father wants that none should perish, but many will. Sadly, many will go to Hell on that last day. That's why when parents don't discipline their children as the Bible urges, it is sad. It is setting children up to think that exceptions can be made for not behaving rightly, and more importantly for not believing rightly in Jesus. Spurgeon explained it this way…even with those entering college, they have found ways that are not a "level playing field." There are back doors into the right colleges through large donations by their parents. There are side doors through fraudulent activities. But on Judgment Day, there is only one Door, and His name is Jesus Christ. (John 10:9) In John 14:6

(NET) Jesus says, *"I am the way, and the truth, and the life. No one comes to the Father except through me."* Pleading moms and dads will not work on that day, so we should *Train a child in the way that he should go*…right here, right now! (Proverbs 22:6) This is the most loving type of parent we can be. Any other kind of parent is selfish, wanting to be loved more than to be loving by training their child in the way they should go.

So many in the world claim they are trying to be a good person. And that's commendable, but not admissible or acceptable on the day of judgment. Luke 18:13 (NET) says, *"God, be merciful to me, sinner that I am!"* We can't be good enough; we need God's mercy. Think about it…you can't apply to a college by saying you have been a good person. They will look at your school records and decide from there. When we stand before God on Judgment Day, we can't plead we've been a good person either. The Father will not be looking at our earthly records and making a decision based on the number of A's, B's and C's we got… This is a pass or fail situation. It's doesn't matter if we got straight A's at feeding the poor, helping the elderly, or even healing the sick through powerful prayers. It doesn't matter if we flunked any of this either. It all adds up to nothing if we haven't called upon Jesus as the Savior of our lives. We need our record to be replaced with Jesus' perfect record. All who call upon Jesus' name will be saved. They PASS! All who don't FAIL! Period.

I always marvel at the two people mentioned in the book of Luke chapter 2. There was Simeon, who had it revealed to him that he wouldn't die before seeing the *Lord's Christ*. And there was the prophetess, Anna, who had been married only seven years before becoming a widow. After that, Anna never left the Temple for 84 years, worshipping and fasting and praying night and day. That would make her easily over 100 years old. These two people knew where their faith was, it was in the Messiah to come. And when Jesus came that day, as a baby in His parents' arms to be circumcised at eight days old, they were there, waiting for Him. Simeon took baby Jesus into his arms and blessed God, saying, *"Now, according to your word, Sovereign Lord, permit your servant to depart in peace. For my eyes have seen your salvation that you have prepared in the presence of all peoples: a light, for revelation to the Gentiles and for the glory of your people Israel."* (Luke 2:29-32 NET) He told

Mary and Joseph that their Child was *"destined to be the cause of the falling and rising of many in Israel and to be a sign that will be rejected. Indeed, as a result of him the thoughts of many hearts will be revealed—and a sword will pierce your own soul as well."* Luke 2:34-35 (NET) Jesus was rejected by many and will continue to be rejected by many more until the end of this age. We can't be surprised by this. But we should be aware of it and not be a part of it. When every knee bows, and every tongue confesses Jesus is Lord, let it be a repeat of what we personally have proclaimed for many, many years on this Earth already, just as it was for Anna and Simeon. They waited patiently for the Lord, and He came!

If we think we have waited a long while, and if every day "sheltering in place" is a struggle for us, we can think about those 84 years Anna spent in the Temple. So many probably thought she should "get a life." But she had chosen her life, and she was rewarded. The Bible says in Luke 2:38 (NET), that Anna came up to Mary and Joseph and *began to give thanks to God and to speak about the child to all who were waiting for the redemption of Jerusalem.* Simeon's and Anna's faith were rewarded on that day, and ours will be, too, when we wait upon the return of our Savior, while hastening the day.

Let's talk now about what that Day of Judgment will be like, even though it's not a pleasant thing to do. Jesus talked more about Hell than any other person in the Bible. In fact, Hell is barely mentioned in any other book other than the Gospels, Matthew, Mark, Luke and John. It is slightly mentioned in the Psalms and a bit in the Epistles, but not much. The prophets barely spoke about it, and in the first five books of the Bible, it's not mentioned much if any at all. It is certainly mentioned in the Revelation of Jesus Christ. It's obvious that Jesus was the greatest authority we could have about Hell, even though today we want to make Jesus into all love, grace, and mercy, and with no judgment included. But Jesus told the Truth. He told both sides of the story…no glossing over it for Him. Hell is real. Heaven is real. Jesus is to be believed, then, now, and forever more!

Revelation 20:11, tells us about a large white throne and the One who is seated on it. I'm not an expert on the book of Revelation, but maybe that's not needed here. What's needed is keeping our focus on what prepares us for the moment when we stand before this throne…the blood of Jesus Christ is how we prepare. When we read about the white throne, we should realize there is judgment coming for all. Unbelievers and believers...the unbelievers whose names are not written in the book of life will be judged according to their deeds to determine the degree of punishment they will receive. Those who are believers, whose names are written in the book of life, will be judged for their deeds in order to determine the rewards they will receive.

When Christ stood before Pilate, He was judged. He knows how that feels. When we stand before God, we will be judged. Why? It says in 2 Corinthians 5:10 (NET), *For we must all appear before the judgment seat of Christ, so that each one may be paid back according to what he has done while in the body, whether good or evil.* That's you and me. That's your sweet grandma, and your long-lost uncle. All of us! For some, it will be a very good day. For others, horrific! If we ever wanted to be the center of attention, we will get our chance. This is why being entertained at church instead of hearing the Truth of the Gospel is so dangerous—it is not loving, it is not kind, it is the greatest injustice done to mankind for the sake of money, popularity, or whatever the reason is.

We are told God is not to be feared but I heard a trusted pastor teach the exact opposite. He said we are to fear God, and I believe he is right. (Chapter Thirteen will dive deeper into the subject of fearing God.) God is love, absolutely! But God is also completely just, and if we are outside of His will, and outside of the love that God wants to pour into our hearts through the death, burial and resurrection of His One and only Son, we should fear God. This pastor said the scariest thing there is, is to know that God is good. Why's that? Because we're not, so what does He do with us?

God says, *"Vengeance is mine, I will repay,"* and again, *"The Lord will judge his people."* Hebrews 10:30 (NET) There's no messing around here! But we need not fear when Jesus is near and we know our faith is in Him. Jesus said to the disciples, *"Where is your faith?"* We need to be clear on where and in whom our faith is focused...then Judgment Day is only Good News for us! It's about our rewards.

There is a throne spoken about in Revelation chapters four and five. This throne includes a rainbow, worship, lightning, and thunder. There were other smaller thrones and crowns being talked about, too. There were torches, and seven spirits, and a sea of glass like crystal. Look at this compared to the white throne in chapter twenty of Revelation…nothing is the same there…no rainbow, no choirs singing "holy, holy, holy". Judgment for God's children is finished when we get to chapter twenty of Revelation. Those with their names written in the Lamb's book of life are ushered into heaven and receive rewards. Those not written in the book of life are thrown into the lake of fire. (Rev. 20:15) This is where the rubber meets the road for all time!

It's hard to believe a loving God would throw anyone into a lake of fire. But He does, because God is a just God. He has to do it. No evil can be allowed into Heaven. It would mess everything up! The only virtue we have on this Earth comes because the Great Restrainer, the Holy Spirit, is here amongst us and living in those who do believe. Any good we see, is God. Anything else, is satanic—and it's pure evil and not fit for the perfection of Heaven. To take a look at ourself apart from Christ, void of the Holy Spirit, is to see someone horrific. We need to give thanks every day for the loving work of God in our hearts and in our world. When the Restrainer is removed…look out! It will be mayhem, and we don't want to be here! *For the hidden power of lawlessness is already at work. However, the one who holds him back will do so until he is taken out of the way.* 2 Thessalonians 2:7 (NET)

Jude verse 21 says that while we are here on earth, we should be *anticipating the mercy of our Lord Jesus Christ that brings eternal life.* When we become a true Christ follower, the reward is Salvation! *…to those who eagerly await him he will appear a second time, not to bear sin but to bring salvation.* Hebrews 9:28b (NET) We can rejoice in what is to come, even when times are hard here. Those who have been through tough times with Jesus, have had their faith tested. It shows faith to be what it is, no more and no less. The Word says you will know them by their Fruit. If tough times bring out the worst in us, that's rotten Fruit showing up. This is not saying that we don't fall from time to time, that we don't have some ugly fruit that appears on our tree here and there…but overall, our life should be an upward movement into Christlikeness when we go through good and difficult times. Storms should refine our faith, not redefine it in ways that aren't Biblical.

And you became imitators of us and of the Lord, when you received the message with joy that comes from the Holy Spirit, despite great affliction.

1 Thessalonians 1:6 (NET)

We are to be imitators of how Paul lived his life out after meeting Jesus.

Walking with Jesus is not for the faint of heart. It's for those willing to give their whole heart to the Lord even when things are looking extremely bleak. Paul was concerned about the Thessalonians. He wrote: *So when I could bear it no longer, I sent to find out about your faith, for fear that the tempter somehow tempted you and our toil had proven useless.* 1 Thessalonians 3:5 (NET) Paul knew as much or more than anyone who has walked on earth, just how the prince of the air works on our hearts and in our lives trying his best to pull us away from the faith we have in Jesus. That's why it takes a true faith in a true Savior to withstand such a pull…this is where the real Jesus and the fake Jesus meet and divide. Only a real Savior can see us through the worst of times, the greatest of fears, the most hurting relationships and bring us out whole, and with a stronger faith. He will *have mercy on those who waver; save others by snatching them out of the fire; have mercy on others, coupled with a fear of God, hating even the clothes stained by the flesh.* Jude 22-23 (NET) By clinging to the real Jesus, we will find solace. The fake Jesus fails, big time, in these areas. It's here where some "seem to be" falling away from their faith. But we have to wonder, where was their faith? Because if it wasn't in the true Jesus, a falling away can be a very good thing. It is best that they go into the wilderness of despair…perhaps it's there they'll find the true Jesus Christ of the Bible.

We ought to thank God always for you, brothers and sisters, and rightly so, because your faith flourishes more and more and the love of each one of you all for one another is ever greater. As a result we ourselves boast about you in the churches of God for your perseverance and faith in all the persecutions and afflictions you are enduring.

2 Thessalonians 1:3-4 (NET)

This is true faith on display. When asked once how I was doing while my son went through chemotherapy, I quickly answered, "Without God, I wouldn't be walking. With God, I can run." I know what faith put to the fire looks and feels like. It hurts. It is hard. But it can flourish, deepen, and help us run the race we have been called to when Jesus is the Source of all comfort and strength. It has been said, "If you have Jesus, you have everything. If you don't, you have nothing. Forsake everything but Him and be saved." It's really all or nothing, truly. And it has nothing to do with what we do, and everything to do with what Jesus has already done! When we begin to grasp our own depravity, we will begin to understand the need for the Cross.

He is the one who saved us and called us with a holy calling, not based on our works but on his own purpose and grace, granted to us in Christ Jesus before time began, but now made visible through the appearing of our Savior Christ Jesus. He has broken the power of death and brought life and immortality to light through the gospel!
2 Timothy 1:9-10 (NET)

During this corona virus, it's not a time to panic. It's a time to wake up and turn to the full true Gospel of Jesus Christ. When a house is built on sand, it shakes. When a house is built on rock, it withstands the storms. The Rock is the Word of God. God never changes, never sways in a strong wind, never shakes when the Earth trembles, never sinks when the floods come...Our Father is the Maker of all, in control of all, and we can rest in all He is every single day.

So I endure all things for the sake of those chosen by God, that they too may obtain salvation in Christ Jesus and its eternal glory.
2 Timothy 2:10 (NET)

Being shut up in our homes is a time to wake up to God. It is important to know God's Word intellectually. It is also very important to know God's Word in a relational way...take a walk, lament, rejoice, and relate to our God. When we read the Word, we should see our life in its pages. We should see our struggles in

David's struggles. We should see our sins in Paul's. Sometimes, we may even recognize we are in a certain place for *just such a time as this* like Esther did. The Bible is real people. Real stories, real people walking with a real God who saves. This is the time for us to get to know where our faith is, and then walk confidently in it like those in the Bible have shown us…then sharing Jesus with others, until we come to Judgment Day. We all want to hear those words, *"Well done, good and faithful servant."* Words very few will hear. Words many will miss. That's sad, but biblical. There is a wide gate and a narrow gate—there are the many, and there are the few. Those are the cold hard facts of life on planet Earth. And if we don't deal with them here and now, they will be dealt with there and then on Judgment Day.

"Enter through the narrow gate, because the gate is wide and the way is spacious that leads to destruction, and there are many who enter through it. How narrow is the gate and difficult the way that leads to life, and there are few who find it!"
Matthew 7:13-14 (NET)

This faith that we are talking about is concerning the Cross at Calvary. Anything less, any other hill, any other cross, will lead us straight to Hell on Judgment Day. To listen to pastors speak about faith, and to hear very little if any teaching on the Cross, is heart wrenching. Too many congregants are hearing words from the Bible, and stories in the Bible, but Jesus is being overlooked. There are those who preach entertaining Old Testament stories that never bring in the light of the Savior. They dance around the subject of the Cross like it's offensive. They exclude the blood, like it's too much. They avoid repentance and confession, preferring to talk about love, grace, and the goodness we can all obtain from God without talking about the faith in Jesus it takes to receive such amazing gifts. The Bible, from front to back, is about Jesus. To leave Him out in either the Old or New Testament, is like leaving out Jesus' resurrection from the dead when talking about His death and burial. Paul said:
"For if only in this life we have hope in Christ, we should be pitied more than anyone."
1 Corinthians 15:19 (NET)

Quoting Michael Green, he says, "The Resurrection, therefore, is the place to begin if you are looking for a satisfying faith on which to base your life. Do not waste a lot of time investigating every religion under the sun from animism to Hinduism. Examine the evidence for the resurrection of Jesus instead. If he is risen, you need look no further."

Let's look no further, because on Judgment Day our Father in Heaven will look no further than His Son. When Jesus turns and says, "He/she is with me," we are in! If Jesus says, *"I never knew you,"* we are out. The corona virus could be more contagious than serious. Our faith in Jesus Christ needs to be both! When the Gospel spreads quickly and powerfully in our walk with Christ, then others can know His Truth is the overwhelming Hope we all need! So many are going to be shocked on the day of judgment. So many have sat in church pews for years hearing heresy, unaware of the consequences they are facing. The pastors preaching such heresy will be held accountable. *Not many of you should become teachers, my brothers and sisters, because you know that we will be judged more strictly.* James 3:1-2 (NET) In Jude 16 it says some *give bombastic speeches, enchanting folks for their own gain.* This should grieve us!

It has been said, "Faith looks back to a crucified Savior. Love looks up to a resurrected glorified crowned Savior. Hope looks forward to a coming Savior." (Harding) We can have great Hope knowing Who Jesus is, knowing He is risen, and knowing He is coming soon! On Judgment Day, where our faith is will be all that matters. *Because I will do this to you, prepare to meet your God, Israel! For here he is!* Amos 4:12-13 (NET) One pastor puts it this way, "After this life there is no more death. But for others, after their death there is no more life."

When John began preaching repentance, he was leveling the playing field. He said, *"Therefore produce fruit that proves your repentance, and don't begin to say to yourselves, 'We have Abraham as our father.' For I tell you that God can raise up children for Abraham from these stones! Even now the ax is laid at the root of the trees, and every tree that does not produce good fruit will be cut down and thrown into the fire."* Luke 3:8-9 (NET)

Spurgeon warns us, "If the imperfect judgment of Earth says, 'I'm vile,' how fearful I must be compared to God's justice." We should never test our worth against the world. The Divine Law of God is the true test. Examining ourselves compared to God's command is a must. Seeing our need of Christ's blood to be the only place where God's wrath will be appeased is more than a religion— it is the Gospel that saves.

What are we clinging to, if not the true Jesus? What little "dabs" have misled us? To quote Spurgeon again, "If your religion cannot stand the test of adversity…in the storms, you would be better off without it. For without it, you might discover your true condition and seek the Lord as a penitent sinner… If a burning house is too much, what will you do in a burning world?"

So listen carefully, for whoever has will be given more, but whoever does not have, even what he thinks he has will be taken from him."
Luke 8:18 (NET)

Real faith will be added to by our wonderful God when trials come. If what we have isn't real faith, it will be taken from us…it will fizzle…it will drown in the storms of life, and for good reason! That false faith, that darkness, needs to go…to make room for the real Jesus, the Light of the world, to stand up and take His place in our hearts instead. God's Word says, *Therefore see to it that the light in you is not darkness.* Luke 11:35 (NET)

Jesus Himself said this about Hell: *But I will warn you whom you should fear: Fear the one who, after the killing, has authority to throw you into hell. Yes, I tell you, fear him!* Luke 12:5 (NET) How many times have we heard this sermon in church? Not enough! We should have a very healthy fear of the only One who has the authority to throw us into Hell. That is the God we should have our faith in!

"Where is your faith?"…"Who then, is this?" These two very important questions are from Scripture. One question is from Jesus, and one is from the disciples. They get us to the bedrock of our faith. Bedrock lies under loose deposits of soil. If we are hearing loose preaching, we won't be able to handle these questions in a way that will usher us into Heaven on Judgment Day. Our faith will be built on shifting sand when it's a faith without repentance and humility.

We have to come to the place that Simon Peter did when he experienced the abundance of Jesus. *But when Simon Peter saw it, he fell down at Jesus' knees, saying, "Go away from me, Lord, for I am a sinful man!"* Luke 5:8 (NET) We have to come to this, placing our faith in Jesus, before every knee bows to the King of kings and Lord of lords, like it or not. Jesus is coming back! He has a big party planned! He's invited us! Let's not miss out!

"Get dressed for service and keep your lamps burning; be like people waiting for their master to come back from the wedding celebration, so that when he comes and knocks they can immediately open the door for him. Blessed are those slaves whom their master finds alert when he returns! I tell you the truth, he will dress himself to serve, have them take their place at the table, and will come and wait on them!
Luke 12:35-37 (NET)

Now to the one who is able to keep you from falling, and to cause you to stand, rejoicing, without blemish before his glorious presence, to the only God our Savior through Jesus Christ our Lord, be glory, majesty, power, and authority, before all time, and now, and for all eternity. Amen.
Jude 24-25 (NET)

Let's pray:
Father, Your judgment is coming. We can be assured of that, and we also have our assurance of forgiveness in Your Son, the Lord Jesus Christ. We can stand confidently before You on Judgment Day when we have known Jesus on this day. We thank You for that, and we rest in it until we meet You face to face. In Jesus' mighty name we hope and pray. Amen.

Chapter Eleven Reflections

1) If we don't have Jesus to call on when Judgment Day comes, we are really in a storm without the Eternal Life Preserver. We HAVE TO KNOW that Jesus is with us, sleeping in the stern of our boat, ready and willing to come to our aid each day, and especially on the final day. (Page 153)

2) If our faith is failing us right now during the pandemic, it can be a very good thing in many instances. Why? Because it may show us that we don't have a true faith to begin with, and we need to know it… It is better to get rid of the fake messiahs right now and find the real one while there is still time. (Page 154)

3) What if this storm, like many storms in our lives, isn't just to rock our boat but to build our faith?—to help us know we have placed our trust in the right Person of Jesus Christ? And why is this so very important? Because as it says in 2 Corinthians 6:2 (NET), *Look, now is the acceptable time; look, now is the day of salvation.* (Page 157)

4) If our repentance/confession deepens and our faith grows strong in the Jesus of the Bible, we can know that we are depending on the right Jesus during difficult times. If our repentance/confession goes missing and/or turns into anger, and our faith wanes or completely gets shoved aside, or we go looking for messiahs/gods elsewhere, we have to ask ourselves what have we been believing in all along? (Page 158)

5) When we begin to understand that without the cleansing blood of Jesus we will be condemned as the worst of all sinners…although I know Paul has already claimed that position…we can begin to see the reason for the Cross, the power of the Cross, and the blessing in the Cross. (Page 159)

6) So many in the world claim they are trying to be a good person. And that's commendable, but not admissible or acceptable on the day of judgment. Luke 18:13 (NET) says *"God, be merciful*

to me, sinner that I am!" We can't be good enough; we need God's mercy. (Page 160)

7) Only a real Savior can see us through the worst of times, the greatest of fears, the most hurting relationships, and bring us out whole and with a stronger faith. (Page 164)

8) The corona virus could be more contagious than serious. Our faith in Jesus Christ needs to be both! When the Gospel spreads quickly and powerfully in our walk with Christ, then others can know His Truth is the overwhelming Hope we all need! (Page 167)

NOTES

(These "Reflections" pages may be duplicated and used for group discussions when needed.)

CHAPTER TWELVE

HELL

Hell…we'll be talking about not so much the place, as the pathway there. What does it look like? What does it consist of? How do we avoid it? How do we warn others of it? Those questions and more are what we will be taking a look at in this chapter along our Truth Journey as we also examine ourselves in preparation for Heaven.

We will be going to the very end of God's book for this chapter— the seven churches listed in Revelation will be our focus, with many other stops along the way as the entire Word of God expounds upon where we DON'T want to be headed. This is a very long chapter as each church is addressed. Think of it as seven chapters in one that point out the ways of distraction/deception happening in the churches, while also pointing the way to Jesus/Truth.

The way to Hell can seem exciting, freeing, and even right…but the end result is not any of those things. I remember telling a friend one day to take a look at the end of the "movie" of the life she was choosing to live. Sometimes it's not easy to see where you are at the moment. But if you can honestly look down the road you might see where you will end up. Why is that? Could it be because Satan is the great deceiver? I believe so.

Deception runs rampant in our world today. But it's nothing new. We are warned all throughout Scripture to be aware of what is going on that is not of God. The problem is many times we aren't listening.

No wonder we are warned: *For if someone merely listens to the message and does not live it out, he is like someone who gazes at his own face in a mirror. For he gazes at himself and then goes out and immediately forgets what sort of person he was.* James 1:23-24 (NET) Plus, too many preachers are no longer warning us about the certainty of judgment and the horrors of Hell. No wonder Jesus had John pen these words to the seven churches, *"The one who has an ear had better hear what the Spirit says to the churches."* These words are included at the end of each and every letter to the seven churches in Revelation. We shouldn't have to wonder if it's important when it's repeated seven times. And with seven being the number of completion in the Bible, it seems to put a huge exclamation point at the end of those combined letters.

John 1:4-5 (NET) says, *In him was life, and the life was the light of mankind. The light shines on in the darkness, but the darkness has not mastered it.* What do we need on a pathway to see where we're going? Light! Jesus Christ is that Light. Not just an enlightenment, but the Light of all mankind. We all have two choices set before us in this life…follow Jesus on the path to Heaven or follow Satan on the pathway to Hell. Seems like a pretty easy choice, doesn't it? But when only four percent of the population believes Hell even exists, and only two percent believe they are going there, most probably don't see a great need for Jesus, for the Cross, or for repentance of any kind. They think Jesus is just a man, and His goal is to stop them from having fun while they're here on earth. How deceptive is that thinking? And yet, if truth be told, we are probably the greatest deceiver to ourselves in all of this…more than any other person or entity in this world. What do I mean? We lie to ourselves and we don't even know that we're doing it. In 1 Corinthians 3:18 (NET) it says, *Guard against self-deception, each of you. If someone among you thinks he is wise in this age, let him become foolish so that he can become wise.* We believe so many of the lies we are told without even realizing it. If we did realize it, we would hopefully stop it. And we also believe so many of the lies we tell ourselves…lies about how nobody loves us, nobody cares, we're not worth as much as the next person, or we're not as smart as we should be. How about the lie that we're not as faithful as we need to be to get into Heaven? Only with the Word that is full of God's Truth can we even start to sort through these deceptions. We will never master this completely while we share this world with the devil. But as believers, we have to, we need to, cling to the Light that shines on in the darkness at all times. This is the only way we will find our way Home to Heaven.

Hell is an eternal place where people are paid back perfectly for the sins they have committed. It has been said, "Hell is perfect pure justice." We serve a just God…a perfect God. And Heaven is a perfect place designed for perfect people. Since the only perfect Person who ever lived was our sinless Savior, the Lord Jesus Christ, we can't get to Heaven without Jesus and His cleansing blood. We have to come to this realization for ourselves while we are still here in this life. One second after we die, it will be too late. One heartbeat after our last one on this earth, we will enter into eternity somewhere. We need to accept the gift now that's offered in Hebrews 10:10 (NET), *By his will we have been made holy through the offering of the body of Jesus Christ once for all.* Why do human beings reject such an amazing blessing? Jesus did this for us, suffered so much, took on the wrath of His Father that we deserved, and yet so many push Jesus aside…doing their own thing and hoping for the best. Too many times people are listening to the lies in this fallen world, and the depravity of their own heart that deceives them, and at the same time thinking they are being good enough to escape Hell if it really does exist. All LIES! The pathway to Hell is paved with deception. Let's get the potholes in our hearts taken care of ASAP! *You lead me in the path of life. I experience absolute joy in your presence; you always give me sheer delight.* Psalm 16:11 (NET) Our enemy is only out to lead us on the path to destruction. Why do we listen to him? We need to listen to, and believe, the words of Jesus!

In the book of John, the word "believe" occurs over 100 times. That's how important it is to believe the Truth of Jesus Christ. Jesus did many miracles, and they were recorded so that we would believe He truly is the Son of God. He wanted us to have life in His name. Oh, our God so wanted that, and still does! (John 20:31) Jesus prayed for you, and for me, and for everyone who lives upon this earth. In John 17:24 (NET), it was recorded that Jesus said, *"Father, I want those you have given me to be with me where I am, so that they can see my glory that you gave me because you loved me before the creation of the world."* We were on Jesus' mind 2,000 years ago. We were on His mind before the creation of the world. *All things were created by him, and apart from him not one thing was created that has been created.* John 1:3 (NET) Jesus created us, He loves us, and He wants us with Him. But many will live eternally without our Lord Jesus and it will be Hell, physically, emotionally, and spiritually. When people get a reality check, a good grip on the severity of Hell, it can be a great motivating factor for a change in thinking and direction…a 180-degree repentance. Those first Holy Spirit-filled believers in Acts 2:37-38 (NET) asked, *"What should we do, brothers?" Peter said to them, "Repent, and each one of you be baptized in the name of Jesus Christ for the forgiveness of your sins, and you will receive the gift of the Holy Spirit."* Repentance is key on the pathway toward Heaven because it's what changes our direction when we realize we're on the pathway to Hell.

Let's take a look at the horrible place we are walking away from when we choose Jesus Christ as our Savior and Lord, and Heaven as our destination. When we turn toward our Messiah, we are turning away from/leaving behind a place that was never designed for us. The Bible says that Hell was prepared for the devil and his angels. (Matthew 25:41) Our Creator never meant for us to end up there. God is called our Creator until we are adopted into the family of God. Then, and only then, does He become our Father. (Gal. 3:26) Our Father wants us Home with Him.

What I'm going to share with you about Hell here is a condensed version of a testimony by a man who says he had a vision of Hell. Whether or not his testimony is valid is immaterial here. You may wonder how that can be so. Because what I gathered from him are mainly the Scriptures that support what he shared—those cannot be argued against when we believe the Bible to be true. What he experienced is interesting. But even he said it doesn't matter if we believe his experience or not; what matters is what God has to say about Hell.

Scripture tells us we must all appear before the judgment seat of Christ. (2 Cor. 5:10-11) Without having salvation through Jesus Christ on Judgment Day, the final destination will be Hell. This will include being imprisoned in a pit, locked up in prison, and punished. (Isaiah 24:22) Hell is below us, probably in the center of the earth, presently. (Proverbs 7:27 and Ez. 26:20) There are barred gates. (Job 17:16) The person will be very weak. (Isaiah 14:10) They will be helpless. (Psalm 88:4) There will be blasphemy and cursing.

(Revelation 13:6) There will be destruction of both body and soul in Hell. (Matt. 10:28) There is no life, because life is in the blood. (Leviticus 17:11) There is no water because water is the rain of Heaven. (Zech. 9:11, Deut. 11:11) There is no mercy when we are not a descendant of the Father. (Psalm 103:17) It is dark. (Jude 13) There is fire and brimstone. (Psalm 11:6) There is no peace. (Isaiah 57:21) There are different levels of torment. (Matthew 10:15) There is no purpose. (Ecclesiastes 9:10) There is no escape. (Job 7:9) It is extremely difficult to breathe since the Lord gives us breath upon the earth, not in Hell. (Isaiah 42:5) There is no rest. (Revelation 14:11) There are maggots and worms that never die. (Isaiah 14:11 and Job 24:20) Those there will be consumed with terrors. (Psalm 73:19) It is an eternal fire that was originally prepared for the devil and his angels. (Matthew 25:41) There is only hatred in Hell because God is love. (1 John 4:16) There is no peace because Jesus is the Prince of Peace. (Isaiah 9:6)

This list could go on and on, but I'm sure this gives us all a glimpse into the place we never want to be. It is said, "When we understand how severe Hell is, we will be much more appreciative of our own salvation." We don't want our worst enemy to end up there, and neither does our Father in Heaven. That is why God sent His One and only Son to this Earth to die on the Cross for our sins. When we humble ourselves, repent, confess, and believe all that the Cross has provided for us, we will not have to go to this terrible place of torment. When we believe that Jesus endured the wrath of His own Father upon that Cross, received all the punishment we were so deserving of, and then gave up His life so we can be declared righteous and live eternally with Him and all other believers in Heaven, then Hell will not be our final destination. We will be spared! When Jesus was buried in the tomb, it proved He actually died. That it was no lie. We read how they didn't even have to break Jesus' legs before taking Him down from the Cross, like they did the other two men that day. Jesus had already given up His Spirit to the Father when they came to examine the bodies. After three days, Jesus rose again, conquering sin and death. Not that we won't die a physical death, but when we do, we will live eternally in Heaven. In a quotation from D. James Kennedy's book, *Why I Believe* it says, "When you have been in hell a hundred billion, trillion eons of centuries, you will not have one less second to be there—to be lost forever." The exact opposite is true about Heaven! We will be in Heaven longer than a hundred billion, trillion eons of centuries and not have one less second to be there…we will be saved forever! Hallelujah!!

It was said, "Plowing the human heart is an absolute necessity in true Gospel preaching." Luke 9:62 (NET) *Jesus said to him, "No one who puts his hand to the plow and looks back is fit for the kingdom of God."* As we take some time with John going through the seven churches in Revelation now, we can plow through our heart, examine our walk with God, and recognize the path that leads to Heaven.

In John 1:19, John the Baptist is asked, *"Who are you?"* He was quick to confess that he was not the Christ. They continued to question him, and he continued to respond telling them that he was not Elijah, or the Prophet. Finally, John said, *"I am the voice of one shouting in the wilderness, 'Make straight the way for the Lord.' "* John 1:23 (NET) How would we respond if asked, "Who are you?" This is talked about in Ephesians chapter one, about our adoption as God's legal heirs. It's interesting that the first letter to the first church in Revelation was to the Church of Ephesus. Let's dive in and examine ourselves further…not as the world would examine us, but as the Word of God would. We have to start at home with our Father. *For it is time for judgment to begin, starting with the house of God. And if it starts with us, what will be the fate of those who are disobedient to the gospel of God?* 1 Peter 4:17 (NET)

What would it benefit us if we saved the whole world, but we were lost ourselves? That's sort of a different way of looking at the verse in Mark 8:36 (NET), *For what shall it profit a man, if he shall gain the whole world, and lose his own soul?* But how many times have we heard a good sermon and longed for someone else we know to be hearing it…because we think they could really use it. Since we are the one sitting there, it very well could be for us! What if we have a log jam in our own eyes while trying to remove the speck from someone else's? *O God, you are aware of my foolish sins; my guilt is not hidden from you…* Psalm 69:5 (NET) But it can be hidden from ourselves! Let's not even trust our own heart and mind since Jesus didn't. It is written in John 2:24-26 that Jesus didn't entrust himself to man *for he knew what was in man.*

Let's take everything to the Cross of Christ, the Word of God, and allow it to examine us. We should take the words of Jesus very seriously in John 3:18 (NET) where it says, *"The one who believes in him is not condemned. The one who does not believe has been condemned already, because he has not believed in the name of the one and only Son of God."* And John 3:36 (NET) says, *"The one who believes in the Son has eternal life. The one who rejects the Son will not see life, but God's wrath remains on him."*

Spurgeon had this to say about the one who realizes his own depravity. "When he is truly awakened to feel his guilt, if you could lay a fortune before him, he would say, 'Take it away: I want to find Him.'" When we do, we will find that Jesus is enough!

John 12:21 (NET) expresses what so many of us feel, *"Sir, we would like to see Jesus."* Oh, how amazing that Philip went and told Andrew, and they both went and told Jesus. One day, we, too, will see Jesus! It's not selfish, but instead vital, to start our search for Jesus at home...with ourselves, in our own hearts, in our own churches, and then to go out from there sharing the Good News Jesus left us with. It was prayed, "Lord, tear the veil in our own heart and mind so we can examine what's hidden there, and then we can be Your light in the world that's so very dark." The veil of deception can be as thick as the one that tore in the Temple when Jesus died on the Cross at Calvary. It's what stands between unbelief and the purity of the Cross. Let's begin with the churches in Revelation now, as these are the letters that warn us, and keep us from Hell, if we will only just believe. (You might want to turn there in your Bible as we go through them in this chapter.)

The Church in Ephesus

When Jesus examined the church in Ephesus in Revelation 2:1-7, we can all find ourselves in the words written there...the good and the bad. This is not so that we will feel horrible thinking we are heading toward Hell. This is so we can be set free through repentance in Jesus Christ each and every day from everything the enemy tempts us with, including the lie that we might be headed to Hell. As children of God, we are going Home to see our Father. That is guaranteed.

This first letter to Ephesus is a "solemn pronouncement" from Jesus, the One who has a firm grasp on the seven stars

(Angels/Pastors) in His right hand. This is written using the words *your* and *you*. That makes it personal. One pastor said about this letter that we should be "listening to it, looking at it, leaning into it, learning from it, and letting it be done in our own lives."

Jesus is commending the Church of Ephesus on their endurance and how they're not tolerating evil. They are testing what's false...all for the sake of Jesus' name. And, they have not grown weary. It's sounding good so far, and I hope we can find ourselves in these commendations. But there is one thing Jesus has against the Church in Ephesus—they departed from their First Love. What does Jesus tell them they are to do about it? Repent! (Rev. 2:5) Repent is spoken of twice in one verse. It has been said, to have hope, peace and encouragement, you must first repent. The reward that comes in hearing this and conquering this is being given permission *to eat from the tree of life that is in the paradise of God.* (v. 2:7) During those eons of years in Heaven, it says we will eat...from the tree of life...in paradise...with God. I'm liking the sounds of that!

But what about our First Love, Jesus Christ? That's what's being addressed here with them, and what we can and should take a look at in our own life. I know during the corona virus season here in the U.S. I do miss baseball...a lot. But do I put baseball above Jesus in my life? I would certainly hope not. Perhaps the virus has come for very good reason...to get our attention focused back on our First Love. I know for me, on a typical pre-virus Sunday after arriving home from church, having a late breakfast, and finding the A's have a game starting at 1:00, I'm a happy camper. But things that sneak in and take a place in our life like baseball, other relationships, other forms of entertainment, shopping, decorating, gardening, reading, and sometimes even a ministry...before time spent with God, are to be looked at closely.

We have to ask ourselves, how important is God in our daily routine? What is our go-to when we have time in our day to choose an activity? Do we quickly bring up Facebook and scan the stories because our phone is usually very accessible? I know I've been guilty of that. If and when that comes before the importance of the Word of God in our life, "Have we lost our First Love?" If we knew Jesus was coming back tonight, what would we be spending our time doing? Praying! Reading the Word! Sharing the Good News of Jesus Christ without pause! Should any other day look different? Probably so, since there are many things that need to be taken care of on any given day…but this is a good check-up on our own relationship with Jesus as we read about the Church in Ephesus. Jesus had John write this letter for a good reason…to get our attention before we do meet Him face to face…theirs and ours!

That's the personal part of this…now what about the church part of this as in the "building" we go to filled with our brothers and sisters in the Lord on Sunday mornings? Let's ask ourselves, why we attend the church we do? What do we want to find when we get there? Do we find warm and welcoming fellowship, people praying for one another, a sermon filled with the Truth of the Gospel, and worship that praises the Lord Jesus? Or have we made Sunday morning more about the clothes we wear, a surface-type of socializing that may take place, entertaining worship that doesn't include the Truth of the Gospel, and a message that makes us feel good and encourages us, but wouldn't save a soul by what's being preached? It's so easy to get distracted by the good and fun things church can be. But if it's merely a distraction and doesn't come close to the Good News being the real reason we are there, repentance/a change is needed.

When we attend church, we have to ask ourselves if it is instrumental in helping us focus on the Cross? Is it teaching us the Word correctly? Is it helping us see our sins and the need for the Savior…always directing us back to the importance of our walk with Jesus each day throughout the week even after it's over? If we don't leave Sunday morning church services challenged in our daily choices, encouraged in our faith, and full of Hope because of everything Jesus died to provide for our eternity, we might want to look elsewhere for a church that helps us in our relationship with our First Love. Is the corona virus a time of our Lord solemnly removing lampstands/our churches from our world? Is God weeding out the false churches, separating the goats and the sheep? Perhaps… It may be a very needed time both personally and for our church community. Thank You, Jesus, for coming down to Earth so You could lift us up to Heaven.

The Church in Smyrna

The second letter to the Church in Smyrna is located in

Revelation 2:8-11. This church is located 35 miles north of Ephesus…which is now modern-day Turkey. Smyrna means "myrrh." It's a resin/balm that comes out of a tree that has been repeatedly struck/wounded. It bleeds the resin. Where have we heard about myrrh before? It was one of the three gifts the Wise Men brought to young Jesus. Myrrh has been used throughout history as a perfume, incense, and medicine, and was used by the Egyptians to embalm the dead. It was also offered to Jesus on the Cross. When it is written that He was given vinegar to drink mingled with gall (Matthew 27:34), it described the drink in Mark as wine mingled with myrrh. (Mark 15:23) It is used as a drug to dull the senses. Nicodemus used myrrh to prepare Christ's body for burial. (John 19:39) It is often associated with bitter circumstances. Since Smyrna was going through difficult times, it is fitting that their name means myrrh.

How is Smyrna doing as a church? There is no criticism or rebuke from Jesus in their letter. The Church in Philadelphia is a close second, with a little more praise but also talks about them having little strength. Will we see ourselves in this church? What kind of letter would Jesus write to us? To our church? This is another solemn pronouncement from Jesus as He describes Himself as the First, the Last, the One who was dead, but came to life. Then He says, *"I know…"* We know Jesus as one acquainted with deepest grief. (Isaiah 53:3) Jesus says here that He knows the distress they are suffering because of their poverty—Jesus had no place to lay His head. He understands. (Luke 9:58) Jesus tells them He knows about the slander that is against them by those who call themselves Jews but are a synagogue of Satan—Jesus could relate. Jesus was betrayed as Satan filled Judas and Judas betrayed Him. Jesus was lied about. (Mark 14:56-58) Jesus goes on to say to the church at Smyrna, the devil was going to have some of them thrown into prison. Jesus, too, was arrested, and thrown into a cell. (John 18) He told them they were going to experience suffering. (2 Timothy 3:12) Jesus encouraged them to remain faithful even to the point of death—Wow, Jesus knew what that would be like. Smyrna would be given the crown that is life itself, as was Jesus when He rose and wore the crown of our eternal King! For those who hear what the Spirit is saying, and conquers, they will not be harmed by the second death—they will not be thrown into Hell when judgment day comes!

Lord, we want to be, and be in, a church like Smyrna! You were pleased. You were saying, *"Well done, good and faithful servant."*

What must we do to be like the church in Smyrna? It's written in John 6:29 (NET), *Jesus replied, "This is the deed God requires—to believe in the one whom he sent."* If we will do this, seeking first the Kingdom of God, all else will be added to our lives. When Jesus is our First Love, we will move from being a church like Ephesus, into a church like Smyrna. John 6:35 (NET), *Jesus said to them, "I am the bread of life. The one who comes to me will never go hungry, and the one who believes in me will never be thirsty."*

The Church in Pergamum

Pergamum is the city that invented papyrus (paper). It was a city where faithfulness and compromise existed side by side. Again, this is a letter to the angel/pastor of the church. It's another solemn pronouncement. 1 John 2:15-17 says, *Do not love the world or the things in the world. If anyone loves the world, the love of the Father is not in him, because all that is in the world (the desire of the flesh and the desire of the eyes and the arrogance produced by material possessions) is not from the Father, but is from the world.*

With this church, there is a double-edged sword involved. We know that involves the Word of God which is sharper than the sharpest two-edged sword. (Hebrews 4:12) Jesus says He knows where they live and it's not a good place from the sounds of it. (Revelation 2:12-17) It's where Satan's throne is. Whoa! But the good news is, Jesus tells them that they do continue to cling to His name and have not denied their faith in Him even though a faithful witness named Antipas was killed. That would strike fear into most anyone, yet they remained faithful. Let that be said of us all!

Now, there is a downturn here…Jesus has some things to address with those in Pergamum. Some of the people there are following wrong teachings coming from Balaam (a pagan prophet who worshipped the gods of the land) which led to eating food sacrificed to idols and committing sexual immorality. Also, some are following the teaching of the Nicolaitans whose ministry style was lording their authority over the people and also taught that Christians could be immoral and not have to deal with the consequences of that. This is not pleasing to God. Jesus urged the people to repent, otherwise the sword of His mouth, that sharp double-edged sword, will be His weapon of war used against them. He asks them to once again hear what the Spirit is saying if they have an ear, which they do… There is a reward for those in Pergamum that Jesus mentions here…there is some hidden manna, which is Jesus, Himself. They were also to be given a white stone. This is to let them know they were going to be given, not only a new life through Jesus Christ, but also a new name. Even though their city/church was filled with sin, those who called Jesus Savior could live in that pagan culture and not compromise because the Holy Spirit of God is the continued power within them to help resist all that surrounded them.

In the city of Pergamum, almost every major deity had a temple. Whatever they needed, the gods offered it in Pergamum. Zeus/god of the sky had all the power. Dionysus/god of wine and revelry was there for drunken orgies. Demeter was a god of food. Asklepion was the healing center. People came from all over the world to be healed. Snakes did the healing in a dark room at night where the people were put into a trance. Snakes would crawl over them in a ritual of healing. That is why the medical rod with the snake dates back to Pergamum. (This is different than the pole Moses lifted up with the bronze snake pointing to Jesus on the Cross.) This pole with a snake is found on the flag for the World Health Organization which chose it as their emblem in 1948. The Hippocratic Oath originally began with, "I swear by Apollo the physician and by Asclepius…and all the gods and goddesses making them." Athena was also in Pergamum as the goddess of wisdom. No wonder Jesus said, "I know where you dwell…" It was definitely where Satan's throne was.

We have to understand, Satan is not in Hell…in Pergamum, that is obvious. Satan is still alive and well, and we have to deal with him here in this world still. But we have the love of God, the strength of God, and the will of God continually showing us the path to Heaven while urging us to repent and turn away from the pathway to Hell that was so evident in Pergamum. These churches will help us see ourselves as we really are. It is biblical to do so. It says in 2 Corinthians 13:5 (NET), *Put yourselves to the test to see if you are in the faith; examine yourselves! Or do you not recognize regarding yourselves that Jesus Christ is in you—unless, indeed, you fail the test.*

We cannot just look at our face in a mirror and forget what we look like. (James 1:24) It is good to put ourselves to the test, especially now while many of us have more time to be still and know that God is God during this pandemic. Some have called it a "plandemic." Perhaps so, by our mighty God who is *not wanting anyone to perish, but everyone to come to repentance.* 2 Peter 3:9 (NIV)

The last four churches we will talk about mention Christ's return. Beginning with the church in Thyatira which is encouraged to: *"Hold fast until I come."* (Rev. 2:25) Sardis is told: *"You will not know what hour I will come."* (3:3) Philadelphia gets to hear: *"Behold, I come quickly."* Laodicea is told: *"Behold, I stand at the door..."* (3:20) The first three churches don't mention this at all.

These admonitions and encouragements written in Revelation are about personalities and changes that take place over a period of time. We can use them to help us know where we stand in our relationship with Jesus Christ on any given day as we grow in our faith and walk in a deeper repentance.

The Church in Thyatira

Let's look at the Church in Thyatira in Revelation 2:18-29 and see where we can find ourselves. The Lord knows us so well...He knows every hair on our head (Luke 12:7), and every anxious thought (Phil. 4:6). Not a sparrow falls from the sky without Him knowing. (Matthew 10:29) Why should we be surprised to find ourselves in the description of each of these churches?

Thyatira is a wealthy town. They are told in this letter that they are doing well in their deeds concerning love, faith, service and steadfast endurance. Sounding good so far, as Jesus solemnly pronounces their characteristics through eyes of fiery flames and with feet like polished bronze. The sights and sounds that John experienced through all of this really were beyond the descriptive words he has to write with. One day, we too will see our Lord!

John wrote, *"When I saw him I fell down at his feet as though I were dead, but he placed his right hand on me and said: 'Do not be afraid! I am the first and the last, and the one who lives. I was dead, but look now I am alive—forever and ever—I hold the keys of death and Hades!'"* Revelation 1:17-18 (NET) That's the God we serve.

The Lord who died for us! The one who we will stand before one day or fall at his feet as though dead. It is interesting that John adds the detail about Jesus' right hand that was placed on him. The right hand conveys authority, blessings, power, and strength. Everything, every word written in the Bible, is significant. If only we had the time to take it word by word...one day we will, when we have all of eternity to spend with our Lord. And we can ask Him for understanding! How awesome that will be!

Sadly, Thyatira had Jezebel, or the spirit that operated through her at least. It's not a good spirit, as it leads people into sexual immorality and eating food sacrificed to idols. Jesus, once again, looking for repentance, has given time for this turn/change to take place. It hasn't. There will be consequences involving suffering and diseases (Covid?) that will help the churches to know that Jesus is the One who searches all hearts and minds. In this searching, Jesus also found those in Thyatira who didn't participate in these sins. They remained faithful. He tells them to hold onto this, what they have, until He comes. There will be rewards for such faithfulness. Just as Jesus was given the right to rule from His Father, He is willing to give it to those who follow Him to the end. Could that be said of us? It's a lofty goal, one only made possible by the power of the Holy Spirit who lives within each believer. On our own, we will fail miserably. With the very power that raised Jesus from the dead living inside of us, we are victorious! Even when we fall, we are lifted up again, shown mercy, forgiven, and helped to carry on.

Why should we listen to what Jesus is saying to these churches? Because it goes way, way back. Let's look at Deuteronomy 18:15 (NET), *"The Lord your God will raise up for you a prophet like me from among you—from your fellow Israelites; you must listen to him."* And now in Revelation we are being told, *"The one who has an ear had better hear what the Spirit says to the churches."* Our God is the same yesterday, today, and forever! That is why we must heed His word on the path that leads to Heaven instead of Hell: *"I am the light of the world! The one who follows me will never walk in darkness, but will have the light of life."* John 8:12 (NET) That path, that very narrow path, with the narrow gate, is the one we are to be searching for. It is the one that leads to Heaven.

Jesus talked about Hell more than anyone else in the Bible. Why? Because He wants us, and our family and friends, to know Him before it's too late. Jesus wasn't worried about offending anyone, or people thinking He's not as loving as the world thinks He should be. Jesus didn't lie to anyone, as many behind the pulpit do today to unsuspecting congregants. Jesus said in John 8:24 (NET), *"Thus I told you that you will die in your sins. For unless you believe that I am he, you will die in your sins."* Do we hear that being said on Sunday morning? If we're not, we should be! Jesus went on to say in John 8:47 (NET), *"The one who belongs to God listens and responds to God's words. You don't listen and respond, because you don't belong to God."* Let that not be said of us! Jesus was the most loving Person to walk the face of this Earth. But He told it like it is, even telling the Judeans in John 8:44 (NET), *"You people are from your father the devil..."* Can you imagine hearing that in church? They ended up telling Jesus He was possessed by a demon. They should have been fearing Him instead! *How blessed is the one who obeys the Lord, who takes great delight in keeping his commands.* Psalm 112:1 (NET)

It's not pleasant to talk about Hell, but it's much more unpleasant to talk of those going there. What's that saying, "An ounce of prevention is worth a pound of cure." With a warning ahead of time, there's not such a mess at the end. That's the whole point of this "Shelter in Place," right? Keep us home, keep us safe. That's how it's being talked about in the media, for the most part. And it has some merit to it. But when we do take a step back, biblically speaking, it has all the earmarks of end times prophecy being fulfilled. Things taking place now line up perfectly with what God told us would happen. Let's keep an eye on what God is doing in this world to bring many to know Him during this time. As in Iran in the last six months...there have been 60,000 downloads of the Bible with a new anonymous app. Iran is ranked ninth as the most dangerous country in which to be a Christian. They are at risk for persecution and imprisonment, but God's Word is on the rise. It's happening!

Jesus talked about Hell, and twenty different times he talked about fire when referring to Hell. We all know the story of the man, Lazarus, in Luke 16, who died and was carried to Abraham's side. Jesus let us know in telling this story that there is no exit door in Hell. There is a great chasm that has been "fixed" between where Abraham was and the rich man who was in Hades. (Luke 16:26)

And in Luke 16:29, Jesus lets us know that the prophets and Moses gave warnings to the people. God is not slipping Hell in on us trying to fool us...we have been told about Hell for thousands and thousands of years. But so many scoff at these warnings from God.

The term "scofflaw" came about during Prohibition in 1920-1933. It was a constitutional ban on the production, importation, transportation, and sale of alcoholic beverages. "Scofflaw" is being used again for those who go to the beach or the park right now during quarantine. It is someone who mocks the law. What about going to church? What about singing in church? Living in America during this pandemic, many feel their rights are being taken away. There is some merit to this in certain situations. We are to follow the law...until it means disobeying God's law that is written on our heart. For those who mock God, who scoff at His laws, there is no merit. God's Word says, *"Be not deceived; God is not mocked; for whatsoever a man soweth, that shall he also reap."* Galatians 6:7 (KJV) Jesus was truly concerned for our eternal destiny, as we should also be for our own and others. It is not to be toyed with! John 5:24 (NET) says, *"I tell you the solemn truth, the one who hears my message and believes the one who sent me has eternal life and will not be condemned, but has crossed over from death to life.* At the present time, there is a way to cross over, there is a way to escape Hell, and His name is Jesus. The Lord Jesus is the door to freedom and an eternity in Heaven.

You may have heard it said that, "Love Wins." It's also the title of a well-known book. This statement is true, true love does win for those who want to be forgiven. John 3:17 (NET), *"For God did not send his Son into the world to condemn the world, but that the world should be saved through him."* But those who say God is too loving to send people to Hell are the very people who help their friends and family find their way there. *"The one who does not believe has been condemned already, because he has not believed in the name of the one and only Son of God."* John 3:18b (NET) It is a choice we all will make.

Jesus referred to Hell as Gehenna which is a valley in Jerusalem. Why would Jesus tie these two places together? Because Gehenna was a place where some of the kings of Judah sacrificed their children to Molech by fire. This place can still be seen today...it is a valley between the New City and the Old City of Jerusalem. It's not much to look at today, but it has a history that should never be forgotten. This valley is said to be cursed and is known as the destination of the wicked. Matthew 10:28 (NET) Jesus said, *"Do not be afraid of those who kill the body but cannot kill the soul. Instead, fear the one who is able to destroy both soul and body in hell."* In Jesus' day, Gehenna was a place of constant fire—bodies of criminals were thrown into this smoldering heap. When Jesus tied Hell and Gehenna together, He was referring to the city dump of eternity. The way there, the pathway to Hell, is there for those who reject Christ as the one and only way to Heaven.

We were made for God and we are hopeless without Him. So many Christian books are about how empty we are. Sadly, the evangelical churches have become more about man and our self-esteem than the Gospel of Jesus Christ. Those little dabs will do us under, if we aren't paying attention to the Truth of God's Word. Apart from Christ, we are empty, lost and afraid. We are on a path of destruction. The only place to find purpose and meaning in life is living for Christ. When our purpose for living is to give God glory, we can have peace knowing we are on the right path toward Heaven.

The Church in Sardis

In Revelation 3:1-6, we move on to the Church in Sardis, which is 50 miles NE of Smyrna. Here we find Jesus urging them to wake up! That's so important for all of us right now in quarantine. Iran is waking up to Jesus. Is America? Revelation 3:1b-2 (NET), Jesus has John write this to the Church in Sardis: *"I know your deeds, that you have a reputation that you are alive, but in reality you are dead. Wake up then, and strengthen what remains that was about to die, because I have not found your deeds complete in the sight of my God."*

America started out as a Christian nation. The birth certificate for our country was called the Mayflower Compact, written by the male passengers of the Mayflower. They were separatists, Puritans, adventurers, and tradesmen fleeing from religious persecution by King James I of England. Our forefathers then wrote a constitution protecting our fundamental and inalienable rights. And now, many of those rights are being taken from us as churches are told to shut their doors during the pandemic. The Bible and prayer have been taken out of our schools even though the Bible was the reason public schools were founded. The Bible used to be the textbook children used in learning to read. This was instituted to combat religious ignorance. In 1949, Bible reading was part of the routine in 37 states in our schools. In 12 states it was legally required. But in 1963, corporate reading of the Bible and the Lord's Prayer were declared unlawful in schools. It seems our country was once alive to the things of God…and now…we could very well fall under the same condition as Sardis.

Jesus urges them to *remember what you received and heard, and obey it, and repent.* We still can, individually and as a country. We have been given time to repent and so many are praying. God is being so very gracious and good to us. But I believe the whole world is being warned if we don't wake up, Jesus will come as a thief against us. (Revelation 3:3) He has every right! Everything we have, including our soul, belongs to God. Jesus came to save our soul…to transform us and usher us into Heaven. Jesus will also come to condemn our soul and throw us into Hell. Luke 12:5 (NET): *But I will warn you whom you should fear: Fear the one who, after the killing, has authority to throw you into hell. Yes, I tell you, fear him!"*

C.S. Lewis put it this way: "There will be those who say, 'Thy will be done' to God. And others to whom God will say, 'Thy will be done.'"

The Church in Sardis has some faithful followers. They are dressed in white and walk with Jesus. (v. 3:4) They are said to be worthy. (3:4) Their name will never be erased from the book of life. He will declare their name before His Father and before His angels. (3:5) Some were doing well and had a good reputation. It was no time to stop. Their deeds weren't complete. It was time to wake up to the things of God and keep going, or they wouldn't be ready for the return of Jesus. This examination is not for condemnation, but for cleansing.

Jesus provided us so much. He is love. And we are loved. We can be transformed by His love just like the blind man in John, chapter nine. It is such an encouraging story. How many times have we wondered why bad things happen? Did we sin? Did our parents sin? And yet here we find a man who was blind since birth and it was neither the fault of his parents nor him. We know this to be true because Jesus Himself said so. Jesus said, *"Neither this man nor his parents sinned, but he was born blind so that the acts of God may be revealed through what happens to him."* John 9:3 (NET) I took great solace in this verse when my own son went Home to Heaven at the age of 16 from leukemia. Now almost 20 years later, I pray the acts of God have been revealed by what happened to my child. I know my life was transformed through those painful years. Before that season of suffering in my life, I was blind to so much of who Jesus was. I knew Jesus, but not like I do now. Now I see Him as I probably never would have without some messy parts of life being smeared on my face to open my eyes to the Father's amazing love and forgiveness. It took the Living Water of Jesus Christ to help me see clearly what the Cross provides for those who turn to Jesus' saving grace.

Jesus' death, burial, resurrection, and soon return is the core of Christianity. Without the Gospel, the heart of our faith is missing, and we have no Hope for eternity. People will live in a terrible state of sin, die in that sin, and live eternally in Hell without the Gospel being declared while there is still time!

John 9:18-20 (NET) says, *Now the Jewish religious leaders refused to believe that he had really been blind and had gained his sight until at last they summoned the parents of the man who had become able to see. They asked the parents, "Is this your son, whom you say was born blind? Then how does he now see?" So his parents replied, "We know that this is our son and that he was born blind."*

His parents went on to say they didn't know how he was now able to see. They said to ask him and let him speak for himself. The parents did this because they were afraid of the Jewish religious leaders. It reminds me of someone asking one of my longtime friends who I was before my son went Home to Heaven. How blind was I? Well, I could physically see, but I could barely physically talk. I was so shy I wouldn't say a word in a group of people. My friends from the past will attest to that, and the change that has come over me. My mother-in-law says while I was dating my husband in high school, the first two years she knew me, all she heard me say was "Hello" upon arriving, and "Good-bye" upon leaving. That is not the person I am today. You can ask her! The people there that day heaped insults on the man who was no longer blind, saying, *"You are his disciple."* (John 9:28) There is no greater privilege than to be called a disciple of Jesus Christ.

If we have the reputation for being alive like Sardis, but inside we feel dead, it's time to take notice and wake up! Jesus tells them to strengthen what remains that was about to die, in verse 3:2 of Revelation. There is still time...there is Hope...it's time to repent...time to change...time to be a disciple of Jesus Christ that lets His light so shine through our testimony that it cannot be ignored. Testimonies don't come without tests that caused lots of moaning... Jesus hears our cries to Him, and He answers them. People are praying for revival. Revival is for the believers to bring back to life what has gone dormant in our own faith, and then to share our life in Christ with others!

For you, O God, tested us; you purified us like refined silver. You led us into a trap; you caused us to suffer. You allowed men to ride over our heads; we passed through fire and water, but you brought us out into a wide open place.
Psalm 66:10-12 (NET)

Hell is not meant for man. It was designed for Satan and his angels. Let's allow God to lead us to the wide-open place of Heaven and enjoy it for all eternity with Him!

The Church in Philadelphia

As we move to the church in Philadelphia in Revelation 3:7-13, the mood seems to lighten a bit. Philadelphia is 27 miles from Sardis. They are given another *solemn pronouncement of the Holy One, the True One, who holds the key of David...* In a time in our world when no one is coming and knocking on our door other than UPS or FedEx dropping off a package—or maybe DoorDash dropping off a meal, it would be a welcome sight to see a friend at our door, or a family member we have been separated from. This pronouncement goes on to say that this is the One who *shuts doors no one can open*...and that He has put before them *an open door that no one can shut.* No one can stop the Lord from coming and going. Not even a "Shelter in Place" order. Jesus tells the Church in Philadelphia that He knows they *have little strength.* He has compassion on them. He understands. And Jesus is pleased that they have obeyed His Word and have not denied His name. That's a huge commendation! Let that, too, be said of us! As Jesus tells them, and as we should know, too, Jesus knows our deeds. Deeds do not pave our way into Heaven. But when we are on the pathway there, deeds will accompany us. We will be known by our fruits…by others, and by our Lord. Jesus was also known by what He did. John 10:25 (NET) *Jesus replied, "I told you and you do not believe. The deeds I do in my Father's name testify about me."* The deeds we do testify about our faith in Him…they show that we have a testimony to begin with. Let's get the cart behind the horse of Salvation…by grace through faith first and then deeds automatically follow. We can ride along that way all the way to Heaven, sharing the Good News.

As one author writes, "What a person has done, that is, what he has worked on in this lifetime, follows him through the grave—either into the Lake of Fire or the Kingdom of God."

The Church in Philadelphia seemed to be hanging in there with their witness even in their weakness. In 2 Corinthians 12:10 (NET) it says, *Therefore I am content with weaknesses, with insults, with troubles, with persecutions and difficulties for the sake of Christ, for whenever I am weak, then I am strong.*

There are times when we just don't feel like trying anymore, or even have the strength to want to feel it. That is called being a human being. That is not an indication of our Salvation. We all feel that way at times. But what we do in those times is an indication of where we are spiritually…do we have an ear that is willing to hear what the Spirit is saying? The choices we make in times like those are an indication of our willingness to listen to the Spirit. Don't you wonder how the writers of the Bible can remember everything that took place, and all the conversations that transpired? Well, it is the same Holy Spirit spoken about in John 14:26 (NET) who lived in them, who now lives in us. It says, *But the Advocate, the Holy Spirit, whom the Father will send in my name, will teach you everything, and will cause you to remember everything I said to you.*

What does this have to do with a dry spell in our life, a weak time, an "I don't feel like doing it" time? EVERYTHING! Because the Holy Spirit never leaves us in those times, and is always there as our Comforter, reminding us of what we have been taught, and urging us on. When we hear that still small voice urging us to pick up our Bible and read even when we don't feel like it, that is God loving us through His Spirit. When we are reminded to pray during those times even when we don't feel like it, that is our loving God wanting us to pour our hearts out to Him and seek His help and healing and strength. When we receive a text or a phone call of encouragement to keep on going during those times, that is the Hand of God operating through those around us to see us through the tough times. We are never alone with our Counselor living within. We can know that, even when we don't feel that.

Jesus told the Church in Philadelphia that they kept His admonition to endure steadfastly. He said He would *keep them from the hour of testing that is about to come on the whole world to test those who live on the earth.* Whether there is a pre-tribulation rapture, a mid-tribulation rapture, or a post-tribulation rapture may not be known for sure. But what we can know for sure is that whatever the end looks like, Jesus will be there to keep us, to hold us, to comfort us, and to strengthen us. The whole world will be tested, but sadly many will not know Jesus or pass the hour of testing. Our responsibility is to endure steadfastly with Him to the end. There is a crown of life waiting, it is ours, even though the wait seems long. Jesus said in Rev. 3:11, *"I am coming soon."* Soon to God looks different than our soon most times, but it can be trusted! In Revelation 3:12 it says for those whose names are written in the Lamb's book of life, Jesus' name will be written on them, and also the name of His city, the New Jerusalem, and His new name as well. He reminds them once again, *"The one who has an ear had better hear what the Spirit says to the churches."*

These letters were written 2,000 years ago on the Island of Patmos which is just there off the coast of present-day Turkey. It's interesting to think of John being there, alone with Jesus, taken up and seeing all that would transpire. To those, then, it seemed His return would be soon. To us today, we can know it is so much sooner. We are not to be distressed about it. Jesus assured us in John 14:2-3 (NET), *"There are many dwelling places in my Father's house. Otherwise, I would have told you, because I am going away to make ready a place for you. And if I go and make ready a place for you, I will come again to take you to be with me, so that where I am you may be too."* What a wonderful assurance we have, that a place is being made ready for us. He's still working on it, getting it just right. But Hell, on the other hand, was prepared for the devil and his angels. It's ready, other than some expansion possibly going on because there are people ending up there who were never meant for that place, as Isaiah 5:14 states. The KJV says, *Therefore hell hath enlarged herself, and opened her mouth without measure.* Other versions just talk of *Death opening up its throat and wide its mouth.* (NET) Either way, we know all the good stays with God, and Hell is left with the dregs of all the bad this world contains. Those that want nothing to do with God here, will get their wish there. But because of Jesus, we don't have to go to that horrible place. This fact of the Bible gives us the Hope we long for, especially on those days when we just don't "feel it". One day, all the pain and distress of our flesh will be done. We will be in our heavenly Home.

God does not send anyone to Hell. But some have such a hostility toward God that they would rather rot away in Hell than give God the glory He so deserves. They are thrown into Gehenna, the garbage dump, only after they have rejected the King of glory. Up until that time, that last day, there are huge signs that point to Jesus. We just have to follow His clear directions to Heaven to avoid the pathway to Hell. Repent, and stay attached to the true Vine. John 15:5-6 (NET) says, *"I am the vine; you are the branches. The one who remains in me—and I in him—bears much fruit, because apart from me you can accomplish nothing. If anyone does not remain in me, he is thrown out like a branch, and dries up; and such branches are gathered up and thrown into the fire, and are burned up."*

Yes, there will be some throwing going on at the end, but only by choice. Not God's choice. He wants us with Him. It's because of everyone's right to choose life or death. There is *no condemnation for those who are in Christ Jesus.* Romans 8:1 (NET) God says in Deuteronomy 30:19 (NET), *"...I have set life and death, blessing and curse, before you. Therefore choose life so that you and your descendants may live!"* We are told these things so we will have joy, today and forevermore. *"But now I am coming to you, and I am saying these things in the world, so they may experience my joy completed in themselves."* John 17:13 (NET) Our Father doesn't want us miserable. He wants us to be filled with His joy, despite the hardships we must endure until Jesus' return. Jesus prays for us to His Father in John 17…He wants us to believe that His Father sent Him. Jesus wants us to know that just as the Father loves Him, the

Father loves us. Why else would the Father send His one and only Son to save us?!

There is a woman many years ago who had a sign in her home. It simply said, "Perhaps Today." It was a reminder to her and all who entered her home that she was awaiting her Lord. Our witness doesn't have to be complicated to be powerful.

The Church in Laodicea

When Jesus had John write to the Church in Laodicea, He made it clear who He was. It is written that Jesus is the *Amen, the faithful and true witness, the originator of God's creation.* (Rev. 3:14) Our witness needs to be either hot or cold to let those around us know where we stand. One man said to me about Jesus when I was sharing the Good News with him…"That's a hard sell." I knew where he stood and so did God. Another person I spoke to when I asked if she knew Jesus, said, "Yes, I do." One was hot, one was cold…but both were very clear…not lukewarm. Are we identified to those around us as on fire for Jesus, or cold as ice concerning Him? Jesus uses words here that we don't want to ever hear in 3:16 of Revelation, *"I will vomit you out of my mouth."*

As we wait for Jesus' return, as we hold on even through this pandemic, what are we doing? I find it interesting that the disciples went fishing after Jesus' resurrection. I guess they tried to go back to a somewhat normal life, as we are hoping to do. Many will return to work soon, we hope…and fishing was their job. *Simon Peter told them, "I am going fishing."* It seems without hesitation, the others said, *"We will go with you."* John 21:3 (NET) …like it was no big deal. They saw Christ crucified, then saw the risen Christ, and now as the 40 days before His ascension were upon them (although they didn't know it would be 40 days yet), they went back to fishing. Let it not be said of us that we just went back to work and forgot this season of the virus, the quarantine, the closed churches, and the world events surrounding all of it. But, should Jesus tarry, sadly most will do just that, just like some did after 9/11.

Jesus appeared to the disciples on the beach that day, just as one day Jesus will appear to us. We read how He lit a fire to cook their fish. Is He perhaps lighting a fire in us right now to not forget our risen Lord? To stay "hot" for Him, and not let this time of quarantine make us "cold"?

Jesus tells Laodicea that although they are rich and have all they need, they don't realize how wretched, pitiful, poor, blind, and naked they are. They were located on a very advantageous position on the trade route and had become one of the most important and flourishing commercial cities of Asia. But Jesus urges them to come to Him to become truly rich. The Lord wants to provide them the clothing necessary for an entrance into Heaven. He wants to give them eye salve so their blindness can be healed. Jesus reminds them that what comes with His love is rebuke and discipline—they are to be earnest and repent. So are we!

Summation of the Seven Churches

Five of the seven church letters include repentance. Only the churches of Smyrna and Philadelphia do not. And then Jesus has John pen these words in Revelation 3:20 to the church in Laodicea, which mean even more during this season in our world: *"Listen! I am standing at the door and knocking. If anyone hears my voice and opens the door I will come into his home and share a meal with him and he with me."* What a welcome sound that would be from a friend, a knock at the door. What a welcome joy that would be, for so many, to have family come through the door and be able to hug them once again. And if one day that knock we hear is our Lord Jesus Christ, we would surely want Him to find a fire burning in our home for Him; one that represents our heart toward Him today— one that didn't miss Him in the trials we are going through. To that person, Jesus says in Revelation 3:21 (NET): *"I will grant the one who conquers permission to sit with me on my throne, just as I too conquered and sat down with my Father on his throne."* Jesus' Father welcomed Him Home when His job on this Earth was finished. The Son had a place to go. Family to be with. Love to be enjoyed. And so do we when our earthly job is finished. We don't know when that day will be, or how it will look. But we do know it is coming and who we will be with as a member of the family of God. We want to be counted among those who have an ear and who have heard what the Spirit is saying to the churches.

We know what the pathway to Hell looks like now after looking at the letters Jesus had John write to these churches…it doesn't include repentance. And we know what the pathway to Heaven looks like…it is narrow, and few find it. But the road Home is there for us to find. When the masses are moving in one direction in this world, we should ask ourselves what path they are on? If it is not Biblical, we are to get off it quickly. We are to repent, and change directions toward Heaven. Yes, it can be like the salmon swimming upstream. It can be difficult. But just like the salmon, it's what we are meant to do. And just as the salmon arrive at their destination and new life is the result, so, too, will we arrive at our destination where a new life will begin. It is what we have been promised, and God keeps His promises. Our God is always with us, He is always in control, He is always good, and He is always watching over us. Talk about being sheltered in the place we stand today! As His children, we truly are!

A Brief Review of the Churches

Church in Ephesus: I know your works, steadfast endurance, and how you don't tolerate evil. But you have departed from your First Love. Repent.

Church in Smyrna: They are enduring distress, slander, prison, and possibly to the point of death. They are told to remain faithful and they will receive the crown that is life itself. Well done. No rebukes.

Church in Pergamum: Jesus said He knew where they lived…it is where Satan's throne is. All the gods/goddesses are there. Some were clinging to their faith, some not. They are to repent. There is hidden manna and a white stone with a new name.

Church in Thyatira: I know your deeds of love, faith, service, steadfast endurance. But some tolerate the same spirit Jezebel had. Repent. God will repay the unfaithful. But the faithful will be given no additional burden.

Church in Sardis: They have a reputation for being alive, but they are dead. They need to repent. They need to wake up, otherwise Jesus will come like a thief. The one who wears white will never have their name erased from the book of life.

Church in Philadelphia: Known by many deeds, but they had little strength. No rebuke. They obeyed God's Word and had not denied His name. Told to hold on to what you have so that no one can take away your crown.

Church in Laodicea: Neither hot nor cold. Lukewarm—vomit you out of my mouth. They need to put their focus on Jesus instead of earthly comforts and property. Be earnest and repent.

To all the churches: The one who has an ear had better hear what the Spirit says to the churches.

Let's Pray:
Father, we want to have an ear and hear what Your Spirit is saying to us. We know the path toward Hell is broad, and too many are on it. The narrow path that leads through Your heavenly gates is where we desire to go. Lead us safely there, as we follow You daily. In Jesus' saving name we pray. Amen.

Chapter Twelve Reflections

1) What do we need on a pathway to see where we're going? Light! Jesus Christ is that Light. Not just an enlightenment, but the Light of all mankind. We all have two choices set before us in this life…follow Jesus on the path to Heaven or follow Satan on the pathway to Hell.
(Page 174)

2) Hell is an eternal place where people are paid back perfectly for the sins they have committed. It has been said, "Hell is perfect pure justice." We serve a just God…a perfect God. And Heaven is a perfect place designed for perfect people….Repentance is key on the pathway toward Heaven because it's what changes our direction when we realize we're on the pathway to Hell.
(Page 175)

3) When we believe that Jesus endured the wrath of His own Father upon that Cross, received all the punishment we were so deserving of, and then gave up His life so we can be declared righteous and live eternally with Him and all other believers in Heaven. Hell will not be our final destination. We will be spared!
(Page 177)

4) When Jesus examined the church in Ephesus in Revelation 2:1-7, we can all find ourselves in the words written there…the good and the bad. This is not so that we will feel horrible thinking we are heading toward Hell. This is so we can be set free through repentance in Jesus Christ each and every day from everything the enemy tempts us with, including the lie that we might be headed to Hell.
(Page 179)

5) These admonitions and encouragements written in Revelation are about personalities and changes that take place over a period of time. We can use them to help us know where we stand in our relationship with Jesus Christ on any given day as we grow in our faith and walk in a deeper repentance.
(Page 185)

6) Why should we listen to what Jesus is saying to these churches? Because it goes way, way back. Let's look at Deuteronomy 18:15 (NET), *"The Lord your God will raise up for you a prophet like me from among you—from your fellow Israelites; you must listen to him."* And now in Revelation we are being told, *"The one who has an ear had better hear what the Spirit says to the churches."* (Page 186)

7) Jesus talked about Hell more than anyone else in the Bible. Why? Because He wants us, and our family and friends, to know Him before it's too late. Jesus wasn't worried about offending anyone, or people thinking He's not as loving as the world thinks He should be. Jesus didn't lie to anyone, as many behind the pulpit do today to unsuspecting congregants.
(Page 187)

8) Jesus' death, burial, resurrection, and soon return is the core of Christianity. Without the Gospel, the heart of our faith is missing, and we have no Hope for eternity. People will live in a terrible state of sin, die in that sin, and live eternally in Hell without the Gospel being declared while there is still time!
(Page 191)

<u>NOTES</u>

*(These Reflection/Note pages may be duplicated
and used for group discussions when needed.)*

CHAPTER THIRTEEN

FEAR

Fear is not a word we like, but peace is a word we all love. Find me a person who doesn't like peace, and I will find you…no one! Peace is a hot commodity! When stocks drop, there is a lack of peace. When jobs are lost, there is a lack of peace. When illness comes, there is a lack of peace. When relationships fail, there is a lack of peace. When hunger strikes, there is a lack of peace. Everything and anything can affect our peace in this world…but what brings us our most deep-seated peace? What if I were to tell you fear does? You probably wouldn't believe me. You might think I have lost my mind. But if we want true peace with God, we have to know a true fear of God. It has been said, "If for etiquettes sake we refuse to explain and illustrate the dark sayings of scripture, then God will not be regarded as holy, men will not understand their dreadful predicament, and the price paid by Christ will never be calculated or appreciated." (Paul Washer) There is a deception surrounding the subject of fear. We are led to believe that fear doesn't bring peace, when actually it can, and does, when it is the right kind of fear.

There is a good fear, an honest fear, and a strengthening fear that brings peace. It is a fear of God—it is a fear that reconciles us with God so that we are no longer His enemies. *And you were at one time strangers and enemies in your minds as expressed through your evil deeds, but now he has reconciled you by his physical body through death to present you holy, without blemish, and blameless before him*— Colossians 1:21-22 (NET) When we have been reconciled with our Father in Heaven by understanding the need to be fearful of the Almighty, then there can be peace in our soul as a result of the blood of the Cross of Jesus Christ. *For God was pleased to have all his fullness dwell in the Son and through him to reconcile all things to himself by making peace through the blood of his cross— through him, whether things on Earth or things in heaven.* Colossians 1:19-20 (NET) When it's not about us and how good we try to be, but instead all about Jesus and His perfect goodness, we can rest in God's peace. All blame is then gone. *For the scripture says, "Everyone who believes in him will not be put to shame."* Romans 10:11 (NET)

In this chapter, we will be looking at the deception surrounding the word fear, and how not fearing God is not Biblical. This needs to be talked about in our churches. We shouldn't be afraid of a Biblical type of fear, we should be embracing it and sharing it with others. *So then, let us pursue what makes for peace and for building up one another.* Romans 14:19 (NET) So why are some Bible translations using a different word for fear…possibly to make them more palatable? I surely hope not, because true fear of the Lord is so needed, especially in a world where fear is everywhere. With a godly fear, it can be the beginning of not fearing anything else. Fearing the One who has absolute control and power over us is humbling ourselves before our Creator—we begin to understand we are nothing without Him, and everything He calls us to be with Him.

We can only have peace with God through our Lord Jesus Christ. When we meet our life's end, when we stand before God on Judgment Day, we can have blameless peace because of the Cross of Christ and how we feared God in this life. A reverent fear? Yes, of course, but also so much more than that. But it gets passed over today so as not to be too hard on those sitting in our churches on Sunday morning. Are we growing soft? Are those little dabs at it again? Yes! We are not being prepared to rejoice in sufferings, not letting God produce in us endurance, and then letting that grow us in a character that produces Hope that does not disappoint us…even in, or especially in, trials and tribulations or a call to obedience? Perhaps. (Romans 5:3-5)

God exalted Jesus to His right hand as *Leader and Savior, to give repentance to Israel and forgiveness of sins.* (Acts 5:31) And yet Jesus also learned about fearing the Lord. It seems strange, doesn't it? But the Bible says Jesus walked this Earth in flesh, as fully God and fully Man, and Jesus suffered, and He prayed… *"He had offered up prayers and supplications, with vehement cries and tears to Him who was able to save Him from death, and was heard because of His godly fear, though He was a Son, yet He learned obedience by the things which He suffered.* Hebrews 5:7-8 (NKJV) Did you see that? Jesus had a "godly fear." We are to obey our parents, and Jesus was no different in that respect. Jesus is God, and He is Son. And we are Jesus' siblings as adopted children of our Father in Heaven. We are now neither Jew nor Gentile…we are all one in Christ Jesus. (Gal. 3:28) And when we come to repentance, to receiving forgiveness of sins, it is the only way to attain true peace each day…otherwise we are fighting against God constantly and we aren't called His children. In Genesis 22:12, Abraham feared and obeyed God. He didn't fight God, even though sacrificing his son, Isaac, didn't make sense. It says: *"Do not harm the boy!" the angel said. "Do not do anything to him, for now I know that you fear God because you did not withhold your son, your only son, from me."(NET)* When we surrender and stop fighting God, then a peace that surpasses understanding is available to us…those who fear the Father with their whole heart, soul and mind and spirit receive this peace.

The Word says, He declared in a loud voice: *"Fear God and give him glory, because the hour of his judgment has arrived, and worship the one who made heaven and earth, the sea and the springs of water!"* Revelation 14:7 (NET) This Judgment Day will come for all mankind…isn't it much better to prepare now? To fear God here and now, and be prepared for there and then? Even those who have worshipped Satan in this life, will fear God when Judgment Day comes. That is also the day when the true believers in Jesus Christ will receive eternal peace because we will stand there blameless. Spurgeon said, "A deep sense of gratitude will nourish Christian zeal. When we reflect on the miry pit from which we were lifted, we find plenty of reason for spending ourselves for God."

Most of us have heard the verse in Psalm 111:10a, *To obey the Lord is the fundamental principle for wise living...* But you might not have recognized it in this translation because the word "fear" has been changed in this translation, as well as others. We know this verse better when we read it in the NKJV, *The fear of the Lord is the beginning of wisdom...* The fear of the Lord is the beginning of so much that we shouldn't miss it in our relationship with Him. Wisdom can mean understanding, knowledge, insight, etc... Things we can all do better with as we walk this earth.

Proverbs 23:17 (NET) says, *Do not let your heart envy sinners, but be zealous for the fear of the Lord all the day.* Zealous for the fear...we have to go after it, seek it, find it, let it change us from the inside out like nothing else can! Proverbs 24:21a (NKJV) says; *My son, fear the Lord and the king.* You may wonder why all this talk of fear in God's Word? Jesus gives us an explanation in Matthew 10:28 (NKJV) that I will repeat once again here: *And do not fear those who kill the body but cannot kill the soul. But rather fear Him who is able to destroy both soul and body in hell.* We need to fear because there is a Hell, and there is One who is able to destroy us there, our Creator. Our Father doesn't want to. He wants us to come to Him, join His family, be loved by Him for all of eternity in Heaven and call Him Father. So, God warns us now, through the prophets and others, and even by His very own Son who tells us to fear God now, while there is still time to repent and be saved. Hebrews 10:30 (NET) says; *For we know the one who said, "Vengeance is mine, I will repay," and again, "The Lord will judge his people." It is a terrifying thing to fall into the hands of the living God.* Knowing this fear and this saving grace is the very place where peace is found on earth. It is the only true place of peace while we are here because Romans 5:1 (NET) says; *Therefore, since we have been declared righteous by faith, we have peace with God through our Lord Jesus Christ.*

When we refuse to fear God, it is called pride. It is rebellion at the core of our being. Romans 1:20-21 (NET) says; *So people are without excuse. For although they knew God, they did not glorify him as God or give him thanks, but they became futile in their thoughts and their senseless hearts were darkened.* We can look at what will come to us if we don't fear God by looking at the opposite of the peace of God in Romans one. God gives people over to a depraved mind it says in Romans 1:28. How depraved? Let's list the characteristics here of just what God is talking about...people will be filled with every kind of unrighteousness, wickedness, covetousness, and malice. They will be rife with envy, murder, strife, deceit, hostility, gossip, slander, hate, insolence, arrogance, boastfulness, and be a contriver of evil. They will be disobedient to their parents, senseless, covenant-breakers, heartless, and ruthless. It goes on to say in Romans 1:32, they will not only do these things, they will also approve of those who practice them. It sounds a lot like our world, doesn't it? Do we see any peace in this list? Absolutely not! So, if they're looking for peace, this is not the direction in which they should be heading. *For I can testify that they are zealous for God, but their zeal is not in line with the truth. For ignoring the righteousness that comes from God, and seeking instead to establish their own righteousness, they did not submit to God's righteousness.* Romans 10:2-3 (NET)

Our Loving Father in Heaven is also a Stern Judge, make no mistake about it. And just as little John Kennedy crawled under his father's desk in the Oval Office without fear, knowing he was loved by the man who sat behind the desk and governed the United States, we, too, want to be able to crawl into our Father's lap without fear on Judgment Day as God's child. The only way to do that is to fear God now, understanding the freedom, peace, and love that come with that fear of our Holy Father. A Therapeutical Gospel says: "God loves me because I am valuable." A Biblical Gospel says: "I am valuable because God loves me." It was not that little John loved his father, but that his father, the president, loved him.

As we take a look at the Ten Commandments, what do we find? Strict rules that no one can follow? Yes, that's true. But what's also true about them is they are a set of rules given to us so that we can live in peace. Jesus came to this world to save us because He knew we could never keep the commandments perfectly. But they were also given to us as a guide to help us live peacefully upon this Earth knowing we need Jesus' help and forgiveness. Without these rules, we wouldn't know which way to turn. We wouldn't understand what sin is. We wouldn't know we are to have no other gods before the Lord God of Heaven. We are not to take God's name in vain. We are to keep the Sabbath holy. We are to honor our mother and father. We are not to kill, commit adultery, steal, lie, or covet our neighbor's wife or goods. Basic, good principles for living life. Principles, when followed, that help us live in peace. God's not making this hard on us. He's making it very clear to fear Him, like we would any good parent, and live within the boundaries set. They are for our own well-being and the well-being of others. But when we fail, because we will, we have a Savior. We know these things, but it does us no harm to go over them again and again. How quickly a young child forgets…how quickly we as the children of God can forget the basics of the Christian life when we aren't reminded of them daily in the Word of God.

I heard it said that there was a man by the name of Dick Lucas. When preaching he would draw a straight horizontal line on a chalk board. He would then draw an arrow pointing up, and one pointing down. The arrow pointing up was leading to fanaticism, teaching Jesus-plus theology. The arrow pointing down indicated liberalism…not living in the revelation of God but instead the speculation of things thought up by man. The horizontal line represented the instructions given in Scripture—not messing with God's Word. He urged his listeners to, "Hold the Line!" (The Ten Commandments are part of that line.) He said we have a great temptation to deviate from it, and we should not! This can be slight, even in changing Scripture just a bit to change the word "fear" in some translations. For whatever reason, it should be cautioned against. If we are to fear God, then let's hold to the line and fear God…for God's sake, and our own good!

Yes, today, and in days gone by, people want to hear only what's easy and pleasing and comfortable. But I would rather fear God any day here, than have to fear Him on Judgment Day. Paul knew what would happen. He wrote in 2 Timothy 4:3 (NET), *For there will be a time when people will not tolerate sound teaching. Instead, following their own desires, they will accumulate teachers for themselves, because they have an insatiable curiosity to hear new things.* They will want to be above the line, or below the line, and will not be satisfied with holding to the line…the Word of God. They will exchange the Truth of God for a lie, and worship and serve the creation rather than the Creator. (Romans 1:25) How peaceful this world would be if we held to the line of God's Word. We need the help and the power of the Holy Spirit within us to even want to hold to that line of Truth.

Martin Luther came up with the concept of "The Great Exchange." He said, "Christ bore the punishment for our sins, thus satisfying God's need for justice, but at the same time credited us Christ's righteousness." We talk about the deal of the century...how about the deal of all eternity! People want justice today. But true justice is only found in our true God. We are not only forgiven, but also given righteousness. That's the best credit, the most loving justice, we could ever receive! And yet so many will not tolerate the sound teaching of the Word of God, and instead want to follow their own desires—when has that ever brought peace to anyone? NEVER! It's a grand illusion that we get sucked into, and before we know it, all peace is gone! Romans 2:5 (NET): *But because of your stubbornness and your unrepentant heart, you are storing up wrath for yourselves in the day of wrath, when God's righteous judgment is revealed!*

Have you ever seen the bumper sticker, "Know Jesus, know peace. No Jesus, no Peace."? Isaiah 28:16b (NET) says; *The one who maintains his faith will not panic.* God's Word spells out clearly where to find peace in Romans 2:6-10 (NET): *He will reward each one according to his works: eternal life to those who by perseverance in good works seek glory and honor and immortality, but wrath and anger to those who live in selfish ambition and do not obey the truth but follow unrighteousness. There will be affliction and distress on everyone who does evil, on the Jew first and also the Greek, but glory and honor and peace for everyone who does good, for the Jew first and also the Greek.*

When we read the familiar Scripture about there is no one righteous, not even one, in Romans 3:10, we should read down to verses 17-18 where it says, *"...and the way of peace they have not known. There is no fear of God before their eyes."* We have to get our focus back on God and not the things of this world. This restores our peace. Without the horizontal line of Scripture, with no fear of God, there is no peace. I know it seems opposite of the way of the world, but isn't most of Scripture? Many in the world live above or below the line, many live following their own desires with an unrepentant heart, storing up wrath for themselves on the day they meet Jesus. If we fear the wrath of God today, we don't need to fear the wrath of God on Judgment Day.

If we are asked, "Do you fear God?" The sensible answer as Christians should be a resounding, "Yes!" Remember Proverbs 1:7, *fearing God is the beginning of wisdom...a wisdom that fools despise.* Isaiah 43:8 (NET) says, *Bring out the people who are blind, even though they have eyes, those who are deaf, even though they have ears.* That would be so much of the world today. People walking around blind and deaf to the things of God. Romans 1:21 talks about becoming futile in their thoughts and with senseless hearts that are darkened. We can only know the way of peace by learning the way of God and walking in it. Even David in Psalm 143 wrote, *Show me the way I should go, because I long for you.* Do we long for the Lord, asking Him to lead us to Him? If we fear God, we will. And if our peace has gone missing, we can ask God as David did in Psalm 143:10, *Teach me to do what pleases you, for you are my God. May your kind presence lead me into a level land.* That's the land where peace is found, no matter the circumstances in life.

Life will always contain turbulence. Even if we're flying in first class…those seated there experience the same bumpy ride as those seated in economy class. Oh sure, first class turbulence is covered over with fancier food, warm nuts, a hot towel, and more space to move around…but life is life, and God is God. Our peace in life only comes from knowing our Savior, from time spent with Him and understanding the best seat of all, the Mercy Seat, that is only accessible through faith in Jesus' death and resurrection. When we come to the Mercy Seat and are cleansed with the blood of Jesus Christ, all the garbage that is piling up can be removed. We can receive forgiveness and start fresh once again. Lamentations 3:22-23 (NET), *The Lord's loyal kindness never ceases; his compassions never end. They are fresh every morning; your faithfulness is abundant!* All may be wrong with the world, all may be wrong with every relationship we have, but when we are right with the Lord, it can smooth out the bumps and make for *level land.* Even if we come to the Mercy Seat kicking and screaming like a child who doesn't want to sit in time out…if we stay long enough and wait on God, we can walk away renewed, refreshed, and at peace with our Father in Heaven. We always have to remember there was only one perfect Child, and that's not us. Jesus Christ was, is, and will always be the perfection we seek for the redemption we need.

It may seem that we don't have time to come to the Mercy Seat, to sit there with Jesus…after all, life is busy! We need to be like Martha and get things taken care of. But I recently heard that "Mary was not praised for sitting still…but for sitting at Jesus' feet." We think of Martha in the kitchen making all the preparations. We see her as being productive, serving Jesus as she felt called to. The activity in itself was not evil, it was a great blessing. But so was the sitting Mary was doing. Mary was actively seeking her Savior. The busier our day, the more we should pray! When we sit with Jesus in prayer, when we pray to Jesus while working in the kitchen, or the office, or while jogging or painting…whatever it is we are doing, we can come to the Mercy Seat and receive from Him. Isaiah 43:25 (NET) says; *I am the one who blots out your rebellious deeds for my sake; your sins I do not remember.* There will be a deeper, more satisfying peace in the activity of prayer than anything else the world can offer us. Because as Romans 5:1-2 (NET) says, *Therefore, since we have been declared righteous by faith, we have peace with God through our Lord Jesus Christ, through whom we have also obtained access into this grace in which we stand, and we rejoice in the hope of God's glory.*

"Blessed are those whose lawless deeds are forgiven, and whose sins are covered." Romans 4:7 (NET) Who doesn't want to live a blessed life eternally, with a good start on that road of faith here and now? Will all our problems be gone? No. But we will know who holds the answers. Peace is a deep longing in the human heart. How do we get there from here? Fear God, bow before Him in submission, and leave our cares at His feet as Mary did. In Acts 9:31 it says the church in the towns *throughout Judea, Galilee, and Samaria experienced peace and were strengthened* while living in the *fear of the Lord and the encouragement of the Holy Spirit. They increased in number.* When the world sees our peace in unsettled times, the Good News is proclaimed without words. Fear of the Lord should never be seen as a bad thing, but instead as something very needed in our Christian walk. Why? Because it's Biblical! It's "Holding the Line," as we talked about earlier! Not having a fear of the Lord would be moving upwards or downwards away from that line. We are not to fear the things of this world. But we are to fear God because when we do, there's nothing else to fear!

Let's look at how many times we read "God-fearing" in the Bible? It's there 17 times! And when someone is said to be, "God-fearing", we know it is a very good thing. We would want the same to be said about us! Cornelius was God-fearing, so was Hananiah in

Nehemiah, Job is included in that group, as is Simeon in Luke 2:25. Some of the Jews were said to be God-fearing, Cornelius, in Acts 10:2, is God-fearing, and he also had a God-fearing soldier in Acts 10:7. There were God-fearing women in Acts 13, and God-fearing proselytes (A person who has converted) in Acts 13:43. Lydia was said to be God-fearing, as well as some God-fearing Greeks in Acts 17:4 and God-fearing Gentiles in Acts 17:17. John 9:31(NASB) says, *We know that God does not hear sinners; but if anyone is God-fearing and does His will, He hears him.* So, if in the future we hear that we are not to fear God, but mainly to revere Him…it is well and good, but not totally correct. Let's "Hold the Line" of Scripture where Peter said: *"I most certainly understand now that God is not one to show partiality, but in every nation the man who fears Him and does what is right is welcome to Him. The word which He sent to the sons of Israel, preaching peace through Jesus Christ (He is Lord of all).* Acts 10:34-36 (NASB) Fear and Peace are both included in this Scripture. Both are needed in true Christianity.

When we talk about fear and peace together, we should also talk about Philippians 4:6-7. This is a very well-known verse where we are told that prayer and petition with thanksgiving bring the peace of God that surpasses understanding. God is the One that guards our hearts and minds in Christ Jesus. There is no other way to real peace other than through Jesus, the only constant in our lives, because everything else can change in an instant. We fear changes that are sudden and bring disaster. Jesus brings peace, whether gentle or sudden. Jesus is always Good News! With faith in Jesus Christ, the fiery arrows aimed at us by Satan can be extinguished. (Eph. 6:16)

Paul knew this well…he had learned contentment no matter what. Paul said he knew what need was, and he knew what plenty was. He learned the secret of being content with either. How is this possible? Paul faced many difficult trials in his life and was shipwrecked more than once. There is a song by The Afters called, "I Will Fear No More." A line from that song says, "Even though I'm in the storm, the storm is not in me." I believe Paul could have written that very sentiment even though there was one thing that did upset Paul—we can read about it in Acts 17:16 (NET); *While Paul was waiting for them in Athens, his spirit was greatly upset because he saw the city was full of idols.* Paul had gotten to know the people there. He went around their city and told them he knew they were very religious. Paul told them in Acts 17:30, there was a time when God overlooked some of these things, but it was now time to repent. He knew better than most anyone, they needed to fear the Lord. Paul had seen Jesus on the road to Damascus! (Acts 9) He had seen Jesus' power to change the human heart. Some chose to believe. Some did not. Paul did what we are still called to do today, he shared the Good News of Jesus Christ, and trusted God with the results. Some will come to Jesus and repent upon hearing the Good News, and some will not. In all this, Paul did not consider his life worth anything. His goal was to finish the task of the ministry that he received from Jesus. (Acts 20:24) Paul had a fear of God, and peace with God, and he wanted others to share the same blessing. This is a peace the world does not know or understand. Paul was concerned though, because he knew that after he was gone, fierce wolves would come in, not sparing the flock. (Acts 20:29) Deception would be everywhere, and he wanted them/us to know it, as does our good Lord Jesus. But when we fear God, the fierce wolves have no power over us. That's why when the "Line" instructs us how to live, we need to listen and obey.

We can know who to fear and why, as did Paul. We should not be afraid of the word fear, we should embrace it when it's meant in the right way. Of course, we are not to have ordinary, earthly fear…the Bible tells us to *fear not* about 365 times! We should not be afraid because God is with us. What we are to fear is a life without God, an eternity that would have us separated from Him. Psalm 119:119-120 says, *You remove all the wicked of the Earthlike slag. Therefore I love your rules. My body trembles because I fear you; I am afraid of your judgments.* Got that right! We should be afraid of the judgments of a just God when we are guilty of many sins. It's only in seeing our true depravity that we see our true need of a Savior and are cleansed of those sins. Can we be a good person without being a Christian? Of course—we are capable of being nice without being motivated by God. Man can do the good he's been taught to do. But all of us are born with the ability to do evil things, and without the grace of God in this world, without the fear of a holy God, there would be a rapid downward spiral into total darkness. God's grace helps us draw a line in the sand…to keep standing on the solid rock of God's Truth and pursuing His light that leads us to a better place when all of this is said and done. *You shall follow the*

Lord your God and fear Him; and you shall keep His commandments, listen to His voice, serve Him, and cling to Him. Deuteronomy 13:4 (NASB) The more we mix the world and its darkness into our Christianity, allowing little dabs of it into our lives and our churches, the less effective we are for the Kingdom of God. *The Lord requires us to do justly, love mercy, and walk humbly with Him.* Micah 6:8 (KJV) This is where true peace and fear mix together properly, and we can learn how to live a holy life.

Let all the Earth fear the Lord; Let all the inhabitants of the world stand in awe of Him.
Psalm 33:8 (NASB)

It has been written about the Gospel that, "It is our task to speak about the one subject that most men would rather forget." Speaking about the fear of God is huge in that regard. The thief on the cross next to Jesus was not afraid to speak out. Let's listen in… *One of the criminals who was hanging there railed at him, saying, "Are You not the Christ? Save Yourself and us!" But the other answered, and rebuking him said, "Do you not even fear God, since you are under the same sentence of condemnation? And we indeed* are *suffering justly, for we are receiving what we deserve for our deeds; but this man has done nothing wrong." And he was saying, "Jesus, remember me when You come in Your kingdom!" And He said to him, "Truly I say to you, today you shall be with Me in Paradise."* Luke 23:39-43 (NET)

Scripture tells us that all men have the knowledge of God. God's eternal power and divine nature have been clearly seen through what has been made. *"So people are without excuse."* Romans 1:20 (NET) *"They exchanged the truth of God for a lie."* Romans 1:25 (NET) It has been said, "Many have chosen a false form of tolerance over the Truth, and a twisted compassion for humanity over the fear of God and fidelity to the Scriptures." One thief chose wisely that day on Calvary—the thief on the cross who spoke about fearing God understood his depravity in that moment. It was making sense to him. He was dying justly. He not only acknowledged God, he knew Jesus was dying unjustly. That thief didn't fully know it at the time, but he was an eyewitness to Romans 5:8 (NET); *But God demonstrates his own love for us, in that while we were still sinners,*

Christ died for us. One thief got it, one didn't. One went to paradise that day...one didn't. One was saved from God's wrath in that moment and he soon knew that the *payoff of sin is death, but the gift of God is eternal life in Christ Jesus our Lord.* (Romans 6:23)

Ever had a war going on in your mind? The war in the one thief's mind was settled on that day. Jesus was Lord. He didn't have much time...some don't...that's why today is the day of Salvation! In Romans 7:23 (NET) Paul said, *"I see a different law in my members waging war against the law of my mind..."* Even though Paul's flesh was pulled toward sin, in his mind he was pulled toward God. Same with the thief. In Romans 8:1, we come to one of the most well-known verses, *There is therefore now no condemnation for those who are in Christ Jesus.* To know that we deserve to be condemned is having a healthy fear of God. The one thief knew that. To know that we are now not condemned because of Christ Jesus is having a healthy view of the Cross. The one thief found that out that day. *For the outlook of the flesh is death, but the outlook of the Spirit is life and peace.* Romans 8:6 (NET)

You might still be wondering, are we really to fear the Lord? It's still going against what you may have always been taught. Well, do we trust that the Word of God speaks truth? Let's continue... In Psalm 19:9, *it says, The commands to fear the Lord are right and endure forever.* Does our Father want us walking around cowering, thinking that lightning is going to strike us at any moment? Absolutely not! But does God want us to take Him seriously? Absolutely yes! This fear of God is not a spirit that we have been given because 2 Timothy 1:7 (NKJV) says, *For God has not given us a spirit of fear, but of power and of love and of a sound mind.* Fearing the Lord is not a demonic fear. It has been said that "God never delivers us from the fear of the Lord." Why would God deliver us from something that brings us so much life?

Let's look at a collection of verses and see what the Word of God says comes from fearing our Lord since Ecclesiastes 12:13 says fearing God is the *whole duty of man:*

Practicing fear gives us a good understanding. Psalm 111:10

Fear is the fountain of life and helps us turn away from the snares of death. Proverbs 14:27

Fear of the Lord helps us to rest satisfied. Proverbs 19:23

His mercy is ours from generation to generation toward those who fear Him. Luke 1:50

We have God's friendship when we fear Him. Psalm 25:14

In the fear of the Lord we have a strong confidence and refuge. Proverbs 14:26

Those who fear God have no lack. Psalm 34:9

We are blessed when we fear the Lord. Psalm 112:1

Fearing God brings holiness to completion. 2 Corinthians 7:1

The rewards of fearing God bring riches, honor, and life. Proverbs 22:4

Going on in the fear of the Lord, our peace is multiplied. Acts 9:31

When fearing God it goes well with us and our descendants. Deuteronomy 5:29

Fearing God helps us not sin. Exodus 20:20

It fulfills desires and God hears our cries and saves us when we fear Him. Psalm 145:19

Fearing our Father makes us acceptable to Him. Acts 10:35

God takes pleasure in us when we fear Him. Psalm 147:10-11

God shows compassion to those who fear Him. Psalm 103:13

Is fear a good thing? When it concerns our relationship with our Father in Heaven it certainly seems so! In the year 2020, during the pandemic, the verse in Exodus 20:20 seems even more impactful: *"Do not fear, for God has come to test you, that the fear of him may be before you so that you do not sin."* Is this pandemic one of those tests we are not to fear? We are to fear God so as not to sin in a world that is so full of sin that evil is now being called good, and good, evil. We all have a choice set before us in 2020…and fearing God is the wise choice. How long should we choose to fear Him? As long as we live on this Earth as children of the King of kings because the Bible says: *If you address as Father the One who impartially judges according to each one's work, conduct yourselves in fear during the time of your stay on earth.* 1 Peter 1:17 (NASB) Otherwise, life is truly futile—with no purpose, no plan, no way to endure, no peace in the midst of crises… Oh, we can fake it for a bit, but we were created by a God who designed our heart to contain His Holy Spirit. Without that integral piece of our God living within us, we are incomplete.

Without our fear of God, we will still live feeling condemned. When we fear, understanding our depravity without the work of Christ on the Cross, we can begin to rest in God's goodness and finally be at peace because of the Cross. This takes time to fully grasp our need to the depth of our soul. We can, at times, still think our goodness has some merit. But when I heard it explained this way, it brought it home for me... Picture your whole life up on a large movie screen for all your friends and family to watch. The movie will include everything you have ever done, thought, and said being there for all to see. Would you be able to sit there, be at peace, not having anything to explain, be embarrassed about, regret, etc…? There would not be one of us who could endure such a display of our sin before those watching. We would even be shocked at some of our own behavior when seen from a distance. Yes, we need to fear a God who loves us so much that this "horror show" doesn't matter to Him because all the wrath that was due to us because of our heinous behavior was put upon His dearly loved Son instead. Picture an old film strip as it heats up in those projectors that we used to watch our family movies on…the film gets stuck in front of the blaring light bulb and is now melting away, being destroyed before our very eyes, never to be watched again… (You might have to be over 50 to know what I'm talking about here.) But what if we see that as our God, His Light burning away our dark sins? *As far as the east is from the west, So far has He removed our transgressions from us.* Psalm 103:12 (NASB). We would all shout out "Hallelujah"! Our defense rests upon Christ's perfection and His completed work on the Cross.

So then, my beloved, just as you have always obeyed, not as in my presence only, but now much more in my absence, work out your salvation with fear and trembling; for it is God who is at work in you, both to will and to work for His good pleasure.
Philippians 2:12-13 (NASB)

The blood of Christ is so much more powerful than the accusations of the devil. God doesn't want us cowering before Satan in fear, God wants us bowing before Him in godly fear so He can gift us with His peace and an eternal life in Heaven. The Holy Spirit then works in our hearts sanctifying us and preparing us to meet our Lord face to face when our time comes. Every knee will bow on that day...ours will do so willingly. We can look forward to meeting our Lord without fear because...*he has reconciled you by his physical body through death to present you holy, without blemish, and blameless before him— if indeed you remain in the faith, established and firm, without shifting from the hope of the gospel that you heard.* Colossians 1:22-23 (NET)

Let's pray:
Father in Heaven, thank You that in fearing You we can live in peace. We can know that Your fear is good for us, and leads us into a closer relationship with You. When we know what we are deserving of, what You have saved us from, we can rest in the comfort of Your love. Thank You, Holy Spirit, for being that comfort as You live in those who do believe in the Lord Jesus Christ. It's in Jesus' name we pray. Amen.

Chapter Thirteen Reflections

1) There is a deception surrounding the subject of fear. We are led to believe that fear doesn't bring peace, when actually it can, and does, when it is the right kind of fear. (Page 203)

2) There is a good fear, an honest fear, and a strengthening fear that brings peace. It is a fear of God—it is a fear that reconciles us with God so that we are no longer His enemies. (Page 203)

3) Jesus had a "godly fear." We are to obey our parents, and Jesus was no different in that respect. Jesus is God, and He is Son. And we are Jesus' siblings as adopted children of our Father in Heaven. (Page 205)

4) You may wonder why all this talk of fear in God's Word? Jesus gives us an explanation in Matthew 10:28 (NKJV) that I will repeat once again here: *And do not fear those who kill the body but cannot kill the soul. But rather fear Him who is able to destroy both soul and body in hell. We need to fear because there is a Hell, and there is One who is able to destroy us there, our Creator.* (Page 206)

5) Yes, today, and in days gone by, people want to hear only what's easy and pleasing and comfortable. But I would rather fear God any day here, than have to fear Him on Judgment Day. (Page 208)

6) Do we long for the Lord, asking Him to lead us to Him? If we fear God, we will. And if our peace has gone missing, we can ask God as David did in Psalm 143:10, *Teach me to do what pleases you, for you are my God. May your kind presence lead me into a level land.* That's the land where peace is found, no matter the circumstances in life. (Page 210)

7) Peace is a deep longing in the human heart. How do we get there from here? Fear God, bow before Him in submission, and leave our cares at His feet as Mary did. (Page 211)

8) Of course, we are not to have ordinary, earthly fear...the Bible tells us to fear not about 365 times! We should not be afraid because God is with us. What we are to fear is a life without God, an eternity that would have us separated from Him. (Page 213)

<u>*NOTES*</u>

*(These Reflection/Note pages may be duplicated
and used for group discussions when needed.)*

CHAPTER FOURTEEN

SIN

Sin...not a fun topic once again, but a much needed one when dealing with deception. But let's remember what 1 Thessalonians 5:23 says about sin; we will *be kept entirely blameless at the coming of our Lord Jesus Christ.*

As talked about in chapter one, sin/deception started in the Garden and continues on to this day. God is not surprised at our sinfulness. He tells us all about it in His Good Book. We can go all the way back to Genesis 4:7 (NET): *"...sin is crouching at the door. It desires to dominate you, but you must subdue it."*

Have you ever felt like Cain did? Angry? Not wanting to do what's right? Not wanting to "subdue" the sin that is lurking and wanting to dominate you? We all have! Cain went with his brother, Abel, out into the field and the very first family had a very bad domestic dispute that didn't end well. One brother killed the other. Should we be surprised that the same sin is still happening today? That, and so much more.

Isaiah tells us in 5:20-21 (NET): *Beware, those who call evil good and good evil, who turn darkness into light and light into darkness, who turn bitter into sweet and sweet into bitter. Beware, those who think they are wise, those who think they possess understanding.* This wise prophet doesn't tell us to be shocked by what is happening, but instead to beware of it. It did happen, it is happening, and it will happen until God creates a New Heaven and a New Earth. And where does that leave us as the children of God? Forgiven! That's where! Hallelujah!

What happened to Jesus on the Cross was seen as good in the eyes of some. In ignorance, they crucified the King of kings thinking He was a false prophet, a blasphemer…someone bringing in a new religion that went against everything they had ever been taught as Jewish people who knew the Torah. They were wrong. Those who were part of the Way, as Christianity was called in the beginning, were thought of as the atheists in their day. Even Saul stood there at the stoning of Stephen thinking his death was justified. Saul, later known as Paul, was ignorant. Earlier, Saul had been sent to Jerusalem to receive his education at the school of Gamaliel. (Acts 22:3) Gamaliel was one of the most noted rabbis in history. Even though we don't hear of Saul until the stoning of Stephen, historians agree Saul was probably in Jerusalem during Jesus' ministry. Saul was also probably in Jerusalem when Jesus was crucified. As a Pharisee, Saul would have heard of Jesus' miracles. He would have been aware of the supernatural events that took place during Jesus' death, i.e. the earthquake, the sky going dark, and the veil in the Temple being torn. This didn't change Saul. But once Saul was informed…transformed…into a follower of the Way…he became one of those he previously hunted down and arrested. Paul became a repentant servant of the Lord Jesus Christ of Nazareth.

Spurgeon said, "We who know by experience the preciousness of this truth, will proclaim it confidently and unceasingly…we will neither dilute it nor change it, nor distort it in any shape or fashion. It shall still be Christ, a positive substitute, bearing human guilt and suffering in the place of man."

When a person repents, it means they change their mind. As mentioned earlier, it means they stop rejecting Christ. Paul certainly changed his mind about Jesus on the road to Damascus when Jesus appeared to him. Paul knew then, without a shadow of a doubt, that he had been wrong about Jesus. Paul understood that he was a sinner who desperately needed a Savior. Paul repented and that was the beginning of a whole new way of living life here on this Earth. Paul discovered the Truth. We all can!

All that is happening on Earth today is not a surprise to God. Ephesians 1:4 (NET) says; *For he chose us in Christ before the foundation of the world that we should be holy and blameless before him in love.* What a relief when we consider how sinful we all are! This can bring us all great peace in Ephesians 1:7 (NET) where it says; *In him we have redemption through his blood, the forgiveness of our offenses, according to the riches of his grace.* Are we saints who sometimes sin? Absolutely! Are we forgiven? Yes, through the blood of Jesus Christ shed for us on the Cross at Calvary. Not only that, *...when you heard the word of truth (the gospel of your salvation)—when you believed in Christ—you were marked with the seal of the promised Holy Spirit, who is the down payment of our inheritance...* Ephesians 1:13-14a (NET) We can know that good things are coming because we are sealed with the indwelling Holy Spirit! Let's hang on to that while we take a closer look at sin so we can honestly examine ourselves, and then begin to fully understand the freedom from sin's destruction that has been offered to us. It's too great of a gift to not appreciate. It is the foundation that our faith rests upon.

Sin is terrible because it is an offense against our holy God. No one on Earth other than Jesus Christ is sinless. Romans 3:23 is a verse many of us know well. It says, *all have sinned and fall short of the glory of God.* So, we have lots of company! This is a fallen world that we are born into and it's the only world we have ever known. No one has to be taught to sin. It comes naturally to all of us. We live in enemy territory, and without the help of the Restrainer, the Holy Spirit, sin will win. Does God know this? Yes! That's why He sent His only Son to save us. Does our Father in Heaven see everything we have ever done and will ever do? Of course! God knows we think it's "all about us". Think of sin as this: **S**elf **I**dolatry **N**oted...from God's perspective. Even many of our new worship songs carry this idolatrous message. Many times, we're no longer singing, "Majesty, worship His majesty". The lyrics are more all about me, myself, and I. Jesus the King of kings is barely there in the lyrics, if at all. Too many of our worship songs are about what we want, what we need, who we are. There are so many little dabs of us, Jesus is barely noticeable. These self-focused songs are very popular in our churches today. Some of them are more blatantly self-focused than others. But what's even more dangerous is the effect they have...what starts in our worship music can then easily move into our pulpits...the feel-good messages about how valuable we are and what we can accomplish if we put our mind to it...instead of how valuable the blood of Jesus Christ is and how much we need His saving grace.

We have to understand that the devil's plan is a counterfeit plan...it runs contrary to God's eternal plan, and he has no originality. Think of it, in Exodus 13:9, it talks about a sign on their hand and forehead, to remind them of the law of the Lord. In Revelation 13:16, there will be a counterfeit sign on hands and foreheads, showing an allegiance to the beast. Satan is always out to steal, kill and destroy all things everywhere, even in our churches. Without the Word of God as our guide, and prayer as our sustaining source of Hope, we will be easy prey for the enemy...and he knows it. And Satan also knows us because he has been around before we were ever born...long before...and he is working hard at making this life as difficult for us as he can. One of Satan's major weapons is making sin so appealing we can be deep into it before realizing the mistakes we are making. Satan won't tell us that *the payoff of sin is death, but the gift of God is eternal life in Christ Jesus our Lord.* Romans 6:23 (NET) Oh no! He lies to us! He doesn't want us to know that right behind the sin being offered to us on a pretty silver platter lurks disaster, not only for us, many times, but for those around us. Yes, sin affects more than just us. It affects all our relationships, our jobs, our health, our finances...gambling addictions, drug and alcohol addictions, pornography, stealing, lying, cheating, anger, unforgiveness... The first steps into these things are ours, usually done in secret. But the last steps into those dark pits not only take us down, they take whole families down for all the world to see.

We've all been there in one form or another, to lesser and greater degrees. To say we have not is to not understand the Gospel of Jesus Christ. If some of us could be good enough for Heaven without Christ's sacrificial love on the Cross, then the Cross would not have been needed. Ephesians 2:1-3 (NET) says, *And although you were dead in your offenses and sins, in which you formerly lived according to this world's present path, according to the ruler of the domain of the air, the ruler of the spirit that is now energizing the sons of disobedience...* This doesn't say some of us, it is for all of us as we will see as we continue on in verse 3: *...among whom all of us also formerly lived out our lives in the cravings of our flesh,* *indulging the desires of the flesh and the mind, and were by nature children of wrath even as the rest...* "All of us...were by nature children of wrath." Whose wrath? God's wrath!

Let's read on in verses four through five about the Good News... *But God, being rich in mercy, because of his great love with which he loved us, even though we were dead in offenses, made us alive together with Christ—by grace you are saved!* The wrath we deserved was poured out on God's only Son. We were saved from all that we were due. Not only that, verses five through seven tell us— *and he raised us up together with him and seated us together with him in the heavenly realms in Christ Jesus, to demonstrate in the coming ages the surpassing wealth of his grace in kindness toward us in Christ Jesus.*

Does this sound too good to be true? It does! But God never, ever, ever, lies! He promises us that...*In him we have redemption through his blood, the forgiveness of our offenses, according to the riches of his grace that he lavished on us in all wisdom and insight.* Ephesians 1:7-8 (NET) Without the cleansing blood of Jesus Christ, we are lost. With it, we can rest, rejoice, pray, and give thanks, and proclaim where our salvation comes from!

This promise is for all who choose to believe in Jesus Christ as their personal Lord and Savior. The Bible tells us over and over we can't keep the law; we all sin, we all fall short. This is very true. But too many times we let the enemy beat us up when we do sin. There is no need for that self-inflicted punishment—not according to God's Word. We are to acknowledge our sin, repent of it, confess it to our Father in Heaven, seek His forgiveness, receive all that Jesus died to give us, and move on, leaving our failures at the foot of the Cross of Christ which was the greatest triumph that ever occurred on planet Earth. Jesus *gave himself for our sins to rescue us from this present evil age according to the will of our God and Father, to whom be glory forever and ever!* Galatians 1:4 (NET) This present evil age is well documented in Scripture. We can read about it in 2 Timothy 3:1-5 (NET): *But understand this, that in the last days difficult times will come. For people will be lovers of themselves, lovers of money, boastful, arrogant, blasphemers, disobedient to parents, ungrateful, unholy, unloving, irreconcilable, slanderers, without self-control, savage, opposed to what is good, treacherous, reckless, conceited, loving pleasure rather than loving God. They will maintain the outward appearance of religion but will have repudiated its power. So avoid people like these.* That's some good advice there!

Sometimes it's hard to see our own sin. We think we're doing okay. But we can be blinded to our own depravity. Paul knew that when he wrote: *So for me, it is a minor matter that I am judged by you or by any human court. In fact, I do not even judge myself. For I am not aware of anything against myself, but I am not acquitted because of this. The one who judges me is the Lord.* 1 Corinthians 4:3-4 (NET) It is good to come to God daily, to repent, to ask Him for help in cleansing ourself from anything that may be offensive to a holy God. The enemy would love to pile things up against us, to create a mountain of garbage so high that it seems overwhelming and hopeless. But when we daily do a "spring cleaning", it can seem much more manageable in our prayer time. This is very important because: *Do you not know that the unrighteous will not inherit the kingdom of God? Do not be deceived! The sexually immoral, idolaters, adulterers, passive homosexual partners, practicing homosexuals, thieves, the greedy, drunkards, the verbally abusive, and swindlers will not inherit the kingdom of God. Some of you once lived this way. But you were washed, you were sanctified, you were justified in the name of the Lord Jesus Christ and by the Spirit of our God.* 1 Corinthians 6:9-11 (NET) It says "some of you once lived this way…" But I would venture to say "all" of us can see ourselves somewhere in the lists the Word of God provides that point out our sins.

The word sin is used over 300 times in the Old Testament and over 100 times in the New Testament. Not surprisingly. What is sin? It is "an immoral act considered to be a transgression against divine law". Sin is all about straying from God's path. The original sin is also called Ancestral Sin. It has existed since the fall of man when Adam and Eve rebelled against God and were disobedient by eating the forbidden fruit from the Tree of the Knowledge of Good and Evil.

Although the Bible doesn't specifically describe a set of "seven deadly sins", the general sins of pride, greed, wrath, envy, lust, gluttony, and sloth are all addressed in the Bible. There are three categories of sin in 1 John 2:16. They are the lust of the flesh, the lust of the eyes, and the pride of life. There is one unforgivable sin:

It is blasphemy against the Holy Spirit. (Mark 3:28-29, Matthew 12:31-32, Luke 12:10.) All these sins can be forgiven except blasphemy. Jesus will save everyone except sons of perdition—a sinner who does not repent to God/puts themselves above God. *Whoever speaks a word against the Son of Man will be forgiven. But whoever speaks against the Holy Spirit will not be forgiven, either in this age or in the age to come.* Matthew 12:32 (NET) That is lasting sin. Once in Hell, there is no reversing it. Once in Heaven, we are there forever and ever.

When it is talked about that sin actually means missing the mark, a term used in archery when the arrow falls short of the bullseye, what are we missing exactly? Isaiah 43:7 says we were created for God's glory. Glory is when the invisible qualities of God are made visible…when His character, His moral laws reflect who He is. When we are obedient to our Father in Heaven, we are reflecting God's glory. When we sin, when we miss the mark, we are doing the opposite of that, we are concealing rather than revealing who God is. Sometimes this involves violating a written command, sometimes it's not doing what we ought to do. (James 4:17) Sin takes many shapes and forms, but the end result is always the same, we are not glorifying God. No amount of excuses will suffice…we all do this at different times, on different days, during different seasons of our lives. *If we say we do not bear the guilt of sin, we are deceiving ourselves and the truth is not in us. But if we confess our sins, he is faithful and righteous, forgiving us our sins and cleansing us from all unrighteousness. If we say we have not sinned, we make him a liar and his word is not in us.* 1 John 1:8-10 (NET)

What is God's will? To forgive us and love us. The only way we miss this tremendous gift is when we refuse to receive it. It's like the best and biggest present ever is offered to us on our birthday and yet there are those who would rather not receive it and unwrap it— they'd rather just sit in a mud puddle and slosh around with the pigs believing it never gets any better than that. It's all or nothing with God concerning sin. There's no middle ground. There's no waiting until the mud dries and we can walk away without slipping and falling into it again. We have to be completely washed clean of all the mud, dried or not…through the blood of Jesus Christ. We have to be made spotless by what Jesus did on the Cross for us before we are allowed entry into the Kingdom of God in Heaven. Will we venture back to the mud puddle from time to time? Yes. But when we do, we are called to recognize it, and once again repent, confess, and allow God's saving grace to bring us back into His light and love and holiness…and cleanliness again. This is a repeated process called sanctification. *And everyone who has this hope focused on him purifies himself, just as Jesus is pure.*1 John 3:3 (NET) Each time we sin, we are to grow, to learn, just as any child does. When we are two, we will run out into the street in front of a moving car. When we are grown, we will know better. If we are not growing and learning in our walk of faith, we need to ask ourselves if we are truly saved to begin with. If we are, then we are being continually sanctified, which is a very good and needed process in this life.

Sin is lawlessness. 1 John 3:4 (NET) says, *Everyone who practices sin also practices lawlessness; indeed, sin is lawlessness.* This does not mean that we can be saved by keeping the law. Far from it! But the desire of our hearts should be to obey because we are already saved through the death and resurrection of Jesus Christ our Lord. When the Holy Spirit is planted in our hearts, the desire to follow God's will is there with us also. And that desire grows through the years into a faith that is strong, mature, and able to be more powerfully shared with those around us. It has been said, "Faith is the root. Obedience is the Fruit." James 2:20-22 (NET) says, *But would you like evidence, you empty fellow, that faith without works is useless? Was not Abraham our father justified by works when he offered Isaac his son on the altar? You see that his faith was working together with his works and his faith was perfected by works.* Abraham knew the promised King was coming, we know the promised King has come. Abraham's faith was perfected by his obedience, as can ours. But we must always remember…*the one who obeys the whole law but fails in one point has become guilty of all of it.* James 2:10 (NET) Once again, that is why we need the Cross of Christ! He was the only perfect human to ever walk the face of this Earth!

But each one is tempted when he is lured and enticed by his own desires. Then when desire conceives, it gives birth to sin, and when sin is full grown, it gives birth to death. Do not be led astray, my dear brothers and sisters.

James 1:14-16 (NET)

The law was given so that we could see what sin is as it tells us in Romans 7:7 (NET): *What shall we say then? Is the law sin? Absolutely not! Certainly, I would not have known sin except through the law.* The "law" helps us to have guidelines. Just as any good parent would set up boundaries for their child, so our Father in Heaven has done. We also are blessed when we keep to God's laws because they are wise instructions for our safety and well-being. Can we sometimes escape the consequences of our sins? Any teenager has their stories that they love to tell their parents once they become adults...ones that we don't appreciate all that much about their exploits, unbeknownst to us, that they got away with. *The sins of some people are obvious, going before them into judgment, but for others, they show up later.* 1 Timothy 5:24 (NET) When sin continues, and sometimes even the very first attempt at breaking the "law" that governs us, there can be consequences of all kinds. Those are the consequences that come to us. God says, *"Indeed, my plans are not like your plans, and my deeds are not like your deeds," says the Lord, "for just as the sky is higher than the earth, so my deed are superior to your deeds and my plans superior to your plans.* Isaiah 55:8-9 (NET) We can't be surprised when we sometimes go astray, when our plans don't exactly follow God's...we can pray, read the Word, and seek His face each day, and still make many mistakes. Once again, thank You, Jesus.

My little children, I am writing these things to you so that you may not sin. But if anyone does sin, we have an advocate with the Father, Jesus Christ the Righteous One, and he himself is the atoning sacrifice for our sins, and not only for our sins but also for the whole world. 1 John 2:1-2 (NET)

How can we recognize sin? We can turn to Proverbs and quickly sum up an answer to that question. God doesn't keep us wondering... *There are six things that the Lord hates, even seven things that are an abomination to him: haughty eyes, a lying tongue, and hands that shed innocent blood, a heart that devises wicked plans, feet that are swift to run to evil, a false witness who pours out lies, and a person who spreads discord among family members.* Proverbs 6:16-19 (NET) And if that's not enough, we can pick up more sin in Galatians...*Now the works of the flesh are obvious:*

sexual immorality, impurity, depravity, idolatry, sorcery, hostilities, strife, jealousy, outbursts of anger, selfish rivalries, dissensions, factions, envying, murder, drunkenness, carousing, and similar things. Galatians 5:19-21a (NET) Tired from all this? Feeling overwhelmed? It's to be expected. But God doesn't put these truths in the Bible to guilt us, He puts them there to help us come to the Cross of Jesus Christ and find our freedom. When we see our own depravity, hopefully we will be drawn to the Light of Jesus. We were bought with a high price, and we are to glorify God. We do that by following Jesus and making Him Lord of our life…not being perfect…that is impossible. But the grace of God trains us to *reject godless ways and worldly desires,* as stated in Titus 2:12.

Now, if we still have doubts as to what God would have us do and not do, we can ask Him. Is it something that God would bless? Is the new job a place where He would be glorified? Is the relationship we are in bringing Him glory? Is the way we are raising our children shining His light into their lives? Are our friends edifying and encouraging us in our relationship with our Savior, and are we doing the same for them? Is our home a place where Jesus could walk in and be fully welcomed in any room of our house, opening any cupboard, looking in any closet, watching our recorded TV shows? Is our church preaching the Gospel message without compromise? Is our music glorifying the Lord? Are the words that we speak and our treatment of others loving, kind, and compassionate? Are we sharing the Truth of the Gospel by the way we live? If not, if there is doubt in any of these areas, we should prayerfully consider what changes God would have us make as we work out our salvation with fear and trembling. Nothing in our life should take priority over Christ Jesus. Our lives should reflect who He is more and more as we learn to walk closer and closer with Him each day until we meet Him face to face.

And we all, with unveiled faces reflecting the glory of the Lord, are being transformed into the same image from one degree of glory to another, which is from the Lord, who is the Spirit.
2 Corinthians 3:18 (NET)

So put to death whatever in your nature belongs to the earth…
Why? *…because of these things the wrath of God is coming on the*

sons of disobedience. Colossians 3:6 (NET) It is! There is no mistake about it! But the wrath is not for us! It is for the "sons of disobedience" who are not covered by the blood of Jesus Christ. Do they care? No. They aren't even thinking about God or what His desire is for their lives. When they get to Hell, they will still be rebelling against God. That is where we come in! We share Jesus with them when we can, wherever we can, however we can…always being ready to give an answer to those who ask about the Hope that we possess. Yet we are to do it with courtesy and respect. (1 Peter 3:15-16)

What is going on in this *world* does not have to live in *us*. The Holy Spirit lives in us. We can read how Lot lived in Sodom, but Sodom didn't live in Lot. Noah lived in a sin-filled world, but Noah obeyed God and built the Ark as instructed—he was given a way of escape from the coming wrath. Lot and Noah put God first in their lives. Ninety-nine percent of all sin is saying "Me first, and I don't care about you." **Self-Idolatry Noted!** We will never be free from sin this side of Heaven, but as Christians when we do sin, there will be genuine sorrow in our heart. The more broken we are over our sin the more godly we can see that we becoming—it will bother us to the core of our being. We will agree with God quickly, we will confess, and we will be forgiven. The only way to sin less in this life is to be in the Word daily and pray more. Otherwise this world's temptation to sin will eat us up and spit us out into that mud puddle! If we are not in the Word and praying, we are opening ourselves up to sin. By opening up the Word and praying, we are building a barrier to stop sin from destroying our lives. It is the wall of protection, the Armor of God, that all Christians need because all Christians will be tempted to sin their entire lives, as will the unbelievers in the world.

The temptations we face are not coming from God, they are coming from our enemy, Satan, just like in the Garden of Eden. *"Did God really say…?"* And when we fall into those temptations, our enemy will be the first one to condemn us for doing so. Not God. God will convict us, call our attention to the error of our ways, and give us a way of escape, offering us forgiveness. The enemy will want to block the way of escape by throwing more sin at us…telling us to just lie about what we've already done, just run deeper into it, just shut out the light… Instead we are to resist the enemy and turn to our Savior with a repentant heart. God loves a contrite and humbled heart. That is where we will find true freedom.

For since he himself suffered when he was tempted, he is able to help those who are tempted.
Hebrews 2:18 (NET)

This talk of sin is not to scare us, it is to prepare us for what's out there in the world we live in. Sticking our head in the sand and trying to ignore the darkness all around us doesn't make it go away, it just gives it more power to operate in our lives.

And no creature is hidden from God, but everything is naked and exposed to the eyes of him to whom we must render an account.
Hebrews 4:13 (NET)

We do not belong to ourselves as believers in Jesus Christ as Lord *...do you not know that your body is the temple of the Holy Spirit who is in you, whom you have from God, and you are not your own? For you were bought at a price. Therefore glorify God with your body.* 1 Corinthians 6:19-20 (NET) We are here to bring God glory, as we talked about earlier. We are to walk closely with our Lord, not spending time messing around in darkness. *I do not want you to be partners with demons. You cannot drink the cup of the Lord and the cup of demons. You cannot take part in the table of the Lord and the table of demons.* 1 Corinthians 10:20b-22 (NET) *We are to do everything for the glory of God.* 1 Corinthians 10:31b (NET)
How do we know our sins are all covered under the blood of Jesus Christ? Because Jesus was raised on the third day after stating on the Cross, *"It is finished."* Jesus' resurrection sealed the deal. Without the resurrection, we would only have a great guy who healed many people and went to the Cross as a sacrifice...*if Christ has not been raised, your faith is useless; you are still in your sins.* 1 Corinthians 15:17 (NET) After His resurrection, Jesus was seen by the disciples, and by over 500 people for good reason. Our Father in Heaven wanted us to know it was truly finished. The Father's wrath was satisfied, and Jesus was alive and well and there to tell us about it before ascending back into Heaven to sit at the Father's right hand. Jesus is our Advocate when sin crouches at our door. He died

on our behalf and helps us distance ourselves from those who want to agree with us in our sin. Jesus convicts us through the Holy Spirit within when we sin, letting us know that the way we are going is not of Him. Jesus is there when we start only caring about ourselves, letting us know that there is more to this life than what is right before us in that moment, luring us into a dark place. Our Savior is there urging us to read our Bible. The Holy Spirit prompts us when we don't want to listen to reason. He is there helping us resist the darkness. Our Lord fills us with strength when we only want to fulfill our own desires. Jesus is there to help us know that we can be dead to sin and alive to Him by the power of the Holy Spirit. He is there to help us know that sin does not have to reign in our bodies, but we can be used as instruments for God's righteousness instead.

Jesus became sin for us on the Cross. I read, "Our Father in Heaven will never hold us accountable after what His Son, Jesus, did for us. If the Father denies Jesus and His suffering, He would be saying Jesus died in vain, and that it wasn't enough. It was." When Jesus hung on the Cross, the Father abandoned Him, God withdrew His presence and crushed His one and only Son. The full wrath of the Father was poured out upon the Son for all the sin of all the world. The Father's wrath was satisfied that dark day. What was due us, Jesus not only took, but His righteousness then became ours. This is our only and best Hope for all of eternity. There is nothing we need to add to this. In fact, if we do add anything to it, those little dabs show we don't believe Jesus is the Son of God. Instead, we make Him into less than He really is, and His death and resurrection do not save us. But when we do believe Jesus is our all in all, then we are born again, made alive, saved, and transformed into a new person. John 3:7 (NET) says, *You must all be born from above.* When we are born from above, we will live in Heaven with our Savior and all the saints for more years than anyone could ever count or even imagine.

For by grace you are saved through faith, and this is not from yourselves, it is the gift of God;
Ephesians 2:8 (NET)

Spurgeon said, "If the grace of God were to leave the best Christian, there is enough sin in his heart to make him the worst of transgressors." A big, wonderful, awesome, amazing gift has been given to us! *For I know that nothing good dwells in me, that is, in my flesh...* Romans 7:18 (NASB) We don't have to work for God's mercy, we don't deserve it, we simply have to believe, repent, and be saved! *At one time, we had no hope and (were) without God in the world.* Ephesians 2:12b (NET) But our Father loves us, and He has made a way for us to be with Him through His Son Jesus. *We were far away (but) have been brought near by the blood of Christ.* We are to *lay aside the old man who is being corrupted in accordance with deceitful desires, to be renewed in the spirit of your mind, and to put on the new man who has been created in God's image—in righteousness and holiness that comes from truth.* Ephesians 4:22-24 (NET)

Sadly, many are Gospel ignorant because the full Truth about sin and redemption is being neglected in too many sermons. Jesus gets tacked on at the end, if at all, and the Cross is not in clear focus. People end up leaving hungry, not only ready for breakfast, but starving spiritually. Salvation is a supernatural work of God, and it's not to be "tacked on" at the end, it is to be shared throughout. If we are only hearing a pep talk on Sunday morning, or Old Testament teachings that don't tie in the Cross of Christ, or talk of miracles, signs and wonders, then we will be starving for the true Gospel that is needed to truly save souls.

We are to learn the Gospel and *Live like children of light— for the fruit of the light consists in all goodness, righteousness, and truth— trying to learn what is pleasing to the Lord.* Ephesians 5:8b,9,10 (NET) Also, *Therefore consider carefully how you live— not as unwise but as wise...* Ephesians 5:15 (NET) *Christ loved the church and gave himself for her to sanctify her by cleansing her with the washing of the water by the word, so that he may present the church to himself as glorious—not having a stain or wrinkle, or any such blemish, but holy and blameless.* Ephesians 5:25b-27 (NET) *For this reason, take up the full armor of God so that you may be able to stand your ground on the evil day, and having done everything, to stand. So, pray at all times in the Spirit, and to this end be alert, with all perseverance and petitions for all the saints.* Ephesians 6:13,18 (NET)

In the end times, especially, many will be led more and more into sin. We need to be given a new heart of flesh for our old heart of stone. Otherwise, we will stay stuck in our old patterns of sin, without joy, without peace, and without Jesus as our Savior. In Matthew 24, it tells us how it will be as people will betray one another and hate one another. There will be false prophets who will deceive many. We can be prepared for those times when we are prepared in our own hearts, knowing the Truth spelled out in the Bible about who we are in Christ Jesus. Yes, we can live in this world, but not be a part of it. Just as Sodom was not in Lot, the world need not be in us when we are filled with the Holy Spirit. When we sin, we can know, *we have an advocate with the Father, Jesus Christ the Righteous One, and he himself is the atoning sacrifice for our sins, and not only for our sins but also for the whole world.* 1 John 2:1-2 (NET) Our *sins have been forgiven because of his name.* 1 John 2:12 (NET)

The Good News is: *"For I will be merciful toward their evil deeds, and their sins I will remember no longer."* Hebrews 8:12 (NET) This is why we need Jesus, the Cross, His crucifixion for our sins, His resurrection, and His coming back again. When we know this Gospel Truth for ourselves, we are then better prepared to share it with others. I hope with **Self-I**dolatry **N**oted.....we can lay it down at the foot of the Cross and walk away into the Light of our Lord and Savior, Jesus Christ.

Let's pray:

Father, Your goodness astounds us. You sent Your Son into this world while we were still sinners, and poured Your wrath onto the One You love because You also love us. Help us to see our sin quickly, and deal with it as You have taught us in Your Word. Your forgiveness is such a precious gift. We accept it and want to walk in obedience to You more and more. Thank You, Lord Jesus. Amen.

Chapter Fourteen Reflections

1) Sin…not a fun topic once again, but a much needed one when dealing with deception. But let's remember what 1 Thessalonians 5:23 says, we will *be kept entirely blameless at the coming of our Lord Jesus Christ.* (Page 223)

2) Paul understood that he was a sinner who desperately needed a Savior. Paul repented and that was the beginning of a whole new way of living life here on this Earth. Paul discovered the Truth. We all can! (Page 224)

3) No one has to be taught to sin. It comes naturally to all of us. We live in enemy territory, and without the help of the Restrainer, the Holy Spirit, sin will win. Does God know this? Yes! That's why He sent His only Son to save us. (Page 225)

4) One of Satan's major weapons is making sin so appealing we can be deep into it before realizing the mistakes we are making. Satan won't tell us that *the payoff of sin is death, but the gift of God is eternal life in Christ Jesus our Lord.* Romans 6:23 (NET) Oh no! He lies to us! He doesn't want us to know that right behind the sin being offered to us on a pretty silver platter lurks disaster, not only for us, many times, but for those around us. (Page 226)

5) *But God, being rich in mercy, because of his great love with which he loved us, even though we were dead in offenses/transgressions, made us alive together with Christ—by grace you are saved!* The wrath we deserved was poured out on God's only Son. We were saved from all that we were due. (Page 227)

6) Sadly, many are Gospel ignorant because the full Truth about sin and redemption is being neglected in too many sermons. Jesus gets tacked on at the end, if at all, and the Cross is not in clear focus. (Page 236)

7) If we are only hearing a pep talk on Sunday morning, or Old Testament teachings that don't tie in the Cross of Christ, or talk of miracles, signs and wonders, then we will be starving for the true Gospel that is needed to truly save souls. (Page 236)

8) In the end times, especially, many will be led more and more into sin. We need to be given a new heart of flesh for our old heart of stone. Otherwise, we will stay stuck in our old patterns of sin, without joy, without peace, and without Jesus as our Savior. (Page 236)

NOTES

*(These Reflection/Note pages may be duplicated
and used for group discussions when needed.)*

CHAPTER FIFTEEN

CULTS

In studying cults for this chapter, I spent many hours listening and reading. I am no expert on the subject, but as I have been doing in previous chapters, I can gather information and pass it along. That is mainly what I am attempting to do here from those who know this subject much better than I. A great deal of what is written here was gathered from a large number of sources as well as from a series by Walter Martin on cults. Sharing the Gospel in the mission field of those caught up in cults was his passion. Before Walter Martin's early death, at the age of 60 from a heart attack, he was one of a very few who chose to battle the enemy in the area of cults. He taught it well, and I hope I have learned it well enough to be able to pass along what I did gain from him and others so that we all can grow in the knowledge and grace of our Lord Jesus Christ. I pray this helps us personally, and in our own mission fields. This is dark territory. But with our focus on the true Jesus Christ, there is no need to fear. God's power is far above every evil spirit, demon, fallen angel, or any other evil spiritual being that exists. *This power he exercised in Christ when he raised him from the dead and seated him at his right hand in the heavenly realms far above every rule and authority and power and dominion and every name that is named, not only in this age but also in the one to come.* Ephesians 1:20-21 (NET)

We will start in Philippians 2:14-15 where it talks about how we live in the midst of a *crooked and perverse society, and we are to shine as lights in the world by holding on to the word of life.* If we were to pick up our Bible right now and hold it in the palm of our hand, we are holding the Word of life. It is the only Book ever written that can give us the Truth, the whole Truth, and nothing but the Truth...so help us God! And oh, how we need God's Truth today when we can't trust what we hear about what's going on in our world anywhere else. Things are so distorted, twisted, confusing, and chaotic as we come through this pandemic and enter into the world of protests, riots, and division in our country and world. Why? Why the mess? Why can't we all just live in peace and harmony? Because deception runs rampant more and more in this fallen/falling world, and it isn't at the bottom yet. So many are not finding a place in their heart for Jesus. They are being deluded and believing what is false...believing those little dabs that will do us under. (2 Thessalonians 2:11)

The antichrists that are here today are getting things ready for "the" antichrist to take the scene. I'm not being overly dramatic here, it is true. *Children, it is the last hour, and just as you heard that the antichrist is coming, so now many antichrists have appeared. We know from this that it is the last hour.* 1 John 2:18 (NET) I'm not making this up! God's Word tells us it's true, and that was 2,000 years ago. We are so much closer now!

If I told you things are working perfectly in the world today, I wouldn't be making that up either, although you may call me crazy. But things are lining up as they need to. We can read about all of what is happening today in God's Word of yesterday...the end of the story has been written. We even know that when the main antichrist takes a seat on the throne in the temple of God in Jerusalem, which is where the abomination of desolation will take place, referred to in Daniel 12:11 and Matthew 24:15, we will know at that point that we have three and a half years to go before the end of the tribulation. All this mess will be finished at last. God has made it clear. Are we awake and paying attention? Because this is all perfectly planned out and the antichrist is playing right into God's hand. What seems chaotic is really order...God's order to bring about the end of this fallen world and the beginning of His New Heaven and New Earth, perfectly prepared for those who believe in

His Son, the Lord Jesus Christ. (Revelation 21:1)

When we read in 1 Peter 1:9 that the *goal of our faith is the salvation of our souls*, we can believe it! There is a goal! And we who have faith in Jesus as our Lord and Savior are headed right toward it! Our souls, although having to live through many trials and tribulations, will ultimately be saved from the wrath of God when day is done! Now, what does all this have to do with cults? Well, cults are the other side of the coin to all of this, so to speak. The *goal* of cults is to distract us from God's *goal*. Satan wants to get us off course, keep us from salvation, and hold us prisoners there for as long as possible…sadly, sometimes he does so, leading people right into eternal destruction in Hell for those who will not come into a grace-filled relationship with Jesus Christ.

In all this, it is said we can't know when the Lord is coming. That is true, and yet not…what are we told to do in Matthew 24:42-44? *Watch therefore, for you do not know what hour your Lord is coming. But know this, that if the master of the house had known what hour the thief would come, he would have watched and not allowed his house to be broken into. Therefore you also be ready, for the Son of Man is coming at an hour you do not expect.* (NKJV) It's time for believers to wake up and watch what is going on in our world so we will be ready. We are told by our Lord to be ready! It is not time to fall into fear, but into faith-filled watching! Because what does faith bring? It brings us to our goal, the salvation of our souls!

Spurgeon wrote: "No Christian enjoys comfort when his eyes are fixed on falsehood—he enjoys no satisfaction unless his soul is quickened in the ways of God."

We can feel that discomfort when we watch the evening news, look at our social media sites, listen to the radio in the car, even talking to others…telling us half-truths/giving us bad, sad, falsehoods! Is some of what is said true? Of course, yes. But is a lot of it falsehood? Yes! That is called heresy in the church. Sometimes heresy is little dabs of Truth with a whole lot of lies. Sometimes it's little dabs of lies with a whole lot of Truth. Either way, it's dangerous! Both ways can do you under! What we need is the complete Truth from God's Word at all times. We are told to *Beware of dogs, beware of evil workers, beware of the mutilation!* Philippians 3:2 (NKJV) If we are listening to the wrong sources, we will be deceived/mutilated by the lies coming at us about what we need to be doing, or don't need to be doing, instead of what Jesus Christ has already done...and too many will believe the misconceptions and be led astray.

Who is being led astray? It is said that 80 percent of those in cults come from a background of Baptists, Presbyterians, Lutherans, etc... Yes, churches where the Word of God should be being taught in full. But is it? Is the Word being taught? That's the question, and the problem. In 1 John 2:19 it says: *They went out from us, but they did not really belong to us, because if they had belonged to us, they would have remained with us. But they went out from us to demonstrate that all of them do not belong to us.* And why do they not belong to us/the body and family of Christ? Perhaps because they didn't learn the Gospel in full to begin with. Or maybe they even knew the "what" of the Gospel, but couldn't explain it because they never really understood why Jesus died on the Cross...or why Jesus rose again...or why Jesus ascended back into Heaven...or why Jesus is coming back again? As we talked about earlier, part of the Gospel is more dangerous than none of the Gospel. With part of the Gospel being taught, we can think we have the whole of it even when we don't. At least those with none of the Gospel aren't being deceived by partial truth. They are the group in full prideful denial of Jesus Christ of Nazareth, and they *know* they are rejecting Christ. If we don't remain in the teaching of Christ, we do not have God. (2 John 9)

Let's step back just a bit and define our "why", and then we can dive into what a cult is. To grasp the Truth first, it helps us to keep standing firm on solid ground. We believe Jesus died on the Cross because we are sinners, and we needed a Savior to take our sin upon Himself. We needed a perfect sacrifice and Jesus is the spotless Lamb of God. Jesus rose on the third day to confirm that the work on the Cross was finished, sin had been conquered, and also death. Will we still die a physical death? Yes. But we will live eternally in Heaven with our Savior because Jesus' blood has washed our sins away. We are ready to enter into the perfection of Heaven through Jesus Christ. Why did Jesus ascend back into Heaven? Heaven is where Jesus came from and returned to, to sit at the right hand of His Father and be an advocate for us...to be the Shepherd who watches over His flock on Earth, and so the Holy Spirit could then be sent to live inside each one who believes in what Jesus accomplished on the Cross. (John 16:7) Why is Jesus coming back again? Because He promised that He was going to prepare a place for us and that He would one day return to take us to where He is. That is the Gospel Truth. Now, what is a cult?

Our Father has made the Gospel pure and simple to remember and share. Cults make things complicated and confusing. A cult is a social group that is defined by its unusual religious, spiritual, or philosophical beliefs. In Christianity, a cult is a new religious movement which has Christianity in its background but deviates theologically from what the Word of God has proclaimed. Many times, they are groups that follow an individual with his/her own interpretation of the Bible that's not accepted by mainstream Christianity. To list just a few of the major cults, they would be Mormons, Jehovah's Witnesses, Christian Scientists, Unitarian Universalism, Scientologists, Seven-Day Adventists, New Age, Eastern Religions, Islamists, and Buddhists. Some of these cults even contain a good amount of truth that is in alignment with the Bible but then veer away from the Word of God into other areas and emphasize them more than the Gospel as a main focus. Whereas the Bible says: *My aim is to know him, to experience the power of his resurrection, to share in his sufferings, and to be like him in his death, and so, somehow, to attain to the resurrection from the dead.* Philippians 3:10-11 (NET) When this is where we're aiming...to know Jesus, we can know we are on the right path.

We are told in Titus one that we are to hold firmly to the message that has been taught so our teaching will be healthy, and we can correct those who speak against God's Word. Titus goes on to say in 1:10-11 that there are many rebellious people, idle talkers, and deceivers who must be silenced because they mislead whole families and teach what ought not be taught. How does this get started? It can seem small and insignificant in the beginning. Did you know that the Mormon religion started in the early 1800's in upstate New York by Joseph Smith with about 30 people, and it had grown to 14.8 million by 2012? If we think what we are doing in sharing the true Word of God with those around us has little impact, we are wrong. What began with Jesus and the twelve has grown in even greater number to what the Mormon church can or ever will do. The number of Christians in the world today is said to be over two billion. It is the world's largest religious group. Well done good and faithful twelve!!

We are to be on guard though, as Jesus warned us in Matthew 7:15 (NET): *"Watch out for false prophets, who come to you in sheep's clothing but inwardly are voracious wolves."* Many can look, act, and sound genuine, but they are really savage wolves in sheep's clothing. They can lead moral and ethical lives, but still be at war with God. Now this is very important—one thing that all cults have in common, from the first to the last, is they **deny Jesus Christ as God's only way of saving souls.** This is where we are to look first and also last when watching out for these false religions. They can even refer to Jesus as Lord, but the meaning has changed. They are talking about another Jesus, another gospel, and it is counterfeit—they make up an imitation Jesus with the intent to deceive. And it is very deceptive, to the point where many don't realize they are being deceived. We have to know who the real Jesus is—the One and only Son of God, the second Person of the Trinity, always fully God and fully man when He walked upon this Earth for starters. Let me give you a few examples of what following another Jesus…another spirit…could sound like.

If you were to read this quote, what would you think of it?

"There are many ways to calm negative energy without suppressing or fighting it. You recognize it, you smile to it, and you invite something nicer to come up and replace it; you read some inspiring words, you listen to a piece of beautiful music, you go somewhere in nature, or you do some walking meditation."

Sounds nice, calming, with some good advice, right? But what is this exactly? This is from Thich Nhat Hanh, a Zen Master and global spiritual leader. It is a substitute…a counterfeit of true spirituality. It's man's ideas superseding God's. Now if he had said, turn to Philippians 4:8 and think about what is pure, true, lovely, etc…so the God of peace will be with you…as it ends in verse nine, then we would have gone to the *source* of our real peace—not a fabricated way to worldly peace thought up by man. Is this dangerous? When it replaces God's Word in our lives it is. Paul said, *I have experienced times of need and times of abundance. In any and every circumstance I have learned the secret of contentment, whether I go satisfied or hungry, have plenty or nothing. I am able to do all things through the one who strengthens me.* Philippians 4:12-13 (NET) Does this mean we can never use another source of wisdom or advice other than the Bible? Of course not. But we should always be aware of where our focus is. Is Jesus Christ our "go to" or are the things of this world our main source of comfort?

Let's try another situation with a different slant to it this time. Here is a quote from a well-known pastor when asked about Hinduism and Christianity.

"Of course, I believe in Christ as the Savior and all, but I think, too...Hindu people are nice kind people that love God as well."

Now, can Hindu people be nice, kind people? Absolutely! Most probably are. But they don't believe the same God of the Bible that Christians do so they can't love someone, a God, they don't know. This pastor is a false teacher, misleading multitudes in one simple statement. He is confusing the body of Christ by not pointing out false religions in answer to the question he had been asked. Hinduism and Christianity can't both be right...one must be wrong. Hindus believe in reincarnation. Christians believe we are appointed to die once as stated in Hebrews 9:27. One religion has the Spirit of Truth, the other a spirit of error. This is happening a lot, and that's a good reason why at least one-half of the New Testament defends the faith and gives reasons why—Paul and others were well-aware of the wolves that would come against sound Gospel teaching.

One more example before we move on. Another well-known pastor was quoted as saying, "You are gods because you came from God. The only human part of you is this physical body you live in. The real me is just like God." Let's be reminded of what happened when Lucifer said, *"I will be like the Most High"* in Isaiah 14:14. Verse 15 in Isaiah tells us, *"Yet you shall be brought down to Sheol, to the lowest depths of the Pit."* It didn't take God any time at all to put Satan in his place when this happened, kicking him out of Heaven along with a third of the angels who wanted to follow him. And we will be put in our place, too, if we think we are a god. Are there other gods? Yes. We worship them like idols. We can even make shopping a god, sports a god, other people a god in our life...we can and do worship things we shouldn't many times. But when we discover that we have, and are, we should repent, confess, seek forgiveness, and walk more closely with our Risen Savior who is the true God of all creation.

Cults of any kind are dangerous. We are to *have mercy on those who waver; save others by snatching them out of the fire; have mercy on others, coupled with a fear of God, hating even the clothes stained by the flesh.* Jude 22-23 (NET) It is so important to preach the full Word of God from the pulpit. We need to hear teachings about the Cross, the blood, repentance, prayer, the Word, and how to walk in God's Truth in today's world. We are bombarded daily with lies that sound so true. We need to be bombarded even more with Truth that will combat those lies. We need to be so full of the Truth about God that it can be our guiding light through the darkness of this life. When we see our Father in Heaven, the Lord Jesus Christ, and the Holy Spirit as the Holy God they really truly are, we can then start to see our great need of redemption from our sinful ways. (Cults rarely if ever deal with this problem of sin.) This will then set us on a path filled with study, fellowship, sermons, worship, prayer, and an ever-deepening repentance and faith. If we are to find true joy in this life, it is only found in Jesus Christ as our Lord and Savior…to know that Jesus died on a Cross for us, took on the full wrath of God in our place, and that He is coming back again, victorious!

Jesus will not come this time to die, but He will return on a white horse and be ready to go to war with Satan to show us all that He truly lives and has provided an eternity with Him. That was promised in the Word, where it says: *Then I saw heaven opened and here came a white horse! The one riding it was called "Faithful" and "True," and with justice he judges and goes to war.* Revelation 19:11 (NET) Amen!

The problem with cults full of false prophets and false teachers is that they can be very alluring. They can be dynamic and dramatic. They can display powerful giftings…but we must always look at their fruit. They can appear to have a Christlike character bearing that fruit, but it is not Christ and it is not real fruit. Counterfeits are not always easy to spot, but we must be on the lookout for them. What's also tough is that sometimes we actually want what they are "selling". We want the feel-good, make-me-rich, heal-me, love-me-just-the-way-I-am-as-I-continue-in-my-sin, type of preaching. We can't be surprised when the Word tells us: *Now the Spirit explicitly says that in the later times some will desert the faith and occupy themselves with deceiving spirits and demonic teachings, influenced by the hypocrisy of liars whose consciences are seared.* 1 Timothy 4:1-2 (NET) But the Word instructs us: *Preach the message, be ready whether it is convenient or not, reprove, rebuke, exhort with complete patience and instruction. For there will be a time when people will not tolerate sound teaching.* 2 Timothy 4:2-3 (NET) Which will it be? What the Word says or what we want to hear? Which will prepare us to stand before our Maker on Judgment Day? That's what we must be most concerned about, not our comfort and pleasure here and now.

When looking and listening for a good, sound teaching, we have to ask ourselves are we seeing and hearing a message of sorrow about our sins, being gentle while also hungering and thirsting for righteousness? Are there divided loyalties between the world and the Word? Is there mercy? Is it a teaching that includes not only the peace and love of Jesus but also the discipline of the Father? Is it a message filled with the heart made pure when the Holy Spirit dwells in a believer, when a person is born again into the family of God? Is persecution not only talked about, but to be expected in this life? Is it a life filled with faith in Jesus while in a world ruled by the prince of the air, Satan? Is there not only endurance being talked about, but also a great hope in what is to come in Heaven? The Word contains the Good News of Jesus Christ and also the reality of living in a fallen world. If we are being promised all goodness and fairy tales, all wealth and prosperity, all healing from every disease and illness…then we are not hearing the full Gospel Truth. We are being flattered and many will be lost as a result. Those who come wanting what they want, and not what God wants, will be sadly disappointed in the end. Because of some pastors not having the guts to tell the Truth, many in our churches today are Gospel ignorant and cult vulnerable. God has a much better plan than these people could ever devise. If we would only follow the instruction manual given to us by our Father more closely, we would see what an amazing God we serve.

Paul, in talking about the knowledge and the mystery of God, namely, Christ, in whom are hidden all the treasures of wisdom and knowledge in Colossians 2:4 (NET) had this to say: *I say this so that no one will deceive you through arguments that sound reasonable.* Paul wants us to know there is no such thing as a prosperity gospel or a social gospel. There is only one true Gospel...when no description is needed, that is the Gospel that saves us through Jesus Christ as Lord of our life. He is the One who is sufficient, who is full of grace and mercy, who helps us in our weakness, and who died for our sins. Jesus is the perfect Lamb of God, the perfect Sacrifice who laid down His life and drank in the full wrath of His Father on the Cross at Calvary. Jesus rose on the third day proving He is King of kings and Lord of lords, victorious over Hell and the grave. God is not impressed with our good works and the ways and plans people come up with in all these cults. The Father is only impressed with His One and only Son, and what He has done to secure our eternal life in Heaven, reconciling us back to the Father. There is no other way, there is no purgatory, no second chances, only being saved or being lost on Judgment Day...only Heaven or Hell.

What can match this clarity and Truth for what is to come? No cult anywhere carries the power of these promises. *Therefore, just as you received Christ Jesus as Lord, continue to live your lives in him, rooted and built up in him and firm in your faith just as you were taught, and overflowing with thankfulness. Be careful not to allow anyone to captivate you through an empty, deceitful philosophy that is according to human traditions and the elemental spirits of the world, and not according to Christ. For in him all the fullness of deity lives in bodily form, and you have been filled in him, who is the head over every ruler and authority.* Colossians 2:6-10 (NET) We can't let anyone tell us that Jesus was just a man "until God touched Him and put the Spirit of the Living God on the inside of Him." This is a lie some pastors try to encourage us with so we will be confident about praying for signs, wonders, and miracles today. But it is demonic, and it is not to be listened to. Can we pray for healing, for deliverance, and see the miracles of God still today? I believe we absolutely can. I believe it's Biblical when Jesus informs us in John 14:12 (NET); *I tell you the solemn truth, the person who believes in me will perform the miraculous deeds that I am doing, and will perform greater deeds than these, because I am going to the Father.* But we can only do these things because *Christ is the one who died (and more than that, He was raised), who is at the right hand of God, and who also is interceding for us.* Romans 8:34 (NET) Jesus was always fully man and fully God. We must never make a mistake about this Truth. We are only fully man with the Holy Spirit living within us. Big difference! We are not a god.

We have to stick to the Truth and only the Truth at all times! Scripture says: *The arrival of the lawless one will be by Satan's working with all kinds of miracles and signs and false wonders, and with every kind of evil deception directed against those who are perishing, because they found no place in their hearts for the truth so as to be saved.* 2 Thessalonians 2:9-10 (NET) So how do we tell the difference when many pastors/churches are promoting heresy in these areas? We have to focus on the Truth, put Jesus first, and when in doubt, do what Jesus told us to do in Luke 10:20 (NET): *"Nevertheless, do not rejoice that the spirits submit to you, but rejoice that your names stand written in heaven."* If we are rejoicing in the miracles more than our risen Lord and our eternal life with Him, we are out of balance—we need to repent and come back to our treasured relationship with Jesus.

Now, it may seem we have gotten off track, from talking about cults, to other forms of heresy. But it's all inclusive. A cults sole/soul purpose is to keep people away from the true Jesus. This "track" is a wide group. How do we get misled down it? Well, Humanism starts with man. Christianity starts with God. When we are focusing too much on ourselves and not enough on the one true God of the Bible, we will get lost along the way.

These cults include everything from Hinduism, New Age, Mysticism, Mormonism, and not excluding other gospels being preached even in Catholic churches, Baptist churches, Charismatic churches, etc… Anything that deviates from the Word of God should not be accepted within Christianity and the Body of Christ. False teachings can be 70 percent Truth and 30 percent false. They are very dangerous and to be rejected! Paul said: *As I urged you when I was leaving for Macedonia, stay on in Ephesus to instruct certain people not to spread false teachings, nor to occupy themselves with myths and interminable genealogies. Such things promote useless speculations rather than God's redemptive plan that operates by faith.* 1 Timothy 1:3-4 (NET) *To do this you must hold firmly to faith and a good conscience, which some have rejected and so have suffered shipwreck in regard to the faith.*

1 Timothy 1:19 (NET)

True faith has certain symptoms, just like a cold is known by its symptoms. True faith has its Hope of eternity in the Gospel. That Hope is a significant symptom of our faith. How does our faith get shipwrecked? *By not being conscientious about how you live and what you teach.* 1 Timothy 4:16a (NET) We have to watch our life and doctrine closely. We get lazy sometimes. Things can sound good. Fancy words can tickle our ears. Feel-good messages can be less "offensive" to listen to, and to then share with others. But 16b goes on to say: *Persevere in this, because by doing so you will save both yourself and those who listen to you.* We have to understand these cults attack our churches. Rarely do we attack them until they invade our sacred ground…we must always stand firm in what we believe when they do. As we have talked about before, we must hold the line of Scripture as sacred—not going above it with Jesus-plus theology, or below it with man's own speculations. Let's look at some of the things man has come up with in these cultish religions. So many include doing more good stuff than bad.

The Jehovah's Witnesses claim that Jesus was the Archangel Michael. The Mormons believe that all male Mormons are supposed to strive to be gods. They believe in grace by faith…after you've done all you can do. Spiritists believe Jesus is an advanced medium in the 6th sphere of the astral projection. Christian Scientists believe Jesus is a divine idea. Unitarians believe Jesus is an extraordinal man whose followers are deified. We, as Christians, believe the Truth of God's Word, that Jesus is the only Son of God, was born of a virgin, conceived by the Holy Spirit, lived as fully God and fully man upon this earth, died, was resurrected, ascended back to Heaven to sit at the right hand of the Father, and is coming back again! This is how Christianity compares to just a few of the millions of cults in the world today. One hundred and fifty years ago there were only about 1,000 cults. Who do we think is on the move big time while his time is short?! Some cults are just repackaged…New Age is from Satanism.

Why is this happening? Why are people attracted to these groups? The world outside of true Christianity is not good at listening to the justice of God. The world only wants to hear about the love of God. We must fight the good fight of faith until Jesus returns. Jude 3 (NET) says: *Dear friends, although I have been eager to write to you about our common salvation, I now feel compelled instead to write to encourage you to contend earnestly for the faith that was once for all entrusted to the saints.* If we ask ourselves what drives us, it should be the commitment we have made to our Lord and Savior. If we ask what drives the cults, it's the forces of darkness. They disguise themselves as angels of light and servants of righteousness. They are counterfeits. We can get sucked into this strong pull, taking us off course, if we are not more strongly sucked into the Word of God. Many cults when asked about Jesus will claim He is the Son of God. But don't stop there! Delve deeper into their answer. Ask, "Are you saying He is the Savior of the World? Is He the second Person of the Trinity? Or is He merely a sign that points the way to god (small "g")?" *...the god of this age has blinded the minds of those who do not believe so they would not see the light of the glorious gospel of Christ, who is the image of God.* 2 Corinthians 4:4 (NET)

I have watched a video that shows a man singing a worship song, and he is very good at it. He knows what he is doing. When asked to sing the same song again, he is asked to now think about why he is singing those words...his "tune" then changes dramatically. It means something to him. He understands. He gets it. It's valuable. This is why we can't just know *what* we believe, we have to know *why* we believe it. What is our reason for believing? What is our need being met? When we aren't taught our need for the blood of Jesus Christ, but only about the blood, it loses its potency in our walk of faith. We can eat the bread and drink the blood plenty easy on a Sunday morning during communion, but when we do this while understanding what Scripture instructs, it goes deeper into our soul. The Word says: *A person should examine himself first, and in this way let him eat the bread and drink of the cup.* 1 Corinthians 11:28 (NET) Jesus was a real Person, and is really God, who came to this Earth to save sinners, of which we are one. His blood was poured out for us on the Cross to cleanse us from our sins. His body was wounded so that we could be made well and whole... We have a great need of a powerful Savior! That is why we are to clean our personal "plate" through repentance and confession before partaking of Him, understanding on our own, we can't be good enough. We need the Cross of Christ.

The Jehovah's Witnesses come to our doors. They are good

people trying to do good. But good doesn't count in God's economy…they are the second largest cult in the world. They have two gods: Jehovah that created everything, and Michael who is a little god. They don't believe in Hell, the resurrection, the Trinity, or the deity of Christ. What is the power that draws people to a cult like this? Those powerful forces of darkness which we can read about in Ephesians 6:12 (NET): *For our struggle is not against flesh and blood, but against the rulers, against the powers, against the world rulers of this darkness, against the spiritual forces of evil in the heavens.* If we don't think dark powers are real, we are mistaken. God's Word is clear that they are. Also, people are needy. Human beings need something, anything, to fill the void within them when the Holy Spirit is not dwelling within. That is why the full Gospel being preached is so very important. Without that firm foundation, the Cornerstone, people will get lost along the way and start grabbing for any light in the darkness. They will take hold of what is being offered, especially if it does sound Biblical. Hence, counterfeit is so important for cults to utilize—make it sound like the real God. Then, when works get thrown into the mix, it is even more appealing. We all like to think we have something to do with saving ourselves! It doesn't take long to pull someone into the darkness, especially if they can "help" god get the task completed. Paul said in Galatians 1:6 (NET); *I am astonished that you are so quickly deserting the one who called you by the grace of Christ and are following a different gospel.* Do you know why the Mormons were told to have many wives? This was new for me. They believe they are making many babies for souls that are already alive in heaven to come and live in, as well as for other reasons. That's why they practiced polygamy. Interesting…it astonishes me what some believe when the Word of God is not believed. They were taught, and believed, they were doing a very good thing…helping out God. Lies.

The gate is narrow, and few find it. Too many are wandering on the wide road of destruction. *For if someone comes and proclaims another Jesus different from the one we proclaimed, or if you receive a different spirit than the one you received, or a different gospel than the one you accepted, you put up with it well enough!* 2 Corinthians 11:4 (NET) Let's be warned! Let's not put up with anything other than the true Gospel of Jesus Christ. To repeat…one very important fact to remember is we are NOT going to become gods. The Bible is clear on that. *This is what the Lord, Israel's king, says, their Protector, the Lord of Heaven's Armies: "I am the first and I am the last, there is no God but me."* Isaiah 44:6 (NET) Satan tried this lie in the Garden with Adam and Eve, *"ye shall be gods"*. (Gen. 3:5) Satan's still spouting the same lies today.

There are many forms that cults take. There are many world views, including Hinduism. They don't pray to God because they believe they are a god/one with God. Whereas "oneness" in Christianity is because the Holy Spirit lives within us. We are not a god. There is spiritism which includes witches, Satan worship, ESP (reception of information not gained through recognized physical senses), and psychic phenomenon (occurrences that appear to contradict physical laws by mental processes). There has always been a great interest in contacting other dimensions. Is it possible? Yes. And it's very dangerous. As Christians, we shouldn't be involved in these things. The Bible speaks against it, and we should listen for our own good—this territory belongs to Satan. God commanded King Saul to destroy all the wizards and mediums. They are the connection between this dimension and the prince of darkness. There was only one time in the Bible where God permitted this, and we can read about it in 1 Samuel where it basically describes a séance in the Bible. God wouldn't answer Saul, so King Saul went to the devil for his answer. *The woman replied, "Who is it that I should bring up for you?" He said, "Bring up for me Samuel."* 1 Samuel 28:11 (NET) We have to take notice that the devil will usually give us the answer we want to hear. The prophets of old, the real prophets, usually came bearing bad news. The false prophets usually came telling lies of good things to come.

In this story of Samuel and the woman, who was the medium, we see she was shocked because **her** demon didn't show up. God intervened and pronounced divine judgment on Saul instead: *The Lord will hand you and Israel over to the Philistines! Tomorrow both you and your sons will be with me. The Lord will also hand the army of Israel over to the Philistines!"* 1 Samuel 28:19 (NET) This was not good news for Saul, and this is not what God wants us doing. This is operating in the dimension of the devil. There are more than a quarter of a million of these types of spiritists in the United States. But Leviticus 19:31 (NET) says: *Do not turn to the spirits of the* *dead and do not seek familiar spirits to become unclean by them. I am the Lord your God.* Sometimes we wonder what God thinks about this or that…but not this! We have a definite answer! We will *become unclean by them.* This can be a tricky business…Spiritists can sound very moral if you listen to their doctrines. But they want nothing to do with Christianity, with the real Jesus Christ, and we should want nothing to do with what they practice.

Witchcraft/Sorcery is any attempt to influence supernatural forces with one's own will or psyche…or supernaturally influencing natural forces. Revelation 21:8 says that those practicing these things will be put into the lake of fire. And in Galatians 5:21, Paul says those practicing, as in continuing on with these things, will not inherit the Kingdom of God. In regards to magic, it is done by magicians who are illusionists, they do tricks. But real magic draws on occult/demonic powers such as is found in lying wonders. This is not to be messed around with! True miracles, on the other hand, are the supernatural work of God.

Astrology is probably the most well-known cult by those of us in the Christian community. We have probably all heard of the Zodiac and reading our horoscopes. Who didn't glance at them when we used to receive the newspaper each day? Some even think of checking with the "wisdom" of the Zodiac signs when deciding who to date. My husband, when asked what his sign is from time to time, will answer, "Neon". We can't confuse astronomy with astrology. Astronomists study the authentic movement of the heavenly bodies. Astrologists study the signs of the Zodiac…a configuration of stars. Some even believe the hour of our birth can determine our whole life pattern. We know that Psalm 139:16 (NET*)* says: *Your eyes saw me when I was inside the womb. All the days ordained for me were recorded in your scroll before one of them came into existence.* We know Who is in control of our days and it's not the stars we were born under or our Zodiac sign. Sadly, there are many so absorbed in themselves and their signs, they have no time to watch the signs for the coming of the Son of God. *"And what will be the sign of your coming and of the end of the age?" Jesus answered them, "Watch out that no one misleads you."* Matthew 24:3-4 (NET) Having our palms read, going to crystal ball sessions, looking into our horoscopes, calling up the dead…these are not God's ways to show us what our lives will hold. In Daniel 1:20 (NET) it is said: *In every* *matter of wisdom and insight the king asked them about, he found them to be ten times better than any of the magicians and astrologers that were in his entire empire.* God's way is so much better!

If this all seems very far outside of the world we live in, I'd like to share what an acquaintance on social media posted. I read, "Some are asking me about virtual tarot readings and services…I haven't forgotten… With how I have been gifted, I've been worn out spiritually. Every time I do readings, I get an interruption. With all that's going on, I feel there is a thin veil and the lines of communication from spirits are vast and open. So, I don't have the energy to provide free services." (Shortened just a bit.) This is a young woman I met years ago, and I keep her on my social site because she gives me glimpses into a life that is very different than my own. She lives in a very dark world. I do not respond to her posts…but we are to be compassionate and prayerful for those whose spiritual lives are empty. Spiritism is what she practices, and it encourages people to probe into the supernatural realm of Satan, the doctrine of demons, which God has forbidden in His Word. James 4:8 (NET) says; *Draw near to God and he will draw near to you. Cleanse your hands, you sinners, and make your hearts pure, you double-minded.* Our single-minded focus should be the Lord Jesus. He alone has the answers we are needing!

There are many other aspects of cults that we will take a look at briefly. If to know about them helps protect us from being drawn into them, we will spend some time talking about them here.

Levitation is when a solid object defies gravity. It does happen, it is real. To many, it is common- place. Apportation is moving a solid object with no physical means. Some have been photographed doing it. It is real. Materialization is a spirit taking on a physical form. Doctors have examined and proved this has happened. Ectoplasm happens in a séance when a departed loved one takes on a physical shape. These are demons, and not the real person. Satan knows our departed loved ones, and he can use his demons as counterfeits. Dream interpretation is when a psychic interprets a dream and it happens. Interpreting dreams should only be done prayerfully. It happens spontaneously by the Spirit of God, not systematically—it's not a fixed spiritual science to be discovered. It is not listed as a gift. God will interpret dreams when the time is right. Astral projection is a state of consciousness of leaving the body and then returning and confirming what was seen.

What does the Bible have to say about these things that cults will use in their defense? Counterfeits always have to have a real source. There are no counterfeit three dollar bills. The Truth is being twisted with cults.

To prove Levitation is of God, they will say that Jesus levitated. Jesus did not. He ascended to Heaven as the Son of God, and He walked ON the water not over it. He created the water. He can walk on it. (Luke 24:51, Matt. 14:25)

In Apportation (moving a solid object with no physical means), the Bible talks about Philip in Acts 8:39. This was not the same as what the cults are doing. Philip was being moved for the purpose of sharing the Gospel not to demonstrate another dimension of a dark reality to get people to put their faith in it.

With Materialization (a spirit taking on a physical form), John's birth was prophesied in Luke 1:13. An angel came to proclaim it. It held great purpose for the Kingdom of God. He was a real man, living in a real day, for a real purpose.

When Interpreting dreams and doing Astral Projection (leaving the body and then returning to tell what was seen), they want to cite 2 Corinthians 12:1-2 (NET): *Though it is not profitable, I will go on to visions and revelations from the Lord. I know a man in Christ who fourteen years ago (whether in the body or out of the body I do not know, God knows) was caught up to the third heaven.* They say it's a demonstration of God's power, it's from God so they can use the Bible as proof that what they are doing originated from God. Paul was making no money doing this. He was not asking for this…it was given to Him from above. Are there actual cases that Astral Projection happens? Yes. But they are not looking to or for Jesus, they are observing mankind instead of being lifted into fellowship with Christ. They want to conquer death and gain power to live their lives. They think they don't have to face judgment or Hell. Many believe in reincarnation also.

These practices within cults are not leading people to God but away from Him. These are cheap imitations of God's divine power *…do you not know that friendship with the world means hostility toward God? So whoever decides to be the world's friend makes himself God's enemy.* James 4:4 (NET) These things are substitutes for real faith. What we receive through Jesus Christ, as Christians, many people are seeking through Satanic means. We need not fear these things. We have faith in the Lord, Jesus Christ. But knowing about them will help us not be deceived by them.

Suppose a prophet or one who foretells by dreams should appear among you and show you a sign or wonder, and the sign or wonder should come to pass concerning what he said to you, namely, "Let us follow other gods"—gods whom you have not previously known—"and let us serve them." You must not listen to the words of that prophet or dreamer, for the Lord your God will be testing you to see if you love him with all your mind and being. You must follow the Lord your God and revere only him; and you must observe his commandments, obey him, serve him, and remain loyal to him. Deuteronomy 13:1-4 (NET)

We are living in a time when Satan doesn't even hide anymore, and the world still can't see him. But ANYTHING that leads us away from the Cross of Jesus Christ is to be quickly discarded!! *For the Lord is great and certainly worthy of praise, he is more awesome than all gods. For all the gods of the nations are worthless, but the Lord made the heavens. Majestic splendor emanates from him, he is the source of strength and joy.* 1 Chronicles 16:25-27 (NET) It doesn't matter how exciting these false things are, how attractive they are, how intriguing, or how powerful they seem, if it is not of God…RUN! We can be deceived! We are not to substitute anything for hearing the voice of our God. *But I am afraid that just as the serpent deceived Eve by his treachery, your minds may be led astray from a sincere and pure devotion to Christ.* 2 Corinthians 11:3 (NET) That is why we are to leave these things alone!

There are many who use these things as a spiritual narcotic. It removes people from reality and then makes them insensitive to the reality of God. This actually makes hearing the voice of God harder because other voices are interfering. We can't think these things aren't real. They are real. There is a dark world with dark forces. But *You are from God, little children, and have conquered them, because the one who is in you is greater than the one who is in the world. They are from the world; therefore they speak from the world's perspective and the world listens to them. We are from God; the person who knows God listens to us, but whoever is not from God does not listen to us. By this we know the Spirit of truth and the spirit of deceit.* 1 John 4:4-6 (NET)

We need to have our spiritual eyes open. We have been warned by our God. Divination (the practice of seeking knowledge of the unknown by supernatural means) in the Old Testament was worthy of the death penalty. Today, witches are gaining traction. There are more witches than Presbyterians by 100,000.

There are some large religions that seem very compatible with Christianity. There are sincere Catholics who love the Lord but the doctrines of the Catholic church point to a work-based religion. Mary is over emphasized and an earthly priest is not necessary as an intermediary between God and man. (1 Timothy 2:5) The Catholic Church has many extra biblical practices that have been added, and this creates a new religion out of Christianity. Unitarianism is a very large cult. It is one of intellect. Some don't even realize they are in this cult, thinking instead they are following Christ. The core of the Gospel is that Christ became a man, died for our sins, and rose from the dead. We can find that quickly in 1 Corinthians 15. Sadly, the Unitarians do not believe Jesus is God. They believe He is a way, but not the way. These days, to become dogmatic (laying down principles as undeniable truth) is to become offensive. We see that more and more. Christians believe we will be known by our fruit. Unitarians believe works are vital, we have to be the right kind of people. But if ethics save a person, we would not need Jesus as our Savior. Many believe by living perfectly, following God's law without exception, they can get to Heaven. They are mistaken. There would have to be more than one Jesus since He was the only perfect Person to ever walk this earth. We have to come through the blood of Jesus, clinging to nothing but the Cross to enter through the Heavenly gates for all of eternity. We can't measure ourselves against other men as so many try to do to prove their goodness. God is our only Judge. Unitarians recognize evil, as do so many in our world, but they don't recognize Jesus as the answer. Too many believe God helps those who help themselves. We see these lies everywhere in our world today. People are listening to them, following them, and claiming to be Christians...but they are not.

A young man who came out of the New Age and into a true relationship with Jesus Christ states, "We have a moral rebellion, a moral resistance to God. We don't want to submit to a holy and righteous God the same way a criminal doesn't want to find a policeman." (And this was before the whole "defund the police" campaign started.)

Here is the Truth: "Christianity is the acceptance of a certain system of beliefs with regard to the personality of Jesus, His relationship to God, and the supernatural effect of His death and resurrection." (Walter Martin)

Here is a Lie: "If Christianity means a respect and reverence for Jesus and what He sought to be and do in His own time…if it means the effort to bring to birth in our lives today something of that spirit that was in Jesus…Unitarians have as good a right as anyone else to call themselves Christians. None of us have achieved this goal. The mark of a sincere Christian is that he seeks to move toward it. (Look Magazine article)

This is what a lot of people think even without calling themselves Unitarians. People are trying to live up to the Golden Rule, or move "toward it"…trying to be like Jesus. This is a major cultic system that is growing immensely. As Christians, we know we need to be born again. We believe the Word of God where *Jesus answered and said to him, "Most assuredly, I say to you, unless one is born again, he cannot see the kingdom of God."* John 3:3 (NKJV)

How do we talk to others about Jesus when they believe their works will get them into Heaven, and Jesus is just a good man who helped some people while He was here? Walter Martin suggests we ask them if they think Jesus was a better person than them when He was here? Was He more ethical, more moral? They will most like say, *Yes.* Then ask them, "Can you give me one reason why I shouldn't believe Him rather than you?"

Many will quote the Bible but ignore its basic message of salvation…wanting to acknowledge Christ but not His teachings. So many want to pick and choose what they like and then present that to the world saying; "Don't confuse me with the facts. I've already made up my mind." That's not the way the Word of God works. It's all or nothing! Take Jesus or leave Him! Heaven or Hell. No middle ground. No compromise. Jesus Christ crucified!

These cults are man-centered practices that eventually leave us feeling empty. The Truth is, "The living Christ saves dying men." Most cults are not concerned with men's souls, they are concerned with themselves. When we accept the premise that there is no absolute authority, we become the absolute authority. We make up a god and worship him. The world today is becoming more and more of this type of so-called Christian. It is not founded on the God of the Bible but the forces of darkness. What are we to do? God has the answer:

And the Lord's slave must not engage in heated disputes but be kind toward all, an apt teacher, patient, correcting opponents with gentleness. Perhaps God will grant them repentance and then knowledge of the truth and they will come to their senses and escape the devil's trap where they are held captive to do his will. 2 Timothy 2:24-26 (NET)

When a person joins any group that denies the centrality of the Gospel, they are in a cult. Plain and simple. When our churches, Bible studies, self-study, and even worship music veers from the Gospel, we are not coming to grips with the problems of the day and meeting them head on with the Truth that rescues and saves lost souls. Many people leave the church because many never found the Truth of God's Word when they came looking. Then cults are there, waiting, with doors wide open, sucking up those who never learned about Biblical historic Christianity from the pulpit. The cults will use the right terminology to deceive multitudes. *For false messiahs and false prophets will appear and perform great signs and wonders to deceive, if possible, even the elect.* Matthew 24:24 (NET) If our Christian churches won't meet the needs of the spiritually hungry, the cults will feed them hearty lies that seem to satisfy.

Being a Christian is not about having an unholy lust for the supernatural/mystical. It's about knowing the Truth. In the 1970's-1980's, Satanism was renamed "New Age". Its roots are in eastern mysticism, and the attempt is to bypass the mind. They teach of a third eye, which gives spiritual light into a mystical universe. The New Age is a compilation of pagan beliefs and practices. They believe they can create reality by what they believe. They attempt to influence supernatural forces with their will and/or psyche. These cults, as well as all sinful behavior, build bridges into and out of the spirit realm where Satan and his demons are. We are not to be ignorant of these schemes. (2 Corinthians 2:11) These are not small, inconsequential things that are happening. Witchcraft even has many cousins such as fortune telling, Ouija boards, Eastern meditation rituals, etc…any practice that dabbles in a power or source other than Jesus Christ is biblically wrong. We don't want to give demons access into our lives by being involved in these things. We have to be on guard because many times they can look like God. Satan masquerades as an angel of light. (2 Corinthians 11:14)

Zen Buddhism is a major world religion today with over 150 million people. It appeals to the American mind by offering nirvana to people, seeing God as a reflection of man. They believe all creation shares in the nature of God. Zen does nothing for the world. It is egocentric. They believe there is unity in identity…they look within. Sin is not dealt with. 1 John 1:8 (NET) says, *If we say we do not bear the guilt of sin, we are deceiving ourselves and the truth is not in us.* It's only when we look to the Cross that sin is conquered. Zen Buddhists follow the noble 8-fold path and there is a chance to do whatever you want because you decide with your own personal enlightenment. This radically opposes the Lord Jesus. This religion is about self-love, and they are parasites that draw everything from society. They don't offer Jesus to the world. They detach, float along, and believe that "the unconscious is the ultimate reality." John 17:3 says, *Now this is eternal life—that they know you, the only true God, and Jesus Christ, whom you sent.* Eastern cults don't know God.

Many times, we can be totally unaware of what comes out of eastern cults…Yoga being one of those practices that's very popular even in the Christian community today. When we don't understand the history behind something, we can unknowingly get caught up in it. God's Word tells us, *Therefore, dear friends, since you have been forewarned, be on your guard that you do not get led astray by the error of these unprincipled men and fall from your firm grasp on the truth. But grow in the grace and knowledge of our Lord and Savior Jesus Christ. To him be the honor both now and on that eternal day.* 2 Peter 3:17-18 (NET) That is what we are doing here in this chapter, and I am so thankful for the teachings of Walter Martin while researching the cults. Through Martin's study, ministry, and teachings on cults, we are able to grow in the grace and knowledge of our Lord.

Now, back to yoga…some think yoga is simply physical for strengthening and improving flexibility. Actually, it is an ancient practice derived from India, believed to be the path to spiritual growth and enlightenment. Yoga means "union", and the yoga philosophy makes no division between God and man. It again, is egocentric...self-worship cloaked as high-level spirituality. Being in an egocentric cult is about the happiness of self instead of going into all the world with the Gospel of Jesus Christ so that all can come to repentance.

Can yoga be used as simply a form of exercise and not spiritually based? It's dangerous territory...leaving the participant open to deception with dark forces that long to turn people away from the true God. Discernment is needed when considering yoga and such...even when wanting to adapt these things to a Christian worldview. Hindu authorities have said there is no Hinduism without yoga, and there is no yoga without Hinduism. We are not to be involved in Hinduism...they have millions of gods with Brahman being supreme. Yoga is a $10 billion industry with 36 million people taking part in it. In an attempt to make it more palatable, Holy Yoga, as it's now called, has moved into our churches. Some claim to use it to manage stress by chanting Bible verses instead of the names of Hindu deities. But since yoga was originally used by pagans, the philosophy of yoga is fundamentally unbiblical. Our focus is to be on the Savior, not self. Holy Yoga comes close to Christian mysticism by exalting experience over traditional prayer and the reading of Scripture. The methods used in yoga such as visualization, controlled breathing, and chanting to clear the mind and connect with God is not taught in Scripture. It is a mind-altering technique used in the New Age movement. As Christians, we should not be using anything from eastern religions in an attempt to truly hear from God. Yoga is a dangerous exercise that Christians should avoid. (If this causes you unease, please, do your own research. Be a Berean.) It's not how we see it, but how God sees it! Our motivation should never be how we can adapt these things to Christianity, but how we can honor God in all that we do and all that we choose not to do.

Therefore "come out from their midst, and be separate," says the Lord, "and touch no unclean thing, and I will welcome you."
2 Corinthians 6:17 (NET)

How do we know that we are surrendered to Christ and not attached to one of these cults...unaware that we are weakening our faith and causing us to be oppressed? We can ask ourselves, what kind of fruit am I bearing in my walk with Christ? Am I bearing the Fruit of the Spirit with Jesus as the Vine? Does my peace come from the one true God? Is the Holy Spirit my true Guide and Comforter? Christianity is not mind-altering, but instead it is an internal transformation that is holy and right when we are born again into the family of God. *Hold to the standard of sound words that you heard from me and do so with the faith and love that are in Christ Jesus. Protect that good thing entrusted to you, through the Holy Spirit who lives within us.* 2 Timothy 1:13-14 (NET)

We need to be familiar with the Truth of God's Word to recognize the lies coming at us every day! The Word is our anchor point...pure and simple. *We have this hope as an anchor for the soul, sure and steadfast...* Hebrews 6:19 (NET) To know the Gospel well is to be protected with the Armor of God. To have the helmet of salvation firmly secured to protect our minds is essential. To know what we believe about salvation and why we believe it is huge! Jude warned us: *For certain men have secretly slipped in among you—men who long ago were marked out for the condemnation I am about to describe—ungodly men who have turned the grace of our God into a license for evil and who deny our only Master and Lord, Jesus Christ.* Jude 4 (NET) Always look for the doctrine of the Trinity when being taught. Always look for the truth of salvation being by grace through faith in Jesus Christ alone. Always understand the Cross and resurrection of Jesus Christ are essential, and His return is imminent. We need to be careful who the influencers are in our lives. Who are we listening to? Learning from? And are we being Bereans? If the large crowds are going one way, if the world is loving it...ask if it's the right way? Repent, if it is not, and get back to the narrow path that leads to our Mighty God. If passion is winning out over reality, dig into the Word. Soak in the Truth, and not in the excitement of some worldly idea. When we have come to know the Truth, we won't be fascinated with what the cults are offering.

The Gospel is the dividing line between Christianity and all cults. Biblical Christianity focuses on knowing God through His Word, and communion with the Holy Spirit through prayer. Christian mysticism is not so much a doctrine but a method of thought, elevating experiential knowledge. Remember, we don't need to know all about these cults, we need to know about Christ. So if the

Gospel is not being taught, and learned, we are vulnerable. We must all be warned: *But false prophets arose among the people, just as there will be false teachers among you. These false teachers will infiltrate your midst with destructive heresies, even to the point of denying the Master who bought them. As a result, they will bring swift destruction on themselves.* 2 Peter 2:1 (NET) The enemy is out to steal, kill, and destroy. Jesus came to give us life. (John 10:10) Guess who's running the cults? Certainly not our God. The enemy is! And he wants to destroy us! We shouldn't be surprised when the Word says, *And many will follow their debauched lifestyles. Because of these false teachers, the way of truth will be slandered.* 2 Peter 2:2 (NET) The enemy is doing his best to get us to deny the Master who bought us! *...you who believe see his value, but for those who do not believe, the stone that the builders rejected has become the cornerstone, and a stumbling-stone and a rock to trip over. They stumble because they disobey the word, as they were destined to do.* 1 Peter 2:7-8 (NET)

We can observe this stumbling in so many ways today. It's even moving into our worship music when the beat, the lyrics, and the performance take center stage over Jesus being exalted. True worship points us to the Truth of Scripture. Also, many are involved in something call QAnon, thinking evil will be exposed and eradicated here on earth. They are trying to get ahead of what God is doing and wishes to reveal. These are useless speculations taking up way too much time in a Christian's life. Another large movement is the NAR, New Apostolic Reformation. This is the spiritual version of QAnon. This group emphasizes experience over Scripture, mysticism over doctrine, and are attempting to pursue cultural and political control in society. There are many followers of the NAR who are not aware and/or unwilling to admit to even being a part of it. There is also the Word of Faith movement that most of us are familiar with. This group tries to treat God as a mechanism to be manipulated. The Charismatic and Pentecostal churches need to be careful in this respect, and not seek experience over Jesus. The verse in Luke 10:20 (NET) says, *"Nevertheless, do not rejoice that the spirits submit to you, but rejoice that your names stand written in heaven."* Let's all take Matthew 7:22 (NET) as a warning, *"On that day, many will say to me, 'Lord, Lord, didn't we prophesy in your name, and cast out demons in your name, and do many powerful deeds in your name?'"* Of course, we are to minister to others, but we are not to go beyond what is written, and not get into fanaticism.

True Biblical meditation/prayer is also something we need to take note of, sadly. We are not to repeat mantras (vain repetitions) that alter our consciences into a translated state, trying to experience God's presence. These mantras can cause a Dopamine release in our brains. It is sometimes called "Mindfulness Meditation." It is a self-focused type of prayer. True, godly prayer is a quiet, private time with a thoughtful concentration on God's Word. During this godly time, we can allow the Word to penetrate our heart and change our life.

Psalm 1:2 (NET) says, *Instead he finds pleasure in obeying the Lord's commands; he meditates on his commands day and night. This is where God's blessings are found.*

If we have stumbled into anything mentioned in this chapter, or anything that I have missed that is less than the Word of God, let's repent, confess, and get back to the Truth. All cults deny Jesus Christ as God's only way of saving souls. But God is merciful. He wants that none should perish but that all should come to repentance. (2 Peter 3:9) Christianity is not a religion; it is having a relationship with God by receiving Jesus Christ as the Savior/Messiah by grace through faith. Jesus is the fulfillment of both religion and spirituality. He is the standard of Truth and all-sufficient.

What we have been taking a look at here in this chapter can in no way cover every area of where all these little dabs of cults are trying to do us under. They have invaded Christ's territory, and new ways of deception are forming every day. When we are in doubt, we are to pray, be in the Word, study, surround ourselves with other strong Bible-believing Christians, and be Bereans. The more Truth we soak in, the less alluring the tempting lies of the enemy will be, and the less we will fall for his schemes. Our Lord is sufficient in all areas. The enemy's day is coming…but until then *…be strong in the grace that is in Christ Jesus. And what you heard me say in the presence of many witnesses entrust to faithful people who will be competent to teach others as well.* 2 Timothy 2:1-2 (NET)

Let's Pray:
Father in Heaven, You desire that we trust in You alone, that we

worship You alone, and that we believe in Your Son as the only way to Heaven. Guide us by Your Holy Spirit, and help us to avoid these pitfalls in the world, and to keep our focus on what is true, right, and holy. In the powerful name of Jesus we pray. Amen.

To review, so you don't have to go digging later on…

Religion: A belief in God or gods to be worshipped.

Biblical Christianity: Focuses on knowing God through His Word and communion with the Holy Spirit through prayer.

Charismatic/Pentecostal Movement: An emphasis on dreams, visions, feelings, experiences, and new revelation. Some go beyond what is written in the Word of God.

Word of Faith: Can be known to treat God as a mechanism that can be manipulated, which is witchcraft and sorcery.

"Christian" Mysticism: Mystical practices and theory within Christianity. Not so much doctrine as a method of thought…elevating experiential knowledge.

New Age: A compilation of pagan beliefs and practices. Roots in Eastern religions. Attempt to bypass the mind. All is God. Create their own reality. Attempt to influence supernatural forces with one's own will or psyche.

Witchcraft: Satan's counterfeit to holy spirituality. Many cousins such as horoscopes, fortune telling, Ouija boards, and Eastern meditation rituals. Any power that dabbles in the occult or a power source other than the Lord Jesus Christ is witchcraft.

Paganism: Any religious ceremony, act, or practice that is not distinctly Christian.

Spiritism: Not a religion but a philosophy and "way of life". Value scientific research over worship. Affirm moral living but not compatible with the Bible. It is spiritually dangerous.

Spirituality: The quality or fact of being spiritual, non-physical, or predominately spiritual in character as shown in thought, life, etc...spiritual tendency or tone. Focused on spiritual things and the spiritual world instead of physical and earthly things.

Divination: To uncover hidden knowledge by supernatural means. Tea leaves, tarot cards, star charts, and more.

Magic: Magicians are illusionists (tricks). Real magic draws on the occult, demonic power, lying wonders.

Satanism: Not easily defined. It is in contrast to Christianity...disagree on very fundamental principles. Satanists argue among themselves whether Satan even exists and whether they are worshipping him or themselves. Confused and bound by lies.

Christianity: Not a religion. It is having a right relationship with God by receiving Jesus Christ as Savior-Messiah, by grace through faith. Jesus is Lord; and is the fulfillment of both religion and spirituality. He is the standard of Truth.

Meditation: Thoughtful contemplation or reflection for a period of time. (Psalm 1:2)

Christian Devotional Meditation (CDM): An attempt to understand one's self and focus on God's presence using a mantra like, "God loves me". Akin to visualization, contemplative prayer, mindfulness meditation—Eastern Mysticism.

True Biblical Meditation: A quiet, private time, thoughtful concentration on God's Word, focusing on Scripture, what it means, and how it applies to your life. Allowing it to penetrate the heart and change your life.

Transcendental Meditation: Shifting your conscience to a trans-like state, experiencing "God's" presence. Dopamine is released. It is a non-ordinary state of mind.

Dream Interpretation: Happens spontaneously by the Spirit of God. Not systematically. It is not a fixed, spiritual science to be discovered. Not listed as a gift.

Egocentric: An unholy lust for the supernatural to better your life.

Acupuncture: Origin is Chinese Taoism. Yin/negative. Yang/positive. It is a mechanism from Taoism to bring the yin and yang of the body into harmony with Tao. Dangerous in that it is a counterfeit religion.

Yoga: Yoga means "union", and the yoga philosophy makes no division between God and man. It is egocentric...self-worship cloaked as high-level spirituality. Hindu authorities have said there is no Hinduism without yoga, and there is no yoga without Hinduism.

Catholic Church: There are sincere Catholics who love the Lord, but the doctrines themselves point to a work-based religion. Many extrabiblical practices have been added to create a different religion out of Christianity such as purgatory and a focus more on Mary than Jesus.

NAR—New Apostolic Reformation: Actually, a very old approach in this unbiblical religious movement emphasizing experience over Scripture, and modern-day apostles over the plain text of the Bible. They have some basis in Scripture concerning spiritual gifts but go beyond what is written. This movement includes a pursuit of cultural and political control in society. Goal is to retake control of the earth.

QAnon: A political version of the NAR...the evil will be exposed and eradicated here on earth. Thus, our planet will get better. Getting ahead of what God wants to reveal.

Worship Music: True worship music exalts the Truth of Scripture and is dedicated to honoring God. The beat, lyrics, arrangement, and performance should not take center stage over Jesus Christ being the

One exalted. Our soulish satisfaction should not become the star. Any song with unbiblical/false teaching should be rejected.

Chapter Fifteen Reflections

1) This is dark territory. But with our focus on the true Jesus Christ, there is no need to fear. Jesus is far above every evil spirit, demon, fallen angel, or any other evil spiritual being that exists. (Page 241)

2) The *goal* of cults is to distract us from God's *goal*. Satan wants to get us off course, keep us from salvation, and hold us there for as long as possible…sadly, sometimes he does so leading people right into eternal destruction in Hell for those who will not come into a grace-filled relationship with Jesus Christ. (Page 243)

3) Who is being led astray? It is said that 80 percent of those in cults come from a background of Baptist, Presbyterians, Lutherans, etc… Yes, churches where the Word of God should be being taught in full. But is it? Is the Word being taught? That's the question, and the problem. (Page 244)

4) Our Father has made the Gospel pure and simple to remember and share. Cults make things complicated and confusing. A cult is a social group that is defined by its unusual religious, spiritual, or philosophical beliefs. In Christianity, a cult is a new religious movement which has Christianity in its background but deviates theologically from what the Word of God has proclaimed. (Page 245)

5) We are to be on guard though, as Jesus warned us in Matthew 7:15 (NET) *"Watch out for false prophets, who come to you in sheep's clothing but inwardly are voracious wolves."* Many can look, act, and sound genuine, but they are really savage wolves in sheep's clothing. They can lead moral and ethical lives, but still be at war with God. (Page 246)

6) …one thing that all cults have in common, from the first to the last, is they **deny Jesus Christ as God's only way of saving souls.** This is where we are to look first and also last when watching out for these false religions. They can even refer to Jesus as Lord, but the meaning has changed. They are talking about another Jesus, another gospel, and it is counterfeit—they make up an imitation Jesus with the intent to deceive. (Page 246)

7) Cults of any kind are dangerous. We are to *have mercy on those who waver; save others by snatching them out of the fire; have mercy on others, coupled with a fear of God, hating even the clothes stained by the flesh.* Jude 22-23 (NET) It is so important to preach the full Word of God from the pulpit. We need to hear teachings about the Cross, the blood, repentance, prayer, the Word, and how to walk in God's Truth in today's world. (Page 248)

8) The Gospel is the dividing line between Christianity and all cults. Biblical Christianity focuses on knowing God through His Word, and communion with the Holy Spirit through prayer. Christian mysticism is not so much a doctrine but a method of thought, elevating experiential knowledge. Remember, we don't need to know all about these cults, we need to know about Christ. (Page 265)

NOTES

CHAPTER SIXTEEN

SUFFERING

As we finish with this last chapter on the subject of suffering, and the deception found in it, it will be a bit more personal. Suffering has come to us all, and it is included in this Truth Journey because little dabs of deception in our pain can do us under...can hinder us on our Christian walk if we're not made aware of what the enemy is doing. I hope by now our discernment has increased, and many of the lies we believed in other areas have been exposed and can be expelled from our lives. Now, we'll do the same with suffering

I like this verse out of Philippians 3:10-11 (NET) which says: *My aim is to know him, to experience the power of his resurrection, to share in his sufferings, and to be like him in his death, and so, somehow, to attain to the resurrection from the dead.* Let this be the goal of all those who call Jesus, Savior. We are to know Jesus, personally. We are to experience the power of the Holy Spirit who lives within us. We are to share in Jesus' sufferings. We are to die a physical death like He did, coming face to face with our Father in Heaven, and attain a resurrected body when the Day of the Lord arrives. This is our great Hope found in Jesus Christ, our Messiah.

But, until then, and along the way...it will be a bumpy road. There will be suffering. All the things stated above are welcomed by us...knowing Jesus, experiencing His power, and being resurrected from the dead. It all sounds great except the suffering and death parts. Unfortunately, like taxes, they can't be avoided. The death rate is 100 percent. I would have to say the suffering rate is the same…no one escapes either. But dying itself, going from your last breath here on Earth to your first breath there in Heaven, is going to be glorious!

When my son was down to his last couple days on Earth after battling leukemia for five-and-a half years, God gave us a wonderful blessing. Phil left for a bit and came back…from Heaven. I was there with him as he was lying in his bed. When he told me he saw a light, I told him to go toward the light. The next thing I knew, Phil's head went back into his pillow and he was taking in a deep breath, exclaiming, "Oh! I thought I was finished! I don't want to be here anymore. I saw Heaven, and it was so beautiful!" It was a moment I will never forget. It was a gift from God that saw me through some of my hardest days of living without Phil…knowing he was where he most wanted to be. But one other thing Phil told me, that I will never forget, was, "Mom, the devil has been lying to me. It doesn't hurt to die." The devil will lie to us every day of our lives. But on this day, with my son, the devil's lie was exposed. God showed Phil he had nothing to fear when he left his sick body behind. Yes, cancer had been a painful and awful process—all the years of treatment that Phil had to endure were hard, but the moment of transitioning from this world to the next, would not be. That was a lie from the pit of Hell aimed at a young boy who loved Jesus.

While living here on Earth, things can be difficult. Many days are not easy to endure. Suffering is not pleasant, and the process of dying can be very painful. But God puts it all to good use. The enemy would rather we not understand that the tough times are a preparation for meeting our Savior. It is a delicate refining process known only to our Father in Heaven. It's a process that helps us appreciate all Jesus died to give us even before our last day comes. For many, it is the suffering that brings us into an initial relationship with Jesus. For others, suffering is what is useful to draw us closer to Jesus even after having already become a Christian at some earlier point in our lives. Trials can show us God's strength when we are weak, His eternal Hope when all earthly hope seems lost, and His light that shines in the darkest of times. Yes, trials and tribulations have a great purpose that the enemy would prefer we not take notice of. Satan would like us to believe his lies about suffering. Probably the number one lie is that God doesn't love us. But God is love. It's not what He does, it's who He is. Hence, we are going to take notice of Satan's lies in this chapter as we walk out the end of this Truth Journey together—until like James, you, too, can *consider it nothing but joy when you fall into all sorts of trials.*

To authentically talk about suffering, it helps to have been through our own trials. That is why I will share some of what we walked through with our son throughout this chapter. To know that someone has "been there" and has come through it and out the other side is what testimonies are about. It's when we talk about all the "monies" that come from all the "tests" (Testimonies), and all that God did in the midst of them…that we see the faithfulness of God along the way. This is what we come to know in the trials. We are going to get rid of those dabs of deception as together we learn to consider suffering *nothing but joy.* If that seems impossible right now, I understand. But, let's begin to dissect this subject and find the Truth hidden in it.

I'll start with the story of Elizabeth Elliot. Her husband, Jim, was murdered in 1956 at the age of 28 while doing missionary work attempting to evangelize the Huaorani people of Ecuador. As a young widow with a small daughter, Elizabeth grieved deeply. But she didn't grieve as one who had no Hope (1 Thess. 4:13). Elizabeth went on with her life, walking it out with Jesus…and He brought her through it. Was her suffering then over? No. She married again some 18 or so years later, only to have her second husband pass away from cancer after just a few years of marriage. Elizabeth did marry a third time and her husband outlived her, but she suffered with Alzheimer's the last ten years of her life. Her husband cared for her throughout. Hers was not an easy life, but it was a life dedicated to the Lord, Jesus. Elizabeth summed up suffering in a very simple way. She said suffering is: "Having what you don't want or wanting what you don't have." I believe if we think about that…we will find that to be true. In her testimony, Elizabeth said that, "Jim's absence thrust me, hurried me, forced me to God…my hope and my only refuge. And I learned in that experience who God is in a way I could never have known otherwise." In her heartbreak, Elizabeth got to know the heart of God and His compassion toward her through it all.

Some books today will tell us we are to "Have our best life now".

This is deception. What we are living in now is the worst of life we will ever experience as believers in Jesus Christ. This world is as far away from God as we will ever be, and as hard as it will ever get…although God never leaves us nor forsakes us. One day, we will meet our Lord face to face and live with Him forever in our Heavenly Home. This, here on Earth, is as bad as our suffering gets for believers. Our best life is truly waiting for us once we leave here where all our suffering will be finished. This is not our best life, nor should we expect it to be. We are told in 1 John 2:15 (NET): *Do not love the world or the things in the world.* Why? Because in 1 John 2:17 (NET) it says, *And the world is passing away with all its desires, but the person who does the will of God remains forever.* Our future, our Hope, is not found here in this life other than putting our faith in Jesus Christ as our Savior. One day, all this will be gone, all the pain, all the suffering, all the tears. 1 John 2:17 (NET) repeats this: *And the world is passing away with all its desires, but the person who does the will of God remains forever.* This is talking about our best life THEN! We will forever remain with God one day! We will be back in the Garden, so to speak, where there are no thorns or thistles like we experience here: *…the ground is cursed because of you; in painful toil you will eat of it all the days of your life. It will produce thorns and thistles for you…* Genesis 3:17b-18 (NET)

Let's face it…we live in a messed-up world. We mess it up. But God sent us help and there's Hope! *And, after you have suffered for a little while, the God of all grace who called you to his eternal glory in Christ will himself restore, confirm, strengthen, and establish you.* 1 Peter 5:10 (NET) The Father sent His Son, Jesus, to save us, to wash us, from all this mess. Jesus was born as a baby and Isaiah prophesied about Him: *For He grew up before Him like a tender shoot, and like a root out of parched ground; He has no stately form or majesty that we should look upon Him, nor appearance that we should be attracted to Him. He was despised and forsaken of men, A man of sorrows and acquainted with grief;* Isaiah 53:2-3a (NASB) Jesus came into this painful, messed-up world to help us get out of here alive. Really! Not that we won't die a physical death. But when we leave here, when we depart from our deathbed, we will be more alive than ever! This is all just a shadow of what is to come! That's why our son, Phil, was astounded at the beauty he saw in Heaven when he left here for a few brief moments!

Therefore do not let anyone judge you with respect to food or drink, or in the matter of a feast, new moon, or Sabbath days—these are only the shadow of the things to come, but the reality is Christ! Colossians 2:16-17 (NET) This isn't it! Heaven is! This is a shadow of the glorious future God has planned for His children, those who call on Jesus to save them! But in the meantime, what we are living in right now is sorrow and suffering—the very things Jesus experienced on this Earth. God is not asking us to go through anything that His Son did not endure as Jesus walked out His life, straight toward the Cross at Calvary. There, Jesus suffered the wrath of His Father, poured out upon Him, crushing Him, and dying of a broken heart for the sins of the world. While on Earth, Jesus knew thirst, betrayal, persecution, pain, torture, loss, grief, heartache, tiredness, even anger…righteous anger as His Father's House was turned into a den of thieves. And Jesus knows physical death, personally, as His body died that day when the sky darkened and the veil in the Temple tore in two. Jesus also knows resurrection…the very power that lives within us, the Holy Spirit, raised Jesus from the dead. Jesus conquered sin and death. Are we going to suffer in our life? Yes. Are we going to die? Yes. Are our loved ones going to suffer and die? Yes. But can we have great Hope in it all? Yes! Because of Jesus! *Moreover if the Spirit of the one who raised Jesus from the dead lives in you, the one who raised Christ from the dead will also make your mortal bodies alive through his Spirit who lives in you.* Romans 8:11 (NET)

How does this look in our own lives? Isn't there an easier way? We all want to avoid suffering, don't we? Yes. But when our soul is down, that is when God lifts us up. When we are struggling, we are more apt to call for help. When we call for that help, Jesus is there. Paul wrote in 2 Timothy 1:8 (NET): *So do not be ashamed of the testimony about our Lord or of me, a prisoner for his sake, but by God's power accept your share of suffering for the gospel.* Sometimes our suffering is brought on by human error, by wrong choices, by our own stupidity. There is no honor in that, but there is forgiveness and mercy and redemption. But many times, our suffering is brought on for the sake of the Gospel, as was Paul's. Sadly, too many teachings from the pulpit and elsewhere today are only trying to make us feel good. But in doing, so they aren't teaching the full Truth. Then, when we don't feel so good, when it seems God has "failed" us and isn't "loving" us…we wonder what happened because this isn't what we heard about on Sunday morning. Those deceptive teachings can actually keep us from the real Jesus, from the One who was personally acquainted with grief and experienced pain. This Jesus is the One we can trust—the One who knows how we feel because He felt it, too. This true Jesus is our Advocate. He sits at the right hand of our Father in Heaven, and He is the One who will be handed the scroll one day, opening the seals, bringing this world to an end, and ushering us into the New Heavens, and the New Earth. (Revelation 5:7) There is no easy way through this life. But take heart, your life looks just like everyone else's…a life that is filled with hardship, trials, sadness, and grief because we live in a fallen world. But, also, when our lives are lived for Jesus, we can be filled with joy in those things because hope, peace, and a wonderful eternal future are there for us. But how do we walk this out when things get really hard? We stay in the Word! We pray, we fellowship with other believers, we keep believing in and sharing the Gospel, and we keep putting one foot in front of the other through good times and bad.

Not long ago, I was a pre-tribulation rapture supporter. I believed we would be leaving this Earth in the rapture before the hard end-times stuff really hits the fan. I've changed my mind. It is a woman's prerogative. As I took a closer look at what Scripture had to say, mainly Matthew 24 and 2 Thessalonians 2, I saw that we Christians could very well still be here living through the last days on this Earth. We quite possibly will experience the intense suffering that will come, and we could possibly see the antichrist rise to power. I don't know what that will look like for Christians, and I could be wrong. There may be a pre-tribulation rapture. But if not, there may be a "passing by" of some of the hardships for us as the Israelites experienced when death passed by their doors in Egypt by placing blood on their doorframes. That may be what is talked about in the letter to the church in Philadelphia in Revelation 3:10 (NET) where it says, *Because you have kept my admonition to endure steadfastly, I will also keep you from the hour of testing that is about to come on the whole world to test those who live on the earth.* This is a very important verse used by those who are in support of the pre-tribulation rapture, saying the "keep you from the hour of testing" means we won't be here. I hope they are right. One pastor who believes in the pre-tribulation belief said, "I'll explain it to you on the way up." That would be wonderful. But what if he is wrong? Are we being prepared to live in the suffering of the last days while awaiting our Savior who will return on His white horse ready for war? Will that be when our trials really do end and we are raptured out of here? Only time will tell, and I may well change my mind again, maybe to a mid-tribulation rapture happening if new information is revealed to me. These are not hills to die on, as far as I know, but simply different interpretations of Scripture. The Gospel stands steadfast in the midst of these secondary issues. All this to say, no one wants to suffer, but we do. Perhaps the suffering of today will just increase slowly, or quickly, until we meet Jesus? Maybe all the suffering we will endure isn't only found in the chapters of Revelation. However, and whatever happens, we can know that God is with us. This is not said to be a downer, but to be a realist, knowing *these are only the shadow of the things to come, but the reality is Christ!*

Where do we go from here? Many times, to go forward, we have to look back. I know this goes against so much of what is happening in America today with those trying to eradicate our history. But history teaches us things. I heard it said, "God isn't just wanting to save America, He is wanting to save Americans." I would add, Danes, Germans, Africans, Australians, Koreans, and everyone He has created. God was always wanting His people to remember what He brought them through as an encouragement for their future and how He would provide. Even Job found a deeper relationship with God after his time of intense suffering. There are few who have had it as bad as Job. God knew in the hurting there would be helping. When the pain of this life cuts deep into our soul, the love of God can penetrate more deeply, too. I found that to be true with the death of our 16-year-old son from leukemia in 2001. I'd never felt such pain. The grief came in tsunami-size waves in the years that followed. As Elizabeth Elliot said about suffering…it is, "Having what you don't want or wanting what you don't have." I wanted what I didn't have, even though I still had so much. Maybe it's like that original Garden problem, *Then the Lord God commanded the man, "You may freely eat fruit from every tree of the orchard, but you must not eat from the tree of the knowledge of good and evil, for when you eat from it you will surely die."* Genesis 2:16-17 (NET) Adam and Eve had everything, but they wanted what they couldn't have. After our son's death, I still had two other wonderful sons, a great husband, a large family, a church family, and a faith that was sustaining me…but I didn't have my youngest son. I was MISERABLE!! It cut to the core of my being as nothing else could. Grief did as it had done in Elizabeth's life, it "thrust me, hurried me, forced me to God…my Hope and my only refuge." Yes, I, too, was deep in a pit of miry clay that seem to stick to my feet as I simply went out for a walk. In those days I walked for sanity's sake while listening to worship music. I tried to regain some peace that seemed to have been ripped out of me when Phil went Home to Heaven. But even in walking, my feet felt like lead, my gait was so slow, it seemed I had nothing left, and yet I had everything. I was so blind, but now I see. God was teaching me how to live life without someone I loved dearly by falling in deeper love with the One who now held Phil in His hands. I also had to be happier for my son being in Heaven than I was sad for me living without him here. It took a great deal of time, and a great deal of effort. Grief is hard work. Suffering is not for wimps. I needed the Gospel like never before…the Good News of Jesus Christ. I knew nothing else would see me through it. That is the great Truth found in suffering.

Now this is the gospel message we have heard from him and announce to you: God is light, and in him there is no darkness at all. If we say we have fellowship with him and yet keep on walking in the darkness, we are lying and not practicing the truth. But if we walk in the light as he himself is in the light, we have fellowship with one another and the blood of Jesus his Son cleanses us from all sin.
1 John 1:5-7 (NET)

I needed God's light, desperately. I quickly slipped into dark places when the waves of grief came. They pounded hard, they knocked me to the ground. I wailed. I wanted to rip my clothing in mourning. I was in agony and there wasn't anything that could change it. My son was gone. I was in my early 40's. I would probably live the next 40 years without him. I told Phil so, encouraging him that he wouldn't be missing us because time in Heaven is different than time on Earth. I couldn't breathe when the waves of grief came. I gasped for air. I didn't want to be walking in darkness. My only escape was to practice walking in the Truth. But to go after it with lead in my shoes was so difficult…so tiring. I lived in the Psalms for months on end. The enemy tried to overpower me with his lies. I resisted, although I do remember a time when I lived without Hope for three days—I must have decided to let go of it. I don't remember now. But I do remember how it felt. I never want to feel that way again. It was a desperate time. After that, I would cling to Hope, if it was all that I could do.

Now by this we know that we have come to know God: if we keep his commandments. The one who says "I have come to know God" and yet does not keep his commandments is a liar, and the truth is not in such a person.
1 John 2:3-4 (NET)

In our times of suffering there are decisions to be made. Holding tightly to our Hope in Jesus is a big one. Suffering helps us know if the Truth is truly in us. Are we really willing to carry our cross and follow Jesus to the depths of our being? Or, have we just been playing church? Playing a Christian? Playing with faith? This doesn't mean we don't cry, mourn, hurt…but it means we allow God to bring us through it and heal us in what we can't change/escape. God will grow us in His time and in His way. How do we keep God's commandments and know that His Truth is in us? We love God and others. That is where we start. Can we be angry at God? Yes. God can take it, and He understands. I remember telling God how much I hated what had happened, but I loved Him. Do we stay angry at God? No. This would only play into the hands of the enemy and harm us more.

As for you, what you have heard from the beginning must remain in you. If what you heard from the beginning remains in you, you also will remain in the Son and in the Father. Now this is the promise that he himself made to us: eternal life. These things I have written to you about those who are trying to deceive you.
1 John 2:24-26 (NET)

In the worst of times, our enemy will be there…continually trying to deceive us. Satan will do whatever he can to keep us away from the Word, from God, and from the Hope we have in Jesus. We have to stay attached to the Vine, Jesus, through it all. It's the only way to combat the lies during our suffering seasons.

I believe in eternal life in Heaven, and I taught my son about eternal life through Jesus Christ. Phil understood what was happening with his cancer, and he believed if God didn't heal him on this Earth he would be going to Heaven. Phil was baptized seven months to the day before he arrived in his heavenly home… God's perfect plan. I was with Phil when he left for Heaven, along with my husband and one of our sons. I told him good-bye and that I would see him again. After Phil was gone, I didn't want the enemy to fill me full of his lies about all that had happened…but he sure tried. So many prayed for our family during that time. Prayers are powerful and appreciated. Unfortunately, when we are on the outside of what someone is suffering through, we can't always know how intimately God is working on the inside providing what is needed…answering all those prayers. We need to keep praying, even when we aren't sure they are making a difference, because they do!

Let's change course here for a few minutes and talk about how our worldview really affects how we go through suffering in this life. Pastor Voddie Baucham said we need to ask ourselves four questions to determine our worldview.

1) Who am I?
2) Why am I here?
3) What's wrong with the world?
4) How can what is wrong be made right?

He went on to say if we answer these questions as the world would, it would be something like this:

1) Who? I'm here by a random evolutionary process.
2) Why? I'm here to get all I can…pursuing pleasure.
3) What? We are not educated or governed as we should be.
4) How? We need more education and government or therapy.

The difference is, believers go to God! But the world goes to man's ways to find some sort of utopia while here on earth. As Christians we are able to understand our world view with Biblical answers to these questions.

1) Who am I? We were created by God. We start with Who God is. Humanism starts with man.
2) Why am I here? We are here to glorify God and bring Him honor.
3) What is wrong in the world? Sin. There was a fall in the Garden. There are highly intelligent and educated people who are still evil. More education will not solve this problem.
4) How can what is wrong be made right? We have to be reconciled to God through Jesus' death on the Cross.

For God was pleased to have all his fullness dwell in the Son and through him to reconcile all things to himself by making peace through the blood of his cross—through him, whether things on Earth or things in heaven.
Colossians 1:19-20 (NET)

No matter what we are going through, we need to flee to Christ and cling to the Cross, because Jesus is our only Hope in this world. Too many times in the last century, the Gospel was not, and is not, being preached in our churches. Christianity has withered to a promise of a better life. That's a secular worldview. With a Biblical worldview, we can stand firm in our Who, Why, What, and How. As Christians, we can have solid answers. In many colleges, they now teach there is no absolute truth. We know that God is Truth. Not that we will understand all the intricacies of all our sufferings, but we know the One who does, and we can hold tightly to Him. When we start with God, life's difficult puzzle pieces will fall into place because each day of our life is known to God before it was ever lived by us. *Your eyes saw me when I was inside the womb. All the days ordained for me were recorded in your scroll before one of them came into existence. How difficult it is for me to fathom your thoughts about me, O God!* Psalm 139:16-17 (NET) When we start with man, we have no idea what the picture on the lid of the puzzle box even looks like. When we start with God, we know He does. He has seen the end from the beginning.

God has made everything fit beautifully in its appropriate time, but he has also placed ignorance in the human heart so that people cannot discover what God has ordained, from the beginning to the end of their lives.
Ecclesiastes 3:11 (NET)

Psalm 139 reminds me of the day I was out walking in my grief. I had taken a seat on a bench and was listening to the worship music coming through my headset. I got up to walk on just as the words in the song quoted this verse in Psalm 139:2, *You know when I sit down and when I get up.* How could I not smile through my tears in that moment knowing God was that intimately involved in my sorrow…watching my every sitting down and getting up? Did it take all my pain away? No. But I knew I was loved and cared for. One pastor said, "We don't come to Jesus for a happy lifestyle. We come because we have sinned against God and we need a Savior to save us from the wrath that is to come upon this world."

James is a book in the Bible that teaches us about suffering. James knows that tribulation drives a true Christian closer to Jesus. Writing 54 imperatives out of 108 verses, James doesn't mess around with our deceptive enemy. He tells us that God allows testing so we will become stronger and demonstrate the genuine nature of our faith. Is our faith real? Does it hold water?

"…but I have prayed for you, Simon, that your faith may not fail. When you have turned back, strengthen your brothers."
Luke 22:32 (NET)

The world is watching us as we suffer…they want to know if our God's grace is sufficient. After being born with a heart of stone, God replaces our heart with a heart of flesh so we will be sensitive to all that He has done and will do for all of eternity. This heart of flesh helps us accept God's love and help toward us in our suffering.

Consider it all joy, my brethren, when you encounter various trials, knowing that the testing of your faith produces endurance.
James 1:2-3 (NASB)

It is interesting to think that James had the same earthy parents as Jesus—Mary and Joseph raised more than one child. Jesus had half-siblings on this earth, and James was one of them. After James got to know his Brother as the Savior of the world, things changed in his heart, just like they will in ours as we come to know Jesus for who He really is. If we live our lives with a man-centered gospel, not knowing the true Jesus of the Bible and the full Gospel, and if we lack repentance, then when hard times come, we will lose our peace and joy. We won't understand that through the hard times, through sin and repentance, our hearts are being prepared, like soil, for the seed of faith to not only be planted, but to take deep root in our souls and grow.

James says we are to think about this, to *consider it nothing but joy*. James 1:2 (NET) He doesn't give us any wiggle room when he writes, "*nothing*". We are to have *joy*. Are we to understand that what God is doing in our life is the best way for it to be done? I believe so. God doesn't make mistakes. James assures us that *when,* not *if,* we fall into *all sorts of trials*—no one will escape. And our trials will have many facets to them…financial, emotional, spiritual, relational, etc… Why? James tells us through the Holy Spirit's inspiration…because it is *testing our faith* as God works on us in a special and unique way as only He can do…refining us…transforming us…getting us ready for meeting Him face to face. This is producing *endurance* in our lives that, in the end, will glorify God. We will shine as His bright lights in a dark world. We will be *perfect and complete*, and not lack *anything*. God is raising us up as His children. He is a perfect Father raising imperfect children in a fallen world. It's not an easy task. We want to throw a fit, scream about it, get what we want, and get it now! As God's child, I wanted to bang my head against the brick wall that stood between my son and myself and have it come tumbling down. I wanted Phil to be standing there when it did. I wanted Phil with me. But as it says about David's son in 2 Samuel 12:23 (NET): "*But now he is dead. Why should I fast? Am I able to bring him back at this point? I will go to him, but he cannot return to me!*" No amount of anything on my part could change what had happened. I needed to not resist it anymore. I needed to allow God to bring me through it and show me how it could best be used to glorify my Lord with each day of the 40 years I would continue to live without my son on this Earth. Instead of counting the days I live without Phil as a deficit, I look at each day as being one day closer to seeing him again. This can be an encouragement to others. Just yesterday, the woman waiting on our table told us her brother had just passed away. When I told her I was 19 years closer to seeing my son again, she said it changed her total outlook on living without her brother. She said it made her day. Praise God!

I have heard we can count these hardships we go through, all this suffering, as deposits in the checkbook of our life…not withdrawals even though things are missing. And as time passes, as endurance builds, as our faith is strengthened, as we grow older, we can begin to start looking back and see all that God has brought us through and how it has changed us and helped us to know Him more. In the beginning, it's so hard. Suffering can blind us for a time. It carries with it many tears, many unknowns. But hearts do heal…not with time alone, but with God and time together. There's a worship song that says, "He gives and takes away." In the beginning I could barely listen to it let alone sing it. Then it got to the point where I could hear it and not cry every time. Eventually I could sing those words softly and then later with greater intensity over time. I came to understand how God does give and take away. But the song goes on to say, "Blessed be the name of the Lord." I don't have to like it. I don't. I miss my son. But I am commanded to love the Lord my God with all my heart, with all my soul, and with all my strength. I work on that every day through repentance, prayer, and time in His Word. This is the only way to dispel the lies that still try to come against me years later. The enemy never gives up, but our God is greater!

Job 42:5 (NET) says, *"I had heard of you by the hearing of the ear, but now my eye has seen you."* We can sit in church on Sunday morning hearing great sermons about God and still be blind to Who He really is. For most of us, it's not until we have lived through some difficult things that we truly begin to see God and His goodness. Psalm 27:13-14 (NET) asks: *Where would I be if I did not believe I would experience the Lord's favor in the land of the living? Rely on the Lord! Be strong and confident! Rely on the Lord!*

How are we to rely on the Lord? How are we to be strong and confident? I was given a book by a good friend when our son was first diagnosed with leukemia at age 10½. The title was, "When

Heaven is Silent". It said, "Don't ask 'Why me'? Ask 'What now'?" Of course, the why me? Why our son? questions did come. I went to the "What now" by clinging to God's Word when lies and deception came full force. As I've written, I especially held onto John 9:2-4a (NLT) where Jesus is asked a question about the "Why." It says: *"Rabbi," his disciples asked him, "Why was this man born blind? Was it because of his own sins or his parents' sins?" "It was not because of his sins or his parents' sins," Jesus answered. "This happened so the power of God could be seen in him. We must quickly carry out the tasks assigned us by the one who sent us."* In just looking at that Scripture now, I see it says, *"we must quickly carry out the tasks assigned us."* Is our suffering an assignment? Perhaps it is. We can't always know the "why" in our suffering. God's Word says, *"Indeed, my plans are not like your plans, and my deeds are not like your deeds," says the Lord.* Isaiah 55:8 (NET) We can't always know the why, but we can know the Who.

Phil was our third son, and a surprise baby. With two sons, we thought we were finished. God had other plans when I became pregnant at a time when we didn't even have medical insurance— money was tight. But God provided in amazing ways. When Phil got sick, and when he was eventually escorted into Heaven after a five-and-a-half-year battle with cancer, it didn't make sense to me. Why had God given us this child, only to take him from us a short 16 years later? But now almost two decades later, I can see God so much better in the story He has written for us. Phil had his own assignment. Some of it, I can see now; some I am yet to see. But I'm confident that Phil's job was finished after 16 years, and then he got to go Home. In those 16 years he accomplished many things, one of which was changing my life forever. I could never again be a lukewarm Christian. I would live out the rest of my days with one foot in Heaven and one foot on Earth. I would be more interested in eternal life through Jesus Christ than ever before because of having a child who lives in Heaven. What the enemy wanted to use for harm was truly used for good because I love God and know I am called according to His purpose. (Romans 8:28)

Do not be conformed to this present world, but be transformed by the renewing of your mind, so that you may test and approve what is the will of God—what is good and well-pleasing and perfect.

Romans 12:2 (NET) When we are broken, God uses our shattered pieces to sculpt us into the likeness of His Son. *Evergreens will grow in place of thorn bushes, firs will grow in place of nettles; they will be a monument to the Lord, a permanent reminder that will remain.* Isaiah 55:13 (NET)

During this time in our country when monuments are being torn down so that what has happened in the past will be removed from our history, as it is said, it only begs history to repeat itself. We must move forward in life by learning from the past, from the hurts, from the suffering, and allow God to build upon what He is doing. We must allow God to heal us, teach us, and renew our minds to know Him more deeply. James 1:12 (NET) tells us: *Happy is the one who endures testing, because when he has proven to be genuine, he will receive the crown of life that God promised to those who love him.* Am I happy today? Yes. I am. The pain is gone but the waves of missing still come from time to time. We are never to forget, but we are to move on and live. I like something that was said during this Covid-19 time. An elderly gentleman said, "Don't keep me alive by keeping me from living." So many are shut in just trying to stay alive. I understand there are those who need to be careful. But that is what we sometimes do in grief…in hard times, and we have to be wise during those times to keep on living. We are tempted to isolate, to become a shut-in…I felt afraid to love deeply again because it might hurt too much if they were to die, too. Honestly, I didn't know if I could take another blow like that in my life. I wanted my heart to shut down, and to not be vulnerable again…to spare myself from future pain. That would have been wrong. That is not living. The enemy wanted me to believe his lies…to believe that my God wouldn't be sufficient. That's deception. God is more than enough. Thankfully, through the years, I resisted that temptation. I did open my heart to love again. I now love six grandchildren with all my heart, and I am thankful. I am living, fully!

"Peace I leave with you; my peace I give to you; I do not give it to you as the world does. Do not let your hearts be distressed or lacking in courage. You heard me say to you, 'I am going away and I am coming back to you.'" John 14:27-28 (NET)

God fulfills the promise of His peace, and He will fulfill the promise of His coming back to us one day. Jesus Christ is our Hope on the worst of days and the best of days, and the Holy Spirit is our strength. God has an end goal, a finish line. None of this will last forever. This world is passing away and so are we. There will be a New Heavens and a New Earth, and we will be made new also.

We can take heart…even in the midst of these battles on Earth. God will provide a time of refreshment. Look for them and enjoy them when they come. Early on, I spent one day emotionally distraught as I cleaned out my son's dresser, bagging up his things for a pick-up the next day. I will never forget it…going through his clothes, drawer by drawer. But I will also never forget how three days later my husband and I were on vacation sitting at a picnic table out in the beautiful warm sunshine in Canada. It made me take notice what a difference just three days could make. The enemy will lie and tell us it will never get any better…little dabs, drop by drop, are trying to do us in…but it will get better. Jesus was laid in a tomb on a dark Friday and He rose three days later on a glorious Sunday by the power of the Holy Spirit. Once again, God was showing up in my personal tragedy at that picnic table, giving me His peace and joy. He will do the same for all of us if we will let Him.

But be sure you live out the message and do not merely listen to it and so deceive yourselves. James 1:22 (NET) Our enemy will deceive us, even about suffering. He wants us to think there is no plan in it, no Hope in it, no love in it. There is! Jesus showed us what His suffering provided for us! Our job now is to live it out like it is true…because it is! Through illnesses, job loss, betrayal, difficult relationships, heartbreak, confusion, fear, worry…we have to believe and let God lift us up out of the muck and mire. He will wash us in the blood of the Hope of the resurrection of Jesus Christ. *So submit to God. But resist the devil and he will flee from you.* James 4:7 (NET) Let's resist the devil and fight the good fight of faith while suffering.

It has been said that, "The best is bought only at the cost of great pain. When it comes time to suffer, can I put myself in God's hands and accept His will?" We might ask, why does our world have to work this way? Remember the Christian's Worldview we talked about earlier? It's because of the fall in the Garden. It is what it is. This isn't Heaven…but we are on our way there as believers in the Lord, Jesus Christ. In the meantime, our biblical worldview should be: We are created by God. We are here to glorify God. Sin is what separates us from God, and Jesus made a way for us to be reconciled to our Father through his death, burial, and resurrection.

The Lord will accomplish what concerns me; Your lovingkindness, O Lord, is everlasting; Do not forsake the works of Your hands.
Psalm 138:8 (NASB)

Voddie Baucham teaches, "The problem on the outside is not solved inside of us. It's the problem on the inside that is solved on the outside by God." Humanism looks inside, to man. Christianity looks outside toward God. Paul Washer explains, "Suffering turns our eyes upward. Ease brings them back down." We want ease, we want a painless life, we want things to go well in all areas, but that's not reality. Our true reality and Hope are found in a strong relationship with our Father in Heaven...and the only way to the Father is through His Son, Jesus. It has been said, "Without God we have no Hope. Without Jesus we have no God. If we want this Hope in God, we have to abandon everything else other than Jesus Christ." Like that old hymn says, "My hope is built on nothing less than Jesus' blood and righteousness. I dare not trust the sweetest frame but wholly lean on Jesus' name."

We all have our unique and personal stories of suffering. A young woman who had a stroke at the age of 26, lived on with disabilities. She said, "The redefined me has become the refined me." She was focused on Jesus. What are we looking at in life? What are we focused on? I read: "Everything about our lives is determined and influenced by our view of God. Once you see God as He is, you'll see your life in a whole new light." How do we attain this view of God? Sadly, many times, through our personal suffering. That is why the enemy would like to deceive us about it, have us blame God for it, and be angry and unforgiving toward God because of it. The enemy doesn't want us to grow in our suffering, he wants us to turn our backs on God and continue to suffer all the days of our life, despairing and depressed. God wants us to grow and see His Son in it, so Jesus can see us through it, and grow us out of it! The Holy Spirit strengthens our hearts during these times through prayer and the Word of God—the Word that tells us the Lord's return is near! In my own suffering/trials right now, as we await Jesus' return, I want to be like a solar panel. I want to soak in the Son of God and let Him fill me full of His Holy Spirit power so I can be His light in a dark world.

Our God does many unpredictable things, but one thing we can have no doubt about, and that is the return of Jesus our Lord. We are not to be blown and tossed around by the wind like the waves of the sea as we await that glorious day. We are to hold steadfast, standing on our Rock, as the winds of life blow. With waves, there is a predictable sequence to them as they get farther from their source…the wind that drags over the ocean pulling up ripples on the surface of the sea causes these waves. In the middle of the wave pattern, they grow larger. With the tremendous waves in our life, we sometimes wonder in the middle of them if we will survive as the intensity builds. But eventually every wave settles upon the shore, flattening out…giving us some rest.

Spurgeon wrote, "Blessed are the waves that wash the mariner upon the rock of Salvation." Life comes in waves as we work out our salvation. *So then, my beloved, just as you have always obeyed, not as in my presence only, but now much more in my absence, work out your salvation with fear and trembling;* Philippians 2:12 (NET)

We can know that our Father in Heaven sets the boundaries of our suffering, just like He did with the seashore upon the land. *He set for the sea its boundary so that the water would not transgress His command, when He marked out the foundations of the earth;* Proverbs 8:29 (NASB)

And also with Job in 1:12 (NET): *So the Lord said to Satan, "All right then, everything he has is in your power. Only do not extend your hand against the man himself!"* Nothing that is happening is out of God's control. We can trust in that. When we take our suffering to God. He alone is able to help us through it, take it from us, and give us peace. So many sit beside the sea searching for peace. The ocean draws people to its shores…but even the waves upon the seashore won't give us the peace we are looking for if Jesus isn't in our hearts. We will walk away still feeling empty until we allow the Holy Spirit to fill us with Himself.

Paul endured many forms of suffering, but all along the way he never forgot his Damascus road experience. Paul saw Jesus for who He really was. Many of us have moments in life that we will never forget. Many times, it comes during a period of great suffering. In that moment, our faith either comes into being, or grows suddenly to a new level of understanding. I remember such a moment as I stood in the hallway of a children's oncology clinic looking at pamphlets on the wall. I had been a Christian for many years. But after reading a pamphlet that explained to me what happens when your child relapses with leukemia, as Phil had just done, I slowly replaced the pamphlet of "bad news" on the rack and went into the small room where my son was receiving chemotherapy. I sat down in a chair and prayed a simple prayer of new understanding in Phil's fight against cancer. I said, "Lord, it doesn't matter if we dot every 'i' and cross every 't', does it. You alone will decide if our son will live or die." I knew in that moment that chemotherapy would not save our son, only God would. God healed Phil by taking him Home to Heaven.

I have learned to live with God's decision, and also that we are given what we need when we suffer…to know Jesus and the power of His resurrection. When we learn this, when we are comforted by this Truth, we can then in turn help others to know and be comforted by it, too. We cannot give away what we do not possess. It has been said we need to behave our faith…live out what it is we believe. In suffering and allowing God to transform our lives, the result/fruit becomes more of a witness than even our words. The enemy doesn't want us to know this.

Blessed is the God and Father of our Lord Jesus Christ, the Father of mercies and God of all comfort, who comforts us in all our troubles so that we may be able to comfort those experiencing any trouble with the comfort with which we ourselves are comforted by God. For just as the sufferings of Christ overflow toward us, so also our comfort through Christ overflows to you.
2 Corinthians 1:3-5 (NET)

It is said God doesn't give us more than we can handle. It has also been said, "God is real, and life is unfair. God has promised a way out through Jesus Christ." Which one do you believe more? What is written by Paul is this: *In fact, we expected to die. But as a result, we stopped relying on ourselves and learned to rely only on God, who raises the dead.* 2 Corinthians 1:9 (NLT) Paul was given more than he could handle—that is the truth. But he was learning to trust in God through it all, and not in himself. So are we! Paul was experiencing *comfort through Christ* that *overflows* to others. This is what he has left us with in his writings. We are here to do the same…to be a peaceful people, filled with the Hope of a Savior that not only sustains us but that can be shared with others. Let's not mistake 1 Corinthians 10:13 to mean that God doesn't give us more than we can handle. Instead, let's understand that what God does give us to go through, He alone provides a way of escape so that we are able to endure it. We need our Savior to help us because it is more than we can, or should try to, handle on our own. As one pastor said, "God is in the business of putting His people in a place where only He can come through for them." Let's keep our eyes on Jesus and watch Him work.

We can pretend to be okay for a while when hard times come. We all have. But when trouble comes and stays much too long, our true self will eventually rise to the surface. If what rises in us is not a Hope in Jesus Christ as our Savior, we are to take note of that, and dive deeper into the Word of God and get to know Him more. This is what will save our souls in times of trials and for all of eternity. Life is all about Jesus, all about the Gospel…anything less is deception from the enemy. Jesus' suffering on the Cross taught us how suffering can be used to glorify our Father. Suffering helps us grow in the grace and knowledge of our Lord and Savior. We don't suffer alone as Christ did on the Cross when the Father poured out His wrath and turned away from His only Son in those moments. No. Instead, we suffer *with* Jesus as He helps us through the things we must face. We have been given the Holy Spirit to strengthen and comfort us. Jesus' death and resurrection gives us full assurance that all He accomplished on the Cross at Calvary is enough. The enemy would have us believe this is all a lie…that we are alone, abandoned, forgotten, and not cared about or loved. Once again, we should resist all the enemy's lies, all those little dabs, and he will flee from us.

Let me bring this chapter to an end with a quote from a friend: "The Cross is put here for all suffering…the Cross ought to reconcile us to troubles and take off the terror of them. They are what we bear in common with Christ…our cross which Infinite Wisdom has appointed for us, and a Sovereign Providence has laid on us as fittest for us. We must so manage an affliction, that it may not be a stumbling block or a hindrance to us in any service we have to do for God…" (K.S.)

Suffering comes to us all and God has a plan that is "fittest for us". The enemy lies to us all the way around and through our suffering. We can expect it. Satan's plan is to steal, kill, and destroy all that God is doing in our lives and the lives of those around us during difficult seasons. We are living in a time now when the whole world is suffering, there is confusion, there is chaos, there is an unknowing of where we go from here… But we can always trust because *we know that God causes all things to work together for good to those who love God, to those who are called according to His purpose.* Romans 8:28 (NASB) The *good* is not wealth, health, and prosperity. The *good* is what is beneficial for the Kingdom of God. That's why it is for those who *love God* and are *called according to His purpose.* All things happen for God's ultimate purpose in bringing people to Him.

As children of the King of kings and Lord of lords, being called according to His purpose, my prayer is that we will be better equipped to unveil and prevail through all the deception we have talked about in this book and even more. This is not the end, but only the beginning, as we take all these little dabs that are there to do us under and live above them in the victorious life Jesus Christ has provided for us. Let's look forward to eternity with our eyes wide open to a God who *never changes or casts a shifting shadow.* James 1:17 (NET)

Let's pray:

Father, as we come to the end of this book, we know it is only the beginning of You and all You have waiting for us in eternity. We know You suffered for us, Jesus. We know it caused You to sweat drops of blood. We know it was not just Your physical death on the Cross, the physical suffering, that saved us…it was Your Father's wrath being put upon You instead of us. You stepped into this world and took all the pain and suffering we were so deserving of. There is none like You, and we can trust You in all things. The Holy Spirit indwells us now, while we wait for Your imminent return. Come quickly, Lord Jesus. But until You do, we will prayerfully endure to the end, and be saved. Thank You for going to the Cross for us, and leaving us with a peace that transcends understanding and a Hope that comes with the gift of faith You have given us. Your love is beyond our comprehension, but we cling to it each day. It's in Your name we always Hope and pray. Amen.

Chapter Sixteen Reflections

1) Suffering has come to us all, and it is included in this Truth Journey because little dabs of deception in our pain can do us under…can hinder us on our Christian walk if we're not made aware of what the enemy is doing. (Page 275)

2) The enemy would rather we not understand that the tough times are a preparation for meeting our Savior. It is a delicate refining process known only to our Father in Heaven. It's a process that helps us appreciate all Jesus died to give us even before our last day comes. For many, it is the suffering that brings us into an initial relationship with Jesus. For others, suffering is what is useful to draw us closer to Jesus even after having already become a Christian at some earlier point in our lives. (Page 276)

3) Trials can show us God's strength when we are weak, His eternal Hope when all earthly hope seems lost, and His light that shines in the darkest of times. Yes, trials and tribulations have a great purpose that the enemy would prefer we not take notice of. Satan would like us to believe his lies about suffering. Probably the number one lie, that God doesn't love us. But God is love. (Page 276)

4) We are going to get rid of those dabs of deception as together we learn to consider suffering nothing but joy. If that seems impossible right now, I understand. But, let's begin to dissect this subject and find the Truth hidden in it. (Page 277)

5) Elizabeth summed up suffering in a very simple way. She said suffering is: "Having what you don't want or wanting what you don't have." I believe if we think about that…we will find that to be true. (Page 277)

6) What we are living in now is the worst of life we will ever experience as believers in Jesus Christ. This world is as far away from God as we will ever be, and as hard as it will

ever get…although God never leaves us nor forsakes us. One day, we will meet our Lord face to face and live with Him forever in our Heavenly Home. (Page 278)

7) God is not asking us to go through anything that His Son did not endure as He walked out His life, straight toward the Cross at Calvary. There, Jesus suffered the wrath of His Father, poured out upon Him, crushing Him, and dying of a broken heart for the sins of the world. (Page 279)

8) In our times of suffering there are decisions to be made. Holding tightly to our Hope in Jesus is a big one. Suffering helps us know if the Truth is truly in us. Are we really willing to carry our cross and follow Jesus to the depths of our being? Or, have we just been playing church? Playing a Christian? Playing with faith? (Page 283)

NOTES

EPILOGUE

With the help of the Holy Spirit, this book has been written. Looking back now, I can see what immense subjects Truth and deception are…not that this is an exhaustive work. There are too many things concerning these subjects for any one book to hold them all, other than the Bible. If I'd seen the mountain of research and writing ahead of me, I don't know that I would have attempted to plow through it. But each day, God made the mountainous work into a mole hill, so this could get written. I have learned so much along the way…about the little dabs of lies that can do us under, and the little dabs of Truth that can make it difficult for the full Gospel to be understood. God will give us His wisdom as we ask, seek, and knock upon His great storehouse.

I heard one author recently share that he is not an expert—many things he writes about, he just learned 20 minutes before writing it. Oh, how I could relate as I looked into each subject contained here. I did the research so, now, you can hopefully find what you are needing without months and months of digging through what is out there. With prayer, the Word, study, videos, sermons, books, conversations, etc…it became this book. Sometimes, I wasn't even able to change how others taught it, because there seemed no better way for it to be explained. But my hope truly is that this will now be some help to you in your personal walk with Jesus…especially in the times we are living in.

These sixteen chapters are my contributions to fighting back at the deception the enemy would so like to trap us in since *false messiahs and false prophets will appear and perform great signs and wonders to deceive, if possible, even the elect.* Matthew 24:24 (NET)

As the elect, be blessed and be as wise as a serpent and as innocent as a dove.

GIVING THANKS

My heart and thanks go first to, Jesus, my First Love which I dare not ever leave. As I sat with God each morning, reading and praying through the books of the Bible, it seemed each one could be woven into the chapter I was writing at the present time. The Word is amazingly wonderful and miraculous. I thank my Father in Heaven, my Lord Jesus Christ, and the Holy Spirit who continually guides me through each day.

To my second love, my husband, Jim, I owe a dept of gratitude. While he continues to work outside of our home bringing in the money to pay the bills, I am blessed to be able to be home and do what I love. I could say I'm a starving artist/writer, but I'm not. I am well taken care of, and so thankful for Jim's love and support.

To the Mustard Seeds, my amazing Bible study group, I am so grateful. As these chapters were being developed, you sat through each lesson and allowed me to share them with you. As I learned, I hope we all learned together about the love and mercy of our Lord Jesus Christ and the ways the enemy tries to steal, kill, and destroy our lives. I love you all. I appreciate your encouragement. And I know as sisters-in-Christ, we have an eternity waiting for us that will be beyond all we can hope or imagine.

My friend, Drue Little, you have taught me so much since we met. We are truly iron that sharpens iron. And when we sat across the table that day and you said, "A little dab will do you under," I knew it was the title to a book. I quickly wrote it down, asking you if I could use it. You said, "Yes". I didn't know what the book would be about on that day, but here it is. Thank you for all you do for me, and so many in this life!

My Beta-reader team and friends, Denise Croghan, Susan Silva, Lynn Tredway, and Karen Williams: How can I thank you enough for taking the time to read through these 110,000 plus words! You each bring something different to the editing process, and it's a joy to see what you catch that needs correction. Thank you for working with me. I never know if I'm going to write another book, but you are always faithful to say you are ready to read them when needed. Your friendship and help are more than I can ask for. Much love and thanks!

Connie Fulmer-Dixon, here we are, still. You told me many, many books ago when I thought I was done writing, that I wasn't. You were right! You are a blessing to me, and such a wonderful far-away-friend. I know we will have lots of time in Heaven to spend together. Thank you for editing what is needed after the Beta team has done their scouring through. I have learned, book by book, that no matter how many times we go through each page, some typos will escape us. But since God is the only perfect One, I am at peace.

ABOUT THE AUTHOR
dianecshore.com

Diane C. Shore lives in San Ramon, CA with her husband Jim of more than 40 years. They are enjoying these years together after raising three sons, and now being the grandparents of six. Writing and sharing stories about God is Diane's passion. God continues to lead her and show her new ways of how He expresses His love toward us each day. Whether it is sitting one-on-one with someone, or speaking to a group, Diane is excited to boldly proclaim the Good News of Jesus Christ and how He works in our daily lives.

OTHER BOOKS BY DIANE C. SHORE

Non-Fiction

Impossible is Nothing
It Started in the Dark
It Ended in the Light

Devotional

The SAND Room

Fiction

ROSIE in the Garden-1
ROSIE on the Plane-2
ROSIE at the Lake 3
ROSIE by the Gate-4
When You Do
What Do I Want

Children's Books

Cooper's Challenge
Amelia's Artistry

Information and free excerpts of these books are available at:

dianecshore.com

www.ingramcontent.com/pod-product-compliance
Lightning Source LLC
Chambersburg PA
CBHW051815090426
42736CB00011B/1486